Portuguese

Marcia Monje de Castro

Brazilian Portuguese phrasebook
3rd edition – October 2003

Published by
Lonely Planet Publications Pty Ltd ABN 36 005 607 983
90 Maribyrnong St, Footscray, Victoria 3011, Australia

Lonely Planet Offices
Australia Locked Bag 1, Footscray, Victoria 3011
USA 150 Linden St, Oakland CA 94607
UK 72-82 Rosebery Ave, London, EC1R 4RW

Cover illustration
Berimbau Beat and the Capoeira Crew by Yukiyoshi Kamimura

ISBN 1 86450 380 7

text © Lonely Planet Publications Pty Ltd 2003
cover illustration © Lonely Planet Publications Pty Ltd 2003

 10 9 8 7

Printed through Colorcraft Ltd, Hong Kong
Printed in China

acknowledgments

This phrasebook swayed along the production esplanade thanks to the deckchair planning of Jim Jenkin, then publishing manager, and the follow-up work of his successor, Peter D'Onghia. Commissioning editors Karina Coates and Karin Vidstrup Monk did a samba through the initial research, with poise and finesse, deftly recruiting translator Marcia Monje de Castro, who even managed to have a *feijoada* party in the middle of it all. Editor Ben Handicott explored all things Brazilian, with assistance from fellow editors Piers Kelly, who proofed and wrote a few words here and there, and Francesca Coles, who chipped in with work on the Phrasebuilder chapter as well as proofing. In a swan-song performance, editor Emma Koch lent a hand, humming quite a few bars of the introduction. Managing editor Annelies Mertens kept her finger on the pulse, discovered it was a bossa nova, and kept everything in time.

Layout artist John Shippick looked up from his beach towel and away from the volleyball long enough to make the book look as beautiful as the girl from Ipanema, who was passing by. Nick Stebbing, technically a genius, provided macro assistance and was way too busy to notice. Layout was checked by Adriana Mammarella, Kate McDonald and Sally Darmody. Series designer Yukiyoshi Kamimura, our resident Brazilian, was inspired by his homeland, and created the illustrations which brighten up the pages and adorn the cover. He was also an invaluable source of language and cultural information – *obrigado!* The map came via cartographic designer Wayne Murphy and managing cartographer Paul Piaia. Overseeing the whole production was an armada of project managers, starting with Charles Rawlings-Way, who filled in for Huw Fowles for a time, who filled in for Fabrice Rocher for a longer time, before Fabrice returned in time for the final hurrah. *Oba!*

make the most of this phrasebook ...

Anyone can speak another language! It's all about confidence. Don't worry if you can't remember your school language lessons or if you've never learnt a language before. Even if you learn the very basics (on the inside covers of this book), your travel experience will be the better for it. You have nothing to lose and everything to gain when the locals hear you making an effort.

finding things in this book

For easy navigation, this book is in sections. The Tools chapters are the ones you'll thumb through time and again. The Practical section covers basic travel situations like catching transport and finding a bed. The Social section gives you conversational phrases, pick-up lines, the ability to express opinions – so you can get to know people. Food has a section all of its own: gourmets and vegetarians are covered and local dishes feature. Safe Travel equips you with health and police phrases, just in case. Remember the colours of each section and you'll find everything easily; or use the comprehensive Index. Otherwise, check the two-way traveller's Dictionary for the word you need.

being understood

Throughout this book you'll see coloured phrases on the right-hand side of each page. They're phonetic guides to help you pronounce the language. You don't even need to look at the language itself, but you'll get used to the way we've represented particular sounds. The pronunciation chapter in Tools will explain more, but you can feel confident that if you read the coloured phrase slowly, you'll be understood.

communication tips

Body language, ways of doing things, sense of humour – all have a role to play in every culture. 'Local talk' boxes show you common ways of saying things, or everyday language to drop into conversation. 'Listen for ...' boxes supply the phrases you may hear. They start with the phonetic guide (because you'll hear it before you know what's being said) and then lead in to the language and the English translation.

contents

5

brazilian portuguese

Caribbean Sea · St Vincent — Barbados · Grenada — · Trinidad & Tobago · Panama · Venezuela · Guyana · Suriname · French Guiana (Fr.) · NORTH ATLANTIC OCEAN · Colombia · Ecuador · Macapá · Belém · São Luís · Fortaleza · Manáus · Teresina · Rio Grande do Norte · Paraíba · Pernambuco · Peru · BRAZIL · Alagoas · Rio Branco · Porto Velho · Palmas · Sergipe · Salvador da Bahia · Cuiabá · Brasília · Bolivia · Belo Horizonte · Campo Grande · Vitória · Chile · Paraguay · Rio de Janeiro · São Paulo · SOUTH PACIFIC OCEAN · Curitiba · Florianópolis · Porto Alegre · SOUTH ATLANTIC OCEAN · Argentina · Uruguay

■ **national language**

For more details see the **introduction**.

Portuguese is spoken by around 190 million people worldwide, 89% of whom live in Brazil. Brazil, the largest country in South America, is the only Portuguese-speaking nation on the continent. Although the country is large, there's very little regional variation, so you'll have no trouble making yourself understood from top to bottom.

The Portuguese arrived in Brazil at the beginning of the 16th century. Speakers from the different regions in Portugal all brought their own dialectal variations. However, as Portuguese colonists came into contact with the Tupi tribes that lived along the Atlantic coast, the Tupi language, along with Portuguese, became the main languages of Brazil. This was mostly due to the Jesuits, who translated prayers and hymns into Tupi and in doing so recorded and promoted the indigenous language. This situation did not last and the use of Tupi was banned in 1759 when the Jesuits were expelled from Brazil and Portuguese was instated as the country's main language.

Portuguese spoken in Brazil was influenced by Tupi and the Bantu and Yoruba languages of African slaves who were brought to Brazil through till the middle of the 19th century. Over a similar period, European Portuguese also underwent linguistic change through

at a glance ...

language name:
  Portuguese
name in language:
  português porr·too·*ges*
language family:
  Romance
key country: Brazil
**approximate number
  of speakers:** 169 million
  in Brazil, 190 million
  Portuguese speakers
  worldwide
close relatives:
  Catalan, Galician, French
  Italian, Occitan,
  Romanian, Spanish
donations to English:
  cashew, ipecac, macaw,
  petunia, piranha, toucan

contact with French. Due to this divergence, Brazilian Portuguese today differs from European Portuguese in approximately the same way that British English differs from American English. European and Brazilian Portuguese have different spelling, different pronunciation and to some extent, different vocabulary. For example, in Portugal, the word for 'train' is *comboio* and in Brazil you'd say *trem*.

This book will ensure not only that you have the right words at your disposal, but that you pronounce them as a true *brasileiro* (if you're a man) or *brasileira* (if you're a woman). Need more encouragement? Remember, the contact you make using Brazilian Portuguese will make your travels unique. Local knowledge, new relationships and a sense of satisfaction are on the tip of your tongue, so don't just stand there, say something!

abbreviations used in this book

m	masculine	**sg**	singular	**pol**	polite
f	feminine	**pl**	plural	**inf**	informal

The pronunciation guide used in this book is based on the pronunciation of Brazilian Portuguese common in urban areas. There are small variations in pronunciation throughout the country, but they cause little difficulty when communicating.

vowel sounds

Vowel sounds are quite similar to those found in English, so you should be able to get talking with confidence. There are some differences of course: the *ay* sound, for example, is much shorter than the English version of it. But with every conversation you have, the sounds will become more familiar and you'll discover ways to make those same sounds yourself.

symbol	english equivalent	brazilian portuguese example
a	run	*camera*
aa	father	*padre*
ai	aisle	*pai*
aw	saw	*nó*
ay	day	*lei*
e	bet	*cedo*
ee	bee	*fino*
o	go	*gato*
oo	moon	*azul*
ow	how	*saudades*
oy	boy	*noite*

A characteristic feature of Brazilian Portuguese is the use of nasal vowels. Nasal vowels are pronounced as if you're trying to force the sound out of your nose rather than your mouth. It's easier than it sounds. English also has nasal vowels to some extent – when you say 'sing' in English, the 'i' is nasalised by the 'ng'. In our pronunciation guide, we've used ng after nasal vowels to indicate that it's nasal. The following is a list of the vowels that you'll normally see with ng in our phonetic guides.

symbol	english equivalent	brazilian portuguese example
ang	-	amanhã
ayng	-	pães
eng	-	tem
eeng	-	muito
ong	-	bom
oong	-	segundo
owng	-	fogão
oyng	-	nações

consonant sounds

The consonant sounds in Brazilian Portuguese are very similar to those of English, and even the rolled 'r' (rr), which doesn't exist in standard English varieties, will be familiar to most people (it's similar to the 'r' in Spanish). Two sounds (ly and ny) which might appear a little strange at first do actually occur in English (eg, 'million' and 'canyon'), but never at the beginning of a syllable as they do in Brazilian Portuguese.

symbol	english equivalent	brazilian portuguese example
b	big	*beber*
d	dig	*dar/dedo*
f	fun	*faca*
g	go	*guia*
h	hat	*resto/serra*
k	kick	*cama*
l	loud	*lixo*
ly	million	*muralhas*
m	man	*macaco*
n	no	*nada*
ny	canyon	*linha*
p	pig	*padre*
r	run	*para*
rr	as the 'r' in run, but stronger and rolled	*ir*
s	so	*grosso*
sh	ship	*chave*
t	tin	*tacho*
v	very	*vago*
w	win	*muito*
z	zoo	*exame*
zh	pleasure	*gentes*

word stress

Stress generally occurs on the second-to-last syllable of a word, though there are exceptions. When a word ends in a written -r or is pronounced with a nasalised vowel, the stress falls on the last syllable. Another exception: if a written vowel has an accent marked on it, the stress falls on the syllable containing that vowel.

In our transliteration system, we have indicated the stressed syllable with italics.

writing

Brazilian Portuguese is written with the latin alphabet, which is given below. For spelling purposes, pronunciation of letters is also provided:

alphabet			
a	a	n	e·ne
b	be	o	aw
c	se	p	pe
d	de	q	ke
e	e	r	e·he
f	e·fe	s	e·se
g	ge	t	te
h	a·gaa	u	oo
i	ee	v	ve
j	jo·ta	w	daa·bee·oo
k	kaa	x	hees
l	e·le	y	eep·see·lon
m	e·me	z	ze

Some letters have accent marks which denote stress, or variations in the sound usually represented. The accent marks used include those used on vowels: the acute (´), grave (`) and circumflex (^), indicating stress; and the tilde (~), indicating nasalisation. You'll also notice the tail (cedilla) sometimes used at the bottom of the letter 'c' – 'ç' is pronounced as s.

This chapter is arranged alphabetically and is designed to help you make your own sentences. If you can't find the exact phrase you need in this book, remember, a couple of well-chosen words, a little grammar and a gesture or two and you'll generally get the message across.

a/an

The Brazilian Portuguese words *um* and *uma* correspond to the English article 'a/an'. Whether you use the article *um* or *uma* depends upon the gender of the thing, person or concept talked about. If what you're referring to is masculine you use *um*, if it's feminine you use *uma*.

I'd like a pastry and a beer.

> *Quero um pastel*   ke·ro oom paas·*tel*
> *e uma cerveja.*   e oo·maa serr·ve·zhaa
> (lit: I-like a pastry and a beer)

Also see **gender.**

adjectives see describing things

any see some

articles see a/an and the

be

Brazilian Portuguese has two words which can be translated as 'be' in English: *ser* and *estar*. Learning to use them perfectly will take some time and effort, but the basic difference in their usage is not too difficult to grasp. They're both irregular verbs (just as 'be' is in English) so you need to remember by heart the various forms they take.

The verb *ser* refers to states that have a degree of permanency or durability about them.

I	am	Australian	*eu*	*sou*	*australiano* m
you sg	are	kind	*você*	*é*	*gentil* m&f
he/she	is	an artist	*ele/ela*	*é*	*artista* m&f
you pl	are	crazy	*vocês*	*são*	*loucos* m
we	are	students	*nós*	*somos*	*estudantes*
they	are	crazy	*eles/elas*	*são*	*loucos/ loucas* m/f

The verb *estar* generally refers to events which are temporary in nature.

I	am	on holiday	*eu*	*estou*	*de férias*
you sg	are	drunk	*você*	*está*	*bêbado* m
he/she	is	sick	*ele/ela*	*está*	*doente* m&f
you pl	are	lost	*vocês*	*estão*	*perdidos* m
we	are	travelling	*nós*	*estamos*	*viajando*
they	are	busy	*eles/elas*	*estão*	*ocupados/ ocupadas* m/f

comparing things

To compare one thing to another, use the words *mais* (more) and *menos* (less) in the following ways:

mais … do que …   mais … do ke …
more … than …

menos … do que …   me·nos … do ke …
less … than …

TOOLS

14

This shirt is nicer than that one.

Esta camisa é mais   es·*taa* kaa·*mee*·zaa e mais
bonita do que esta.   bo·*nee*·taa do ke es·taa
(lit: this shirt is more nice of
  that this)

To refer to something as the most or least (eg, biggest) use
mais (more) and *menor* (less) in the following ways:

o/a … mais … m/f   o/aa … mais …
the … most …

o/a … menor … m/f   o/aa … me·*nor* …
the … least …

I'd like the cheapest room.

Quero o quarto mais   *ke*·ro o *kwaar*·to mais
barato.   baa·*raa*·to
(lit: I-like the room most cheap)

demonstratives see this & that

describing things

Adjectives are generally placed after the noun. They vary in
form depending on the gender and number of the noun that
they describe:

the pretty young woman

a jovem bonita   aa *zho*·veng bo·*nee*·taa
(lit: a young-woman beautiful)

the pretty young women

as jovens bonitas   as *zho*·vengs bo·*nee*·taas
(lit: the young-girls beautiful)

the handsome young man

o rapaz bonito   o haa·*paas* bo·nee·to
(lit: a young-man handsome)

the handsome young men

os rapazess bonitos   os haa·*paa*·zes bo·*nee*·tos
(lit: the young-men handsome)

Here are the various endings that adjectives take to agree with the nouns that they describe:

	singular	plural
masculine	-o	-os
feminine	-a	-as

feminine see gender

gender

All nouns are either masculine or feminine. They determine the endings used on adjectives that describe them as well as which forms of the Portuguese equivalents of the articles 'a/an' and 'the' are used. The gender that a given noun takes is often arbitrary. For example, there's no reason why the noun *sol* 'sun' is masculine while *praia* 'beach' is feminine. The dictionary will tell you what gender a noun is, but here are some guidelines for taking a guess at the gender of a noun (there are exceptions though):

often masculine	often feminine
nouns referring to male persons (or male animals)	nouns referring to female persons (or female animals)
nouns ending in -o	nouns ending in -a
nouns ending in -ema, -oma and -ama	nouns ending with -dade

Also see **a/an**, **the** and **describing things**.

have

Possession can be indicated using the verb *ter* 'to have' which is an irregular verb.

I have a flight at 6pm.

Tenho um vôo às seis   te·nyo oom *vo*·o aas says
da noite.   da *noy*·te
(lit: I-have a flight at-the six
  of-the night)

I	have	a ticket	eu	tenho	uma pasagem
you sg	have	the bill	você	tem	a conta
he/she	has	water	ele/ela	tem	água
we	have	the key	nós	temos	a chave
you pl	have	a letter	vocês	têm	uma carta
they	have	the menu	eles/elas	têm	o cardápio

masculine see gender

more than one

You can make a noun plural by adding *-s*:

| book | *livro* m | books | *livros* m pl |
| bed | *cama* f | beds | *camas* f pl |

If the noun ends in *-s*, *-z* or *-r*, and the final syllable is stressed, then the plural is formed by adding *-es*:

singular	plural	singular	plural
portuguese	*português*	portuguese	*portuguêses*
youth	*rapaz* m	youths	*rapazes* m pl
flower	*flor* f	flowers	*flores* f pl

Remember when using plural nouns to change the articles and adjectives used with these nouns to their corresponding plural forms too.

There are some exceptions and additional rules for making nouns plural – they can't all be covered here, so consult a grammar of Portuguese if you'd like to know more.

Also see **a/an**, **describing things**, **some**, and **the**.

my & your

Like English, Brazilian Portuguese uses pronouns to indicate possession. In the table below are the equivalents for the English possessive pronouns. To express possession you place them before the noun they describe and make them agree in number (plural or singular) and gender (masculine or feminine) with the noun.

	singular		plural	
	masculine	feminine	masculine	feminine
	map	letter	maps	letters
my	meu mapa	minha carta	meus mapas	minhas cartas
your sg&pl	seu mapa	sua carta	seus mapas	suas cartas
his/her/ its	seu mapa	sua carta	seus mapas	suas cartas
our	nosso mapa	nossa carta	nossos mapas	nossas cartas
their	seu mapa	sua carta	seus mapas	suas cartas

Here's how you'd use possessive pronouns to say that something is yours.

It's my ticket.
   É a minha pasagem.   e a *mee*·nya pa·*saa*·zheng
   (lit: it-is the my ticket)

A simple statement of possession (eg, 'It's mine') is formed by using *É* ('it is') with the possessive pronoun (to agree with the thing possessed).

It's mine.
É meu.   e *me·oo*
(lit: it-is mine)

negative

To make a sentence negative, just add the word *não* (no), before the main verb:

I don't want to walk any more.
Não quero andar mais.   nowng *ke·ro* ang·*daar* mais
(lit: no I-want to-walk more)

The double negative isn't only acceptable, but correct:

I can't see anything.
Não vejo nada.   nowng *ve·*zho *naa·*daa
(lit: no I see nothing)

negative words		
never	*nunca*	*noong·*kaa
no/not	*não*	nowng
nobody	*ninguém*	neeng·*geng*
none sg	*nenhum/ nenhuma* m/f	neng·ee·*oom/* neng·ee·*oo·*maa
nor	*nem*	neng

nouns see gender

number see more than one

planning ahead

The future is usually expressed by using the present tense of the verb *ir*, (go), plus another verb. It's equivalent to 'going to …' in English:

I'm going to come back next week.

Vou voltar na semana   vo vol·*taarr* na se·*ma*·naa
que vem.   ke veng
(lit: I-go to-come-back
   in-the week which comes)

I	vou	we	vamos
you	vai	you	vão
he/she/it	vai	they	vão

Just like in English, you'd also be understood when expressing your plans, if you use the present tense with some indication of time referring to the future:

I'm going to Rio tomorrow.

Vou para o Rio   vo *paa*·ra o *hee*·o
amanha.   aa·*ma*·nyang
(lit: I-go to the Rio tomorrow)

plural see more than one

pointing something out

The easiest way to point something out in Portuguese is to start your phrase with *É …* (lit: It-is …).

That's a beautiful building.

É um edifício bonito.   e oom e·dee·*fee*·syo bo·*nee*·to
(lit: it-is a building beautiful)

Also see **this & that**.

possession see have, my & your and somebody's

There are a number of ways to indicate possession in Brazilian Portuguese. The easiest way is by using the verb *ter* (see **have**). You could also use possessive pronouns (see **my & your**) or, simplest of all, use the preposition *de* (of) followed by the possessor (see **somebody's**).

To find out who's the owner of something, you can use the simple phrases *De quem é isto ...?* (of whom it-is this ...?) for a single thing, or *De quem são estes/estas ...?* m/f (of whom are-they these ...?) for plural things:

Whose seat is this?

De quem é este assento?   de keng e *es·*te aa·*seng·*to
(lit: of whom it-is this seat)

pronouns

Subject pronouns corresponding to 'I', 'you', 'he', 'she', 'it', 'we' and 'they' are often omitted, as verb endings make it clear who the subject is. Use them if you want to emphasise the subject.

	singular			plural	
I	*eu*	e·oo	**we**	*nós*	nos
you	*você*	vo·se	**you**	*vocês*	vo·ses
he /it m	*ele*	e·le	**they** m or m&f	*eles*	e·les
she/it f	*ela*	e·laa	**they** f	*elas*	e·laas

Note that unlike in other romance languages (and even the Portuguese spoken in Portugal), Brazilian Portuguese does not commonly distinguish between formal and informal forms of 'you'.

question words

who	quem	keng
Who are you?	Quem é você?	keng e *vo*·se
what	(o) que	(o) ke
What's wrong?	O que é que há?	o ke e ke a
which/what	qual/quais sg/pl	kwow/kais
What's the best restaurant in the city?	Qual é o melhor restaurante da cidade?	kwow e o me·*lyorr* hes·tow·*rang*·te daa see·*daa*·de
where	onde	*ong*·de
Where is the Australian Embassy?	Onde fica a embaixada Australiana?	*ong*·de fee·kaa aa eng·bai·*shaa*·daa ows·traa·lee·*a*·na
when	quando	*kwang*·do
When is the flight?	Quando sai o vôo?	*kwang*·do sai o *vo*·o
how/by what means	como é que	*ko*·mo e ke
How do I find the bus station?	Como é que vou para a rodoviária?	*ko*·mo e ke vow *paa*·raa aa ho·do·vee·*aa*·ryaa
how much/ how many?	quanto/a m/f quantos/quantas m/f pl	*kwang*·to/*kwang*·taa *kwang*·tos/ *kwang*·taas
How much is it?	Quanto custa?	*kwang*·to koos·taa
why	por que	porr ke
Why are we stopping here?	Por que estamos parando aqui?	porr ke es·*ta*·mos paa·*raang*·do aa·*kee*

some

The plural forms of the words for 'a/an' (*um* and *uma*) are used to express the English 'some'. If what you're referring to is masculine plural, use *uns*, and if it's feminine plural, use *umas*.

I'd like some headache pills.
   Quero uns comprimidos   *ke·ro oongs kong·pree·mee·dos*
   para dor de cabeça.   *paa·raa dorr de kaa·be·saa*
   (lit: I-like some pills for
   pain of head)

I've had a few to drink.
   Tomei umas e outras.   *to·may oo·maas e o·traas*
   (lit: I-drank some and
   others)

Also see **a/an** and **gender**.

somebody's

The simplest way of indicating possession is by using the preposition *de* (from), followed by the person who's the owner of the thing. You can only do this with proper nouns (for people or places).

It's Carla's backpack.
   É a mochila de Carla.   *e aa mo·shee·laa de karr·laa*
   (lit: it-is the backpack
   of Carla)

See also **possession**.

the

There are four words that correspond to the English article 'the'. The form you use is determined by the gender and number of the noun the article is used with:

masculine	o sg	o trem o treng	the train
	os pl	os trens os trengs	the trains
feminine	a sg	a mochila a mo·shee·la	the backpack
	as pl	as mochilas a mo·shee·la	the backpacks

Also see **gender** and **more than one**.

this & that

To refer to or point at a person or object, use one of the following forms (known as demonstratives) before the noun, depending on whether the person or object you're referring to is close or further away, masculine or feminine, and singular or plural:

	singular		plural	
	masculine	feminine	masculine	feminine
close	este	esta	estes	estas
away	aquele	aquela	aqueles	aquelas

Is this seat free?
Este lugar está vago?   es·te loo·gaarr es·taa vaa·go
(lit: this seat it-is free)

This view is wonderful.
> *Esta vista é*   *es·taa vees·taa e*
> *maravilhosa.*   *maa·raa·vee·lyo·zaa*
> (lit: this view it-is wonderful)

These forms can also be used on their own without an accompanying noun – meaning 'this (one)', 'that (one)', 'these' and 'those'.

Does this market open every day?
> *Este mercado abre todos*   *es·te merr·kaa·do aa·bre to·dos*
> *os dias?*   *os dee·aas*
> (lit: this market open all
> the days)

Those are Brazilian.
> *Aqueles são brasileiros.*   *a·ke·les sowng braa·zee·lay·ros*
> (lit: those they-are
> Brazilians)

Also see **pointing something out**.

verbs

Brazilian Portuguese has three types of verbs: those ending in *-ar* (eg, *morar*, 'to live'), those ending in *-er* (eg, *comer*, 'to eat') and those ending in *-ir* (eg, *partir*, 'to leave'). Despite this, the present tense verb endings for each person ('I', 'you', 'we' etc) are very similar for all three so you can recognise them easily:

	-ar	-er	-ir
I		-o	
you/he/she/it	-a	-e	
we	-amos	-emos	-imos
you/they	-am	-em	

As in any language, some verbs are irregular in Brazilian Portuguese. The most important ones are *ser*, *estar* and *ter* (see **be** and **have**).

word order

Generally, the word order of a sentence is the same as in English (subject-verb-object).

I'd like a room.

Eu quero um quarto.　　　　　*e·oo ke·ro oom kwaarr·to*
(lit: I I-like a room)

yes/no questions

When asking a question, simply make a statement, but raise your intonation inquisitively towards the end of the sentence, as you would in English.

Do you speak English?

Você fala inglês?　　　　　*vo·se faa·laa eeng·gles*
(lit: you speak-you English)

If what you're doing is really making a statement but you're requesting confirmation or agreement, you can put the tag *não é* (lit: not it-is) on the end.

John lives in Rio, doesn't he?

João mora no Rio,　　　　　*zho·owng mo·raa no hee·o*
não é?　　　　　nowng e
(lit: John lives-he in Rio
　not it-is)

In rapid everyday speech the tag *não é* sounds more like ne.

Do you speak (English)?
Você fala (inglês)?
vo·*se faa*·laa (eeng·*gles*)

Does anyone speak (English)?
Alguém aqui fala (inglês)?
ow·*geng* aa·*kee faa*·laa (eeng·*gles*)

Do you understand?
Você entende?
vo·*se* eng·*teng*·de

Yes, I understand.
Sim, entendo.
seeng eng·*teng*·do

No, I don't understand.
Não, não entendo.
nowng nowng eng·*teng*·do

I speak (English).
Eu falo (inglês).
e·oo *faa*·lo (eeng·*gles*)

I don't speak (Portuguese).
Eu não falo (português).
e·oo *faa*·lo (porr·too·*ges*)

I speak a little.
Eu falo um pouquinho.
e·oo *faa*·lo oom po·*kee*·nyo

I (don't) understand.
Eu (não) entendo.
e·oo (nowng) eng·*teng*·do

What does 'bem-vindo' mean?
O que quer dizer 'bem-vindo' ?
o ke kerr dee·*zerr* beng *veeng*·do

How do you ...?   *Como se ...?*   *ko*·mo se ...
   pronounce this   *pronuncia isto*   pro·noong·*see*·aa *ees*·to
   write 'ajuda'   *escreve 'ajuda'*   es·*kre*·ve aa·*zhoo*·daa

Could you please …?	Você poderia … por favor?	vo·*se* po·de·*ree*·aa … porr faa·*vorr*
repeat that	*repetir isto*	he·pe·*teerr ees*·to
speak more slowly	*falar mais devagar*	faa·*laarr* mais de·vaa·*gaarr*
write it down	*escrever num papel*	es·kre·*verr* noom paa·*pel*

false friends

Beware of false friends – words which can look and sound like English words but have a different meaning altogether.

atualmente   ak·twow·*meng*·te   nowadays
not 'actually' which is *na verdade*, na verr·*da*·de

longe   *long*·zhe   far away
not 'long' which is *comprido* m, kong·*pree*·do or *comprida* f, kong·*pree*·daa

magazine   ma·ga·*zeen*   department store
not 'magazine' which is *revista*, he·*vees*·ta

novela   no·*ve*·la   soap opera
not 'novel' which is *romance*, ho·*mang*·se

pretender   pre·*teng*·de   intend
not 'pretend' which is *fingir*, feeng·*geer*

puxar   poo·*shaarr*   pull
not 'push' which is *empurrar*, eng·*poo*·raarr

sorte   *sorr*·te   luck
not 'sort' which is *typo*, *tee*·po

cardinal numbers

números cardinais

0	zero	ze·ro	6	seis	says
1	um	oom	7	sete	se·te
2	dois	doys	8	oito	oy·to
3	três	tres	9	nove	naw·ve
4	quatro	kwaa·tro	10	dez	dez
5	cinco	seeng·ko			

11	onze	ong·ze
12	doze	do·ze
13	treze	tre·ze
14	quatorze	kaa·torr·ze
15	quinze	keeng·ze
16	dezesseis	de·ze·says
17	dezesete	de·ze·se·te
18	dezoito	de·zoy·to
19	dezenove	de·ze·naw·ve
20	vinte	veeng·te
21	vinte e um	veeng·te e oom
22	vinte e dois	veeng·te e doys
30	trinta	treeng·taa
40	quarenta	kwaa·reng·taa
50	cinquenta	seen·kweng·taa
60	sessenta	se·seng·taa
70	setenta	se·tena·taa
80	oitenta	oy·teng·taa
90	noventa	no·veng·taa
100	cem	seng
200	duzentos	doo·zeng·tos
1,000	mil	mee·oo
1,000,000	um milhão	oom mee·lyowng

ordinal numbers

1st	*primeiro/primeira* m/f	pree·*may*·ro/pree·*may*·raa
2nd	*segundo/segunda* m/f	se·*goong*·do/se·*goong*·daa
3rd	*terceiro/terceira* m/f	terr·*say*·ro/terr·*say*·raa
4th	*quarto/quarta* m/f	kwaarr·to/kwaarr·taa
5th	*quinto/quinta* m/f	keeng·to/keeng·taa

fractions

frações

a quarter	*um quarto*	oom *kwaarr*·to
a third	*um terço*	oom *terr*·so
a half	*metade*	me·*taa*·de
three-quarters	*três quartos*	tres *kwaarr*·tos
all (of it)	*inteiro/inteira* m/f	eeng·*tay*·ro/eeng·*tay*·raa
all (of them)	*tudo/tuda* m/f	*too*·do/*too*·daa
none	*nenhum*	ne·*yoom*

useful amounts

quantias & quantidades úteis

How much?	*Quanto?*	*kwang*·to
How many?	*Quantos/Quantas?* m/f	*kwang*·tos/*kwan*·taas
Please give me ...	*Por favor me dê ...*	porr faa·*vorr* me de ...
a few	*alguns*	ow·*goons*
(just) a little	*(só) um pouquinho*	(saw) oom po·*kee*·nyo
a lot	*muito*	*mweeng*·to
less	*menos*	me·nos
many	*muitos/muitas* m/f	*mweeng*·tos/*mweeng*·taas
more	*mais*	mais
some	*um pouco*	oom *po*·ko

telling the time

dizendo a hora

The 24-hour clock is usually used when telling the time in Brazilian Portuguese. Alternatively, you can add *da manhã* (in the morning), *da tarde* (in the afternoon), or *da noite* (in the evening) to specify the exact time.

Time is given using a plural form of the verb 'be', *ser* (*são*), except in the case of 1 o'clock, when the singular form (*é*) is used.

What time is it?	*Que horas são?*	ke *aw*·raas sowng
It's (one) o'clock.	*É (um) hora.*	e (oom) *aw*·raa
It's (ten) o'clock.	*São (dez) horas.*	sowng (des) *aw*·raas
Five past (ten).	*(Dez) e cinco.*	(des) e *seeng*·ko
Quarter past (ten).	*(Dez) e quinze.*	(des) e *keeng*·ze
Half past (ten).	*(Dez) e meia.*	(des) e *may*·aa

After the half hour, state the number of minutes to the next hour until that hour arrives.

Quarter to (ten).	*Quinze para as (dez).*	*keeng*·ze paa·raa aas (des)
Twenty to (ten).	*Vinte para as (dez).*	*veeng*·te paa·raa aas (des)
in the morning	*da manhã*	daa ma·*nyang*
in the afternoon	*da tarde*	daa *taarr*·de
in the evening	*da noite*	daa *noy*·te
At what time ...?	*A que horas ...?*	aa ke *aw*·raas ...
At (ten).	*Às (dez).*	aas (des)
At (7.57pm).	*Às (sete e cinquenta e sete da noite).*	aas (*se*·te e seeng·*kweng*·taa e *se*·te daa *noy*·te)

days of the week

Monday	segunda-feira	se·*goong*·daa·*fay*·raa
Tuesday	terça-feira	terr·saa·*fay*·raa
Wednesday	quarta-feira	kwaarr·taa·*fay*·raa
Thursday	quinta-feira	keeng·taa·*fay*·raa
Friday	sexta-feira	ses·taa·*fay*·raa
Saturday	sábado	saa·baa·doo
Sunday	domingo	do·*meeng*·go

the calendar

o calendário

months

January	janeiro	zha·*nay*·ro
February	fevereiro	fe·ve·*ray*·ro
March	março	marr·so
April	abril	aa·*bree*·oo
May	maio	*maa*·yo
June	junho	zhoo·nyo
July	julho	zhoo·lyo
August	agosto	aa·*gos*·to
September	setembro	se·*teng*·bro
October	outubro	o·*too*·bro
November	novembro	no·*veng*·bro
December	dezembro	de·*zeng*·bro

dates

What date is it today?
Qual é a data de hoje?   kwow e aa *daa*·taa de o·zhe

It's (18 October).
Hoje é dia (dezoito de   o·zhe e *dee*·aa (de·*zoy*·to de
outubro).   o·*too*·bro)

seasons

summer	*verão* m	ve·*rowng*
autumn	*outono* m	o·*to*·no
winter	*inverno* m	een·*verr*·no
spring	*primavera* f	pree·maa·*ve*·raa
... season	*época* f de ...	e·po·kaa de ...
dry	*seca*	*se*·kaa
monsoon	*monção*	mong·*sowng*
wet	*chuvas*	*shoo*·vaas

present

now	*agora*	aa·*go*·raa
this ...		
afternoon	*esta tarde*	es·taa *taarr*·de
morning	*esta manhã*	es·taa ma·*nyang*
month	*este mês*	es·te mes
week	*esta semana*	es·taa se·*ma*·naa
year	*este ano*	es·te *a*·no
today	*hoje*	o·zhe
tonight	*hoje à noite*	o·zhe aa *noy*·te

past

(three days) ago	*(três dias) atrás*	(tres *dee*·aas) aa·*traas*
day before	*antes de*	*ang*·tes de
yesterday	*ontem*	*ong*·teng
yesterday	*ontem*	*ong*·teng
last		
month	*mês passado*	mes paa·*saa*·do
night	*noite passada*	*noy*·te paa·*saa*·daa
week	*semana passada*	se·*ma*·naa paa·*saa*·daa
year	*ano passado*	*a*·no paa·*saa*·do

since (May)	desde (Maio)	des·de (maa·yo)
yesterday ...	ontem ...	ong·teng ...
afternoon	à tarde	aa taarr·de
evening	à noite	aa noy·te
morning	de manhã	de ma·nyang

future

futuro

day after	depois de	de·poys de
tomorrow	amanhã	aa·ma·nyang
in (six days)	daqui a	daa·kee aa
	(seis dias)	(says dee·aas)
tomorrow	amanhã	aa·ma·nyang
next ...	... que vem	... ke veng
month	mês	mes
week	semana	se·ma·naa
year	ano	a·no
tomorrow ...	amanhã ...	aa·ma·nyang ...
afternoon	à tarde	aa taarr·de
evening	à noite	aa noy·te
morning	de manhã	de ma·nyang
until (June)	até (junho)	aa·te (zhoo·nyo)

during the day

durante o dia

afternoon	tarde f	taar·de
day	dia m	dee·aa
evening	noite f	noy·te
midday	meio dia m	may·oo dee·a
midnight	meia noite f	may·aa noy·te
morning	manhã f	ma·nyang
night	noite f	noy·te
sunrise	nascer m do sol	naa·serr do sol
sunset	pôr m do sol	porr do sol

How much is it?
Quanto custa?   kwang·to koos·taa

Can you write down the price?
Você pode escrever o preço?   vo·se po·de es·kre·verr o pre·so

That's too expensive.
Está muito caro.   es·taa mweeng·to kaa·ro

I don't want to pay the full price.
Não quero pagar o   nowng ke·ro paa·gaarr o
preço todo.   pre·so to·do

Do you accept ...?	*Vocês aceitam ...?*	vo·ses aa·suy·tang ...
credit cards	*cartão de crédito*	kaarr·towng de kre·dee·to
debit cards	*saque eletrônico*	sa·kee e·le·tro·nee·ko
travellers cheques	*traveller cheque*	tra·ve·ler she·kee

I'd like to ...	*Gostaria de ...*	gos·taa·ree·aa de ...
cash a cheque	*descontar um cheque*	des·kon·taarr oom she·kee
change a travellers cheque	*trocar traveller cheques*	tro·kaarr traa·ve·ler she·kes
change money	*trocar dinheiro*	tro·kaar dee·nyay·ro
get a cash advance	*fazer um saque adiantado*	fa·zerr oom saa·ke aa·dee·an·taa·do
withdraw money	*retirar dinheiro*	he·tee·raarr dee·nyay·ro

Can I use my credit card to withdraw money?

	Posso usar o meu	*po·so oo·zaarr o me·oo*
	cartão de crédito para	kaar·*towng* de kre·dee·to *paa·*raa
	retirar dinheiro?	he·tee·*raarr* dee·*nyay*·ro

Where's …?	*Onde tem …?*	*ong·*de teng …
an automatic	*um caixa*	oom *kai·*shaa
teller machine	*automático*	ow·to·*maa·*tee·ko
a foreign	*uma loja de*	oo·maa lo·zhaa de
exchange office	*câmbio*	kam·bee·o

What's the …?	*Qual …?*	kwow …
exchange rate	*o câmbio do*	o *kang·*byo do
	dia	dee·aa
charge for	*a taxa*	aa taa·shaa
that	*cobrada*	ko·*braa·*daa

I'd like …, please.	*Gostaria de …*	gos·taa·*ree·*aa …
a refund	*ser*	serr
	reembolsado	he·eng·bol·*saa·*do
my change	*ter o meu troco*	terr o me·oo tro·ko
to return this	*devolver isto*	de·vol·*verr* ees·to

Could I have a …,	*Pode me dar …,*	*po·*de me daarr …
please?	*por favor?*	porr faa·*vorr*
bag	*um saco*	oom *saa·*ko
receipt	*o recibo*	o he·*see·*bo

getting around

andando por aí

Which ... goes to (Niterói)?	Qual o ... que vai para (Niterói)?	kwow o ... ke vai paa·raa (nee·te·roy)
boat	barco	baarr·ko
bus	ônibus	o·nee·boos
plane	avião	aa·vee·owng
train	trem	treng

When's the ... (bus)?	Quando sai o ... (ônibus)?	kwang·do sai o ... (o·nee·boos)
first	primeiro	pree·may·ro
last	último	ool·tee·mo
next	próximo	pro·see·mo

What time does it leave?
A que horas sai? aa ke *aw*·raas sai

What time does it get to (Paraty)?
A que horas chega em (Paraty)? aa ke *aw*·raas she·gaa eng (paa·*raa*·tee)

How long will it be delayed?
Quanto tempo vai atrasar? kwang·to teng·po vai aa·traa·zaarr

Is this seat free?
Este lugar está vago? es·te loo·gaarr es·taa vaa·go

That's my seat.
Este é o meu lugar. es·te e o me·oo loo·gaarr

Please tell me when we get to (Búzios).
Por favor me avise quando chegarmos à (Búzios). porr faa·vor me aa·vee·ze kwang·do she·gaarr·mos aa (boo·zee·os)

Please stop here.
Por favor pare aqui. por faa·*vorr* paa·re aa·*kee*

How long do we stop here?
Quanto tempo ficaremos kwang·to teng·po fee·ka·*re*·mos
parados aqui? paa·*raa*·dos aa·*kee*

tickets

Where do I buy a ticket?
Onde que eu compro a ong·de ke e·oo kong·pro aa
passagem? paa·*sa*·zheng

Do I need to book?
Preciso reservar? pre·*see*·zo he·zer·*vaarr*

A ... ticket (to Petrópolis).	Uma passagem de ... (para Petrópolis).	oo·maa paa·*sa*·zheng de ... (*paa*·raa pe·*tro*·po·lees)
1st-class	primeira classe	pree·*may*·raa klaa·se
2nd-class	segunda classe	se·*goom*·daa klaa·se
child's	criança	kree·*ang*·sa
one-way	ida	ee·daa
return	ida e volta	ee·daa e vol·taa
student's	estudante	es·too·*dang*·te

I'd like a/an ... seat.	Gostaria de um lugar ...	gos·taa·*ree*·aa de oom loo·*gaarr* ...
aisle	no corredor	no ko·he·*dorr*
(non-)smoking	na área de (não) fumantes	na *aa*·re·aa de (nowng) foo·*mang*·tes
window	na janela	naa zhaa·*ne*·laa

Is there (a) ...?	Tem ...?	teng ...
air- conditioning	ar condicionado	aarr kong·dee·syo·*naa*·do
blanket	cobertor	ko·berr·*torr*
toilet	banheiro	ba·*nyay*·ro

I'd like to … my ticket, please.	Gostaria de … minha passagem, por favor.	gos·taa·*ree*·aa de … *mee*·nya paa·*saa*·zheng porr faa·*vor*
cancel	cancelar	kang·se·*laarr*
change	trocar	tro·*kaarr*
confirm	confirmar	kong·feerr·*maarr*

How long does the trip take?

Quanto tempo de viagem?	*kwang*·to *teng*·po de vee·*aa*·zheng

Is it a direct route?

É uma rota direta?	e *oo*·maa *ho*·taa dee·*re*·taa

luggage

bagagem

Where can I find …?	Onde posso encontrar …?	*onq*·de *po*·so eng·kon·*traarr* …
a luggage locker	um guarda volumes	oom *gwaarr*·daa vo·*loo*·mes
a trolley	um carrinho	oom kaa·*hee*·nyo
the baggage counter	o balcão de bagagem	o baal·*kowng* de baa·*gaa*·zheng
the left-luggage office	o balcão de guarda volumes	o baal·*kowng* de *gwaarr*·daa vo·*loo*·mes

My luggage	Minha	mee·nya
has been ...	bagagem foi ...	baa·gaa·zheng foy ...
damaged	danificada	da·nee·fee·kaa·daa
lost	perdida	perr·dee·daa
stolen	roubada	ho·baa·daa

That's (not) mine.
Isto (não) é meu. ees·to (nowng) e me·oo

Can I have some coins/tokens?
Pode me dar umas po·de me daarr oo·maas
moedas/fichas? mo·e·daas/fee·shaas

plane

Where does flight (RG 615) arrive/depart?
De onde sai/chega o vôo de ong·de sai/she·gaa o vo·o
(RG 615)? (e·he ge say·sen·tos e keen·ze)

Where's ...?	Onde fica ...?	ong·de fee·kaa ...
arrivals	portão de	porr·towng de
	chegada	she·gaa·daa
departures	portão de	porr·towng de
	partida	paarr·tee·daa
gate (20)	portão (vinte)	porr·towng (veeng·te)
the airport	o ônibus do	o o·nee·boos do
shuttle	aeroporto	aa·e·ro·porr·to

For phrases about getting through customs, see **border crossing**, page 49.

boat

barco

What's the sea like today?
Como está o mar hoje?   ko·mo es·*taa* o maarr o·zhe

Are there life jackets?
Tem colete salva-vidas?   teng ko·*le*·te sow·vaa·*vee*·daas

What island/beach is this?
Que ilha/praia é esta?   ke ee·*lyaa*/*prai*·aa e es·taa

I feel seasick.
Estou enjoado/   es·to eng·zho·*aa*·do/
enjoada. m/f   eng·zho·*aa*·daa

cabin	*cabine* f	kaa·*bee*·ne
car deck	*deck* m *de carro*	de·kee de *kaa*·ho
captain	*capitão* m	kaa·pee·*towng*
deck	*deck* m	de·kee
ferry	*barca* f	*baarr*·kaa
hammock	*rede* f	he·de
lifeboat	*barco* m	*baarr*·ko
	salva-vidas	sow·vaa·*vee*·daas
life jacket	*colete* m	ko·*le*·te
	salva-vidas	sow·vaa·*vee*·daas
yacht	*iate* m	ee·*aa*·te

bus & coach

How often do buses come?
*Qual a frequência dos
ônibus?*
kwow aa fre·*kweng*·see·aa dos
o·nee·boos

Is this the bus to (Campinas)?
*Este ônibus vai para
(Campinas)?*
es·te o·nee·boos vai *paa*·raa
(kang·*pee*·naas)

Does it stop at (Ilhéus)?
Ele para em (Ilhéus)?
e·le *paa*·raa eng (ee·*lye*·oos)

What's the next stop?
*Qual é a próxima
parada?*
kwow e aa *pro*·see·maa
paa·*raa*·daa

I'd like to get off at (Ipanema).
*Gostaria de saltar
em (Ipanema).*
gos·taa·*ree*·aa de sow·*taarr*
eng (ee·paa·*ne*·maa)

city/local bus	*ônibus* m *local*	o·nee·boos lo·*kow*
intercity bus	*ônibus* m	o·nee·boos
	inter urbano	eeng·terr oorr·*ba*·no

train

What station is this?
Que estação é esta?   ke es·taa·*sowng* e es·taa

What's the next station?
Qual é a próxima   kwow e aa *pro*·see·maa
estação?   es·taa·*sowng*

Does it stop at (Ouro Preto)?
Ele pára em (Ouro Preto)?   e·le *paa*·raa enq (o·ro *pre*·to)

Do I need to change?
Preciso trocar de trem?   pre·*see*·so tro·*kaarr* de treng

Is it direct/express?
É direto/rápido?   e dee·*re*·to/*haa*·pee·do

Which carriage is ...?	*Qual o vagão ...?*	kwow o vaa·*gowng* ...
1st class	*de primeira classe*	de pree·*may*·raa *klaa*·se
for (Sabará)	*para (Sabará)*	*paa*·raa (saa·baa·*raa*)

taxi

I'd like a taxi ...	*Gostaria de marcar um táxi ...*	gos·taa·*ree*·aa de maarr·*kaarr* oom *taak*·see ...
at (9am)	*para as (nove da manhã)*	*paa*·raa aas (*naw*·ve daa ma·*nyang*)
now	*agora*	aa·*go*·raa
tomorrow	*amanhã*	aa·ma·*nyang*

Where's the taxi rank?
Onde fica a fila de   ong·de *fee*·kaa aa *fee*·laa de
táxi?   *taak*·see

Is this taxi free?
Este táxi está livre?   es·te *taak*·see es·*taa lee*·vre

Please put the meter on.
Por favor ligue o taxímetro.
porr fa·*vorr* lee·ge o taak·*see*·me·tro

How much is it to …?
Quanto custa até …?
kwang·to koos·taa aa·*te* …

Please take me to (this address).
Me leve para este endereço por favor.
me le·ve paa·raa es·te eng·de·*re*·so porr faa·*vorr*

Please …	*Por favor …*	porr faa·*vorr* …
slow down	*vai mais devagar*	vai *mais* de·vaa·*gaarr*
stop here	*pare aqui*	paa·re aa·*kee*
wait here	*espere aqui*	es·pe·re aa·*kee*

car & motorbike

carro & motocicleta

hire

I'd like to hire a/an …	*Gostaria de alugar …*	gos·taa·*ree*·aa de aa·loo·*gaarr* …
4WD	*um carro quatro por quatro*	oom *kaa*·ho *kwaa*·tro porr *kwaa*·tro
automatic	*um automático*	oom ow·to·*maa*·tee·ko
car	*um carro*	oom *kaa*·ho
manual	*um manual*	oom ma·noo·*ow*
motorbike	*uma motocicleta*	*oo*·ma mo·to·see·*kle*·taa
with …	*com …*	kong …
a driver	*motorista*	mo·to·*rees*·taa
air-conditioning	*ar condicionado*	aarr kong·dee·syo·*naa*·do

PRACTICAL

44

kaar·*tay*·raa de	*carteira de*	**drivers**
mo·to·*rees*·taa	*motorista*	**licence**
kee·*lo*·me·tros	*kilômetros*	**kilometres**
lee·vre	*livre*	**free**
paarr·*kee*·me·tro	*parquímetro*	**parking meter**

How much for daily/weekly hire?
Quanto custa para
alugar por dia/
semana?

kwang·to *koos*·taa *paa*·raa
aa·loo·*gaarr* porr *dee*·aa/
se·*ma*·naa

Does that include insurance/mileage?
Inclui seguro e
kilometragem?

eeng·*kloo*·ee se·*goo*·ro e
kee·lo·me·*traa*·zheng

Do you have a guide to the road rules in English?
Você teria um guia
de ruas em inglês?

vo·*se* te·*ree*·aa oom *gee*·aa
de *hoo*·aas eng eeng·*gles*

Do you have a road map?
Você teria um mapa
de ruas?

vo·*se* te·*ree*·aa oom *maa* paa
de *hoo*·aas

on the road

Is this the road to (Salvador)?
Esta é a estrada
para (Salvador)?

es·*taa* e aa es·*traa*·daa
paa·raa (sow·*vaa*·dorr)

Where's a petrol station?
Onde tem um posto de
gasolina?

ong·de teng oom *pos*·to de
gaa·zo·*lee*·naa

Please fill it up.
Enche o tanque, por favor.   *eng*·she o *tang*·ke porr *faa*·*vorr*

I'd like (30) litres.
Coloque (trinta) litros.   ko·*lo*·ke (*treen*·ta) *lee*·tros

diesel	*diesel* m	*dee*·sel
LPG	*gás* m	gas
unleaded	*gasolina* f *comum*	gaa·zo·*lee*·naa ko·*moong*

Can you check the ...?	Pode checar ...?	po·de she·kaarr ...
oil	o óleo	o o·lyo
tyre pressure	os pneus	os pee·ne·oos
water	a água	aa aa·gwaa

What's the speed limit?

Qual o limite de velocidade? — kwow o lee·mee·te de ve·lo·see·daa·de

(How long) Can I park here?

(Quanto tempo) Posso estacionar aqui? — (kwang·to teng·po) po·so es·taa·syo·naarr aa·kee

Do I have to pay?

Tem que pagar? — teng ke paa·gaarr

signs

Entrada	eng·traa·daa	Entrance
Estrada dê Preferência	es·traa·daa de pre·fe·reng·syaa	Give Way
Mão Única	mowng oo·nee·kaa	One-way
Pare	paa·re	Stop
Pedágio	pe·daa·zhyo	Toll
Proibido Entrar	pro·ee·bee·do eng·traarr	No Entry
Rua Sem Saída	hoo·aa seng saa·ee·daa	No Through Road
Saída	saa·ee·daa	Exit (freeway)

problems

The car has broken down (at Manaus).

O carro quebrou (em Manaus). — o kaa·ho ke·bro (eng maa·nows)

The motorbike won't start.

A motocicleta nâo está pegando. — a mo·to·se·kle·taa nowng es·ta pe·gang·do

I need a mechanic.

Preciso de um mecânico. — pre·see·so de oom me·ka·nee·ko

I've had an accident.
  Sofri um acidente.   so·*free* oom aa·see·*deng*·te

I have a flat tyre.
  Meu pneu furou.   me·oo pee·*ne*·oo foo·*ro*

I've lost my car keys.
  Perdi a chave do carro.   perr·*dee* a *shaa*·ve do *kaa*·ho

I've locked the keys inside.
  Tranquei a chave dentro   trang·*kay* aa *sha*·ve *deng*·tro
  do carro.   do *kaa*·ho

I've run out of petrol.
  Estou sem gasolina.   es·*to* seng gaa·zo·*lee*·naa

Can you fix it (today)?
  Você pode consertar   vo·*se po*·de kong·serr·*taarr*
  (hoje)?   (o·zhe)

How long will it take?
  Quanto tempo vai levar?   kwang·to *teng*·po vai le·*vaarr*

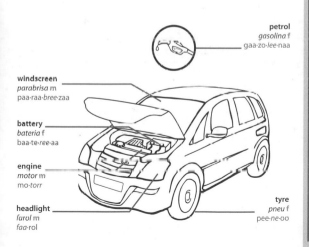

petrol
gasolina f
gaa·zo·*lee*·naa

windscreen
parabrisa m
paa·raa·*bree*·zaa

battery
bateria f
baa·te·*ree*·aa

engine
motor m
mo·*torr*

headlight
farol m
faa·*rol*

tyre
pneu f
pee·*ne*·oo

bicycle

I'd like ...	Queria ...	ke·*ree*·aa ...
my bicycle repaired	consertar a minha bicicleta	kong·serr·*taarr* a *mee*·nyaa bee·see·*kle*·taa
to buy a bicycle	comprar uma bicicleta	kong·*praarr* oo·maa bee·see·*kle*·taa
to hire a bicycle	alugar uma bicicleta	aa·loo·*gaarr* oo·maa bee·see·*kle*·taa

I'd like a ... bike.	Queria uma bicicleta ...	ke·*ree*·aa oo·maa bee·see·*kle*·taa ...
mountain	de montanha	de mong·*ta*·nya
racing	de corrida	de ko·*hee*·daa
second-hand	de segunda mão	de se·*goong*·daa mowng

How much is it per ...?	Quanto custa por ...?	*kwang*·to koos·taa porr ...
day	dia	*dee*·aa
hour	hora	*aw*·raa

Do I need a helmet?
Preciso usar capacete?
pre·*see*·so oo·*zaarr* kaa·paa·*se*·te

Is there a bicycle-path map?
Existe algum mapa de rotas para bicicleta?
e·*zees*·te ow·*goom* maa·paa de ho·taas paa·raa bee·see·*kle*·taa

I have a puncture.
Furou o pneu.
foo·*ro* o pee·*ne*·oo

I'm …	*Estou …*	es·to …
in transit	*em trânsito*	eng *trang·*zee·to
on business	*à negócios*	aa ne·*go·*syos
on holiday	*à turismo*	aa too·*rees·*mo

I'm here for …	*Vou ficar por …*	vo fee·*kaarr* porr …
(10) days	*(dez) dias*	(dez) *dee·*aas
(two) months	*(dols) meses*	(doys) *me·*ses
(three) weeks	*(três) semanas*	(tres) se·*ma·*naas

I'm going to (Recife).
Estou indo para (Recife)   es·to *eeng·*do paa·raa (he·*see·*fe)

I'm staying at the (Ipanema Hotel).
Estou no (Hotel Ipanema).   es·to no (o·*tel* ee·pa·*nee·*maa)

The children are on this passport.
As crianças estão neste passaporte.   aas kree·*ang·*saas es·*towng* *nes·*te paa·saa·*porr·*te

I have nothing to declare.
 Não tenho nada a declarar.   nowng *te*·nyo *naa*·daa aa de·klaa·*raarr*

I have something to declare.
 Tenho algo a declarar.   *te*·nyo *ow*·go aa de·klaa·*rarr*

Do I have to declare this?
 Preciso declarar isto?   pre·*see*·so de·klaa·*raarr* ees·to

That's (not) mine.
 Isto (não) é meu.   ees·to (nowng) e me·oo

I didn't know I had to declare it.
 Não sabia que tinha que declarar isto.   nowng saa·*bee*·aa ke *tee*·nyaa ke de·klaa·*raarr* ees·to

signs		
Alfândega	aal·*fang*·de·gaa	**Customs**
Controle de	kong·*tro*·le de	**Passport**
Passaporte	paa·sa·*porr*·te	**Control**
Free-shop	free·shop	**Duty-free**
Imigração	ee·mee·graa·*sowng*	**Immigration**
Quarentena	kwaa·reng·*te*·naa	**Quarantine**

Where's ...?	Onde fica ...?	ong·de fee·kaa ...
a bank	o banco	o bang·ko
a market	o mercado	o merr·kaa·do
the tourist	a secretaria	aa se·kre·taa·ree·aa
office	de turismo	de too·rees·mo

Can you show me (on the map)?
Você poderia me — vo·se po·de·ree·aa me
mostrar (no mapa)? — mos·traarr (no maa·paa)

What's the address?
Qual é o endereço? — kwow e o eng·de·re·so

How far is it?
Qual a distância — kwow aa dees·tang·syaa
daqui? — daa·kee

How do I get there?
Como é que eu chego lá? — ko·mo e ke e·oo she·go laa

It's ...	Fica ...	fee·kaa ...
behind ...	atrás ...	aa·traaz ...
close	perto	perr·to
here	aqui	a·kee
in front of ...	na frente de ...	naa freng·te de ...
near ...	perto ...	perr·to ...
next to ...	ao lado de ...	ow laa·do de ...
on the corner	na esquina	na es·kee·naa
opposite ...	do lado oposto ...	do laa·do o·pos·to ...
straight ahead	em frente	eng freng·te
there	lá	laa

north	norte	norr·te
south	sul	sool
east	leste	les·te
west	oeste	o·es·te

by bus	de ônibus	de o·nee·boos
by taxi	de táxi	de taak·see
by train	de trem	de treng
on foot	a pé	aa pe

Turn ...	Vire ...	vee·re ...
at the corner	à esquina	aa es·kee·naa
at the	no sinal de	no see·now de
traffic lights	trânsito	trang·zee·to
left	à esquerda	aa es·kerr·daa
right	à direita	aa dee·ray·taa

What ... is this?	Que ...?	ke ...
avenue	avenida	aa·ve·nee·daa
	é esta	e es·taa
lane	travessa é esta	traa·ve·saa e es·taa
street	rua é esta	hoo·aa e es·taa
village	vilarejo	vee·laa·re·zho
	é este	e es·te

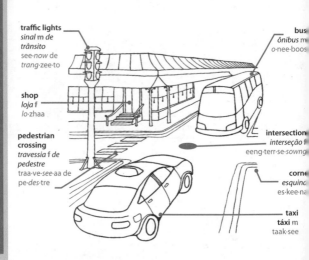

traffic lights
sinal m *de trânsito*
see·*now* de *trang*·zee·to

shop
loja f
lo·zhaa

pedestrian crossing
travessia f *de pedestre*
traa·ve·*see*·aa de pe·*des*·tre

bus
ônibus m
o·nee·boos

intersection
interseção f
eeng·terr·se·sowng

corner
esquina
es·kee·na

taxi
táxi m
taak·see

finding accommodation

buscando hospedagem

Where's a …?	*Onde tem …?*	ong·de teng …
bed and breakfast	*uma pensão*	oo·maa peng·*sowng*
camping ground	*um local para acampamento*	oom lo·*kow paa*·raa aa·kang·paa·*meng*·to
guesthouse	*uma hospedaria*	*oo·*maa os·pe·daa·*ree*·a
hotel	*um hotel*	oom o·*tel*
room	*um quarto*	oom *kwaarr*·to
youth hostel	*um albergue da juventude*	oom ow·*berr*·ge daa zhoo·veng·*too·*de

Can you recommend somewhere …?	*Você pode recomendar algum lugar …?*	vo·se po·de he·ko·meng·daarr ow·*goom* loo·gaarr …
cheap	*barato*	baa·*raa*·to
good	*bom*	bong
luxurious	*de luxo*	de *loo·*sho
nearby	*perto daqui*	perr·to daa·*kee*
romantic	*romântico*	ho·mang·tee·ko

What's the address?
Qual é o endereço?   kwow e o en·de·*re*·so

For responses, see **directions**, page 51.

booking ahead & checking in

Do you have a … room?	*Tem um quarto de …?*	teng oom *kwaarr*·to de …
double	*casal*	kaa·*zow*
single	*solteiro*	sol·*tay*·ro
twin	*duplo*	*doo*·plo

How much is it per …?	*Quanto custa por …?*	*kwang*·to *koos*·taa porr …
night	*noite*	*noy*·te
person	*pessoa*	pe·*so*·aa
week	*semana*	se·*ma*·naa

I'd like to book a room, please.
Eu gostaria de fazer
uma reserva, por favor.
e·oo gos·taa·*ree*·aa de faa·*zerr*
oo·maa he·*zer*·vaa porr faa·*vorr*

I have a reservation.
Eu tenho uma reserva.
e·oo te·nyo oo·maa he·*zerr*·vaa

My name's …
Meu nome é …
me·oo *no*·me e …

For (three) nights/weeks.
Para (três) noites/
semanas.
paa·raa (tres) *noy*·tes/
se·*ma*·naas

From (July 2) to (July 6).
De (dois de julho) até
(seis de julho).
de (doys de *zhoo*·lyo) aa·*te*
(says de *zhoo*·lyo)

Can I see it?
Posso ver?
po·so verr

I'll take it.
Eu fico com ele.
e·oo *fee*·ko kong e·lee

signs

Banheiro	ba·*nyay*·ro	**Bathroom/ Toilet**
Não Tem Vaga	nowng teng *vaa*·gaa	**No Vacancy**
Tem Vaga	teng *vaa*·gaa	**Vacancy**

Do I need to pay upfront?

Tem que pagar		teng ke paa·*gaarr*
adiantado?		aa·dee·ang·*taa*·do

Can I pay …?   *Posso pagar*   po·so paa·*gaarr*
               com …?   kong …

by credit	*cartão de*	kaarr·*towng* de
card	*crédito*	kre·dee·to
by travellers	*travellers cheque*	tra·ve·lers she·kee
cheque		
in (US)	*dólar*	do·laarr
dollars	*(americano)*	(aa·me·ree·ka·no)

For other methods of payment, see **money**, page 35.

For other methods of payment, see **money**, page 35.

listen for …		
paa·raa kwang·taas noy·tes	*Para quantas noites?*	**How many nights?**
he·se·pee·sowng	*recepção*	**reception**
paa·saa·porr·te	*passaporte*	**passport**
shaa·ve	*chave*	**key**
shay·o	*cheio*	**full**

requests & queries

When/Where is breakfast served?

Onde/Quando é servido	ong·de/kwang·do e serr·*vee*·do
o café da manhã?	o kaa·fe daa ma·*nyang*

Please wake me at (seven).

Por favor me acorde	porr faa·vor me aa·kor·de
às (sete).	aas (se·te)

Can I use the …?   *Posso usar …?*   po·so oo·*zaarr* …

kitchen	*a cozinha*	aa ko·*zee*·nyaa
laundry	*a lavanderia*	aa laa·vang·de·*ree*·aa
telephone	*o telefone*	o te·le·*fo*·ne

Do you have a/an ...?	Tem ...?	teng ...
elevator	elevador	e·le·vaa·dorr
laundry service	serviço de lavanderia	serr·vee·so de laa·vang·de·ree·aa
message board	quadro de recados	kwaa·dro de he·kaa·dos
safe	cofre	ko·fre
swimming pool	piscina	pee·see·na

Do you ... here?	Vocês ...?	vo·ses ...
arrange tours	organizam passeios	orr·ga·nee·zang paa·say·os
change money	trocam dinheiro	tro·kang dee·nyay·ro

Could I have ..., please?	Pode me dar ..., por favor?	po·de me daarr ... porr faa·vorr
a mosquito net	um mosquiteiro	oom mos·kee·tay·ro
a receipt	um recibo	oom he·see·bo
an extra blanket	um outro cobertor	oom o·tro ko·berr·torr
my key	minha chave	mee·nyaa shaa·ve

local talk

dive	porcaria f	porr·kaa·ree·aa
rat-infested	infestado de rato	eeng·fes·taa·do de haa·to
top spot	ótimo lugar m	o·tee·mo loo·gaarr

Is there a message for me?

Tem recado para mim?   teng he·kaa·do paa·raa meeng

Can I leave a message for someone?

Posso deixar um   po·so day·shaarr oom
recado para alguém?   he·kaa·do paa·raa ow·geng

I'm locked out of my room.

Fiquei preso/presa fora   fee·kay pre·so/pre·saa fo·raa
do quarto. m/f   do kwaarr·to

complaints

It's too ...	É muito ...	e mweeng·to ...
bright	*claro*	klaa·ro
cold	*frio*	free·o
dark	*escuro*	es·koo·ro
expensive	*caro*	kaa·ro
noisy	*barulhento*	baa·roo·lyeng·to
small	*pequeno*	pe·ke·no

This (pillow) isn't clean.
Este (travesseiro) está   es·te (traa·ve·say·ro) es·taa
sujo.   soo·zho

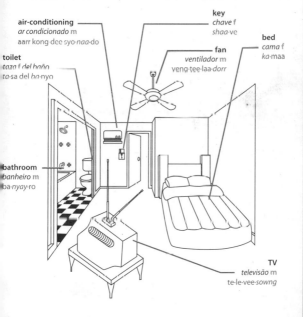

air-conditioning
ar condicionado m
aarr kong dee syo·naa·do

key
chave f
shaa·ve

fan
ventilador m
veng·tee·laa·dorr

bed
cama f
ka·maa

toilet
taza f *del baño*
ta·sa del ba·nyo

bathroom
banheiro m
ba·nyay·ro

TV
televisão m
te·le·vee·sowng

The ... doesn't work.	O ... não está funcionando.	o ... nowng es·*taa* foong·syo·*nang*·do
air-conditioning	*ar condicionado*	aarr kong·dee·syo·*naa*·do
fan	*ventilador*	veng·tee·laa·*dorr*
toilet	*banheiro*	ba·*nyay*·ro

Who is it?
Quem é?   keng e

Just a moment.
Um minutinho.   oom mee·noo·*tee*·nyo

Come in.
Pode entrar.   po·de eng·*traarr*

Come back later, please.
Volte mais tarde, por favor.   *vol*·te mais *taarr*·de porr faa·*vorr*

checking out

fazendo o check out

What time is checkout?
A que horas é o check out?   aa ke *aw*·raas e o shek owt

Can I have a late checkout?
Posso fazer o check out mais tarde?   po·so faa·*zerr* o shek owt mais *taar*·de

Can you call a taxi for me (for 11 o'clock)?
Pode chamar um taxi para mim (para às onze horas)?   po·de shaa·*maarr* oom *taak*·see *paa*·ra meeng (*paa*·raa aas *ong*·ze *aw*·raas)

I'm leaving now.
Estou indo embora
agora.

es·to eeng·do eng·bo·raa
aa·go·raa

Can I leave my bags here?
Posso deixar minhas
malas aqui?

po·so day·shaarr mee·nyaas
maa·laas aa·kee

There's a mistake in the bill.
Houve um erro na conta.

o·ve oom e·ho naa kong·taa

I'll be back ...
  in (three) days
  on (Tuesday)

Estarei de volta ...
  em (três) dias
  na (terça-feira)

es·taa·ray de vol·taa ...
  eng (tres) dee·aas
  naa (terr·saa·fay·raa)

Could I have
my ..., please?
  deposit

  passport

  valuables

Pode devolver ...,
por favor?
  o meu
  depósito
  o meu
  passaporte
  os meus
  objetos de
  valor

po·de de·vol·verr ...
por faa·vorr
  o me·oo
  de·po·zee·to
  o me·oo
  paa·saa·porr·te
  os me·oos
  o·bee·zhe·tos de
  vaa·lorr

I had a great stay, thank you.
Foi ótima a estadia,
obrigado/obrigada. m/f

foy o·tee·ma aa es·taa·dee·aa
o·bree·gaa·do/o·bree·gaa·daa

I'll recommend it to my friends.
Vou recomendar aos
meus amigos.

vo he·ko·meng·daarr ows
me·oos aa·mee·gos

camping

Do you have …?	Tem …?	teng …
a laundry	uma lavanderia	oo·maa laa·vang·de·ree·aa
a site	um lugar	oom loo·gaarr
electricity	eletricidade	e·le·tree·see·daa·de
shower facilities	chuveiro	shoo·vay·ro
tents for hire	barracas para alugar	baa·haa·kaas paa·raa aa·loo·gaarr

How much is it per …?	Quanto custa por …?	kwang·to koos·taa porr …
person	pessoa	pe·so·aa
tent	barraca	baa·haa·kaa
vehicle	veículo	ve·ee·koo·lo

Can I …?	Posso …?	po·so …
camp here	acampar aqui	aa·kang·paarr aa·kee
park next to my tent	estacionar ao lado da minha barraca?	es·taa·see·o·naarr ow laa·do daa mee·nyaa baa·haa·kaa

Who do I ask to stay here?
    A quem eu peço para ficar aqui?   aa keng e·oo pe·so paa·raa fee·kaarr aa·kee

Is the water drinkable?
    A água é potável?   a aa·gwaa e po·taa·vel

Is it coin-operated?
    Isto funciona com moedas?   ees·to foong·syo·naa kong mo·e·daas

Could I borrow (a mallet)?
    Posso pegar (um isqueiro) emprestado?   po·so pe·gaarr (oom ees·kay·ro) eng·pres·taa·do

renting

I'm here about the … for rent.

Estou aqui por causa do …	es·*to* aa·*kee* porr *kow*·zaa do …
para alugar.	*paa*·raa aa·loo·*gaarr*

Do you have a/an … for rent?

Você tem … para	vo·*se* teng … *paa*·raa
alugar?	aa·loo·*gaarr*

apartment	*apartamento* m	aa·paarr·taa·*meng*·to
cabin	*cabine* f	kaa·*bee*·ne
house	*casa* f	*kaa*·zaa
room	*quarto* m	*kwaarr*·to
(partly)	*(parcialmente)*	(paarr·see·ow·*meng*·te)
furnished	*mobiliado/*	mo·bee·*lyaa*·do/
	mobiliada m/f	mo·bee·*lyaa*·daa
unfurnished	*sem mobília*	seng mo·*bee*·lyaa

---

tongue torture

Tongue twisters are very popular in Brazil, and they're not a bad way to get your mouth around a new language. Try these for a bit of r practice:

O rato roeu a roupa do rei de Roma.
o *haa*·to ro·e·oo aa *ho*·paa do re de *ro*·maa
(The rat chewed the clothes of the king of Rome.)

Três pratos de trigo para três tigres tristes.
tres *praa*·tos de *tree*·go *puu*·raa tres *tee*·gres *trees*·tes
(Three plates of wheat for three sad tigers.)

staying with locals

Can I stay at your place?
Posso ficar na sua
casa?
po·so fee·*kaarr* naa *soo*·aa
kaa·zaa

Is there anything I can do to help?
Posso ajudar em
alguma coisa?
po·so aa·zhoo·*daarr* eng
ow·*goo*·maa *koy*·zaa

I have my own ...	Tenho o meu próprio ...	*te*·nyo o *me*·oo *pro*·pree·o ...
mattress	colchão	kol·*showng*
sleeping bag	saco de dormir	*saa*·ko de dorr·*meerr*

Can I ...?	Posso ...?	po·so ...
bring anything for the meal	trazer alguma coisa para a refeição	traa·*zerr* ow·*goo*·maa *koy*·zaa *paa*·raa aa he·fay·*sowng*
do the dishes	lavar a louça	laa·*varr* aa *lo*·saa
set/clear the table	arrumar/ limpar a mesa	aa·hoo·*maarr*/ leeng·*paarr* aa *me*·zaa
take out the rubbish	jogar o lixo fora	zho·*gaarr* o *lee*·sho *foo*·raa

Thanks for your hospitality.
Obrigado/Obrigada
pela hospitalidade. m/f
o·bree·*gaa*·do/o·bree·*gaa*·daa
pe·laa os·pee·taa·lee·*daa*·de

For dining-related expressions, see **eating out**, page 141.

looking for ...

procurando por ...

Where's ...?	*Onde fica ...?*	ong·de fee·kaa ...
a bookshop	*a livraria*	aa lee·vraa·ree·aa
a department store	*a loja de departamentos*	aa lo·zhaa de de·paarr·taa meng·tos
a supermarket	*o supermercado*	o soo·perr·merr·kaa·do

Where can I buy (a padlock)?
Onde posso comprar (um cadeado)?
ong·de po·so kong·praarr (oom kaa·de·aa·do)

For more shops, see the **dictionary** and for phrases on asking and giving directions, see **directions**, page 51.

making a purchase

fazendo compras

I'd like to buy (an adaptor plug).
Gostaria de comprar (um adaptador).
gos·taa·ree·aa de kong·praarr (oom aa·daa·pee·taa·dorr)

How much is it?
Quanto custa?
kwang·to koos·taa

Can you write down the price?
Você pode escrever o preço?
vo·se po·de es·kre·verr o pre·so

Do you have any others?
Você tem outros?
vo·se teng o·tros

Can I look at It?
Posso ver?
po·so verr

I'm just looking.
Estou só olhando.
es·to so o·lyang·do

Do you accept ...?	Vocês aceitam ...?	vo·ses aa·say·tang ...
credit cards	cartão de crédito	kaarr·towng de kre·dee·to
debit cards	saque eletrônico	sa·kee e·le·tro·nee·ko
travellers cheques	traveller cheque	tra·ve·ler she·kee

Could I have a ..., please?	Pode me dar um ..., por favor?	po·de me daarr oom ... porr faa·vorr
bag	saco	saa·ko
receipt	recibo	he·see·bo

Could I have it wrapped?
Pode embrulhar? — po·de eng·broo·lyaarr

Does it have a guarantee?
Tem garantia? — teng gaa·rang·tee·aa

Can I have it sent overseas?
Vocês podem enviar parao exterior? — vo·ses po·deng eng·vee·aarr paa·raa o es·te·ree·orr

Can you order it for me?
Pode fazer o pedido para mim? — po·de faa·zerr o pe·dee·do paa·raa meeng

Can I pick it up later?
Posso pegar mais tarde? · — po·so pe·gaarr mais taarr·de

It's faulty.
Está com defeito. — es·taa kong de·fay·to

I'd like ..., please.	Gostaria de ...	gos·taa·ree·aa de ...
a refund	ser reembolsado	serr he·eng·bol·saa·do
my change	ter o meu troco	terr o me·oo tro·ko
to return this	devolver isto	de·vol·verr ees·to

bargaining

That's too expensive.
Está muito caro.　　　　　　es·taa mweeng·to kaa·ro

Can you lower the price?
Pode baixar o preço?　　　　po·de bai·shaarr o pre·so

I don't want to pay the full price.
Não quero pagar o　　　　　nowng ke·ro paa·gaarr o
preço todo.　　　　　　　　pre·so to·do

Do you have something cheaper?
Tem uma coisa mais　　　　teng oo·maa koy·zaa mais
barata?　　　　　　　　　　baa·raa·taa

I'll give you (five reals).
Dou (cinco reais).　　　　　do (seeng·ko he·ais)

local talk		
bargain	*pechincha* f	pe·sheeng·shaa
rip-off	*roubo* m	ho·bo
sale	*liquidação* f	lee·kee·daa sowng
specials	*preço* m	pre·so
	especial	es·pe·see·ow

clothes

Can I try it on?
Posso experimentar?　　　　po·so es·pe·ree·meng·taarr

My size is (14).
Meu número é (quatorze).　　me·oo noo·me·ro e (kaa·torr·ze)

It doesn't fit.
Não cabe.　　　　　　　　　nowng kaa·be

For clothing items, see the **dictionary**.

repairs

Can I have my (backpack) repaired here?
Vocês consertam a   vo·*ses* kong·*serr*·tang aa
(mochila)?   (mo·*shee*·laa)

When will my ... be ready?	*Quando ...?*	*kwang*·do ...
camera	*fica pronta a câmera*	*fee*·kaa *prong*·taa aa *ka*·me·raa
(sun)glasses	*ficam prontos os óculos (de sol)*	*fee*·kang *prong*·tos os *o*·koo·los (de sol)
shoes	*fica pronto o sapato*	*fee*·kaa *prong*·to o saa·*paa*·to

darn holes

buttons	*botões* m pl	bo·*toyngs*
needle	*agulha* f	aa·*goo*·lyaa
scissors	*tesoura* f	te·*zo*·raa
thread	*linha* f	*lee*·nya

hairdressing

I'd like (a) ...	*Gostaria de ...*	gos·taa·*ree*·aa de ...
blow wave	*secar*	se·*kaarr*
colour	*pintar*	peeng·*taarr*
haircut	*cortar*	korr·*taarr*
my beard trimmed	*aparar a barba*	aa·paa·*raarr* aa *baarr*·baa
shave	*fazer a barba*	faa·*zerr* aa *baarr*·baa
trim	*aparar*	aa·paa·*raarr*

Don't cut it too short.
Não corta muito.   nowng *korr*·taa *mweeng*·to

Shave it all off!
Raspa tudo!   *haas*·paa *too*·do

Please use a new blade.
Por favor use uma   por fa·*vorr* oo·ze oo·maa
gilete nova.   zhee·*le*·te *no*·vaa

I should never have let you near me!
Não deveria nunca   nowng de·ve·*ree*·aa *noong*·kaa
ter deixado você   terr day·*shaa*·do vo·*se*
chegar perto de mim!   she·*gaarr* perr·to de meeng

For colours, see the **dictionary**.

books & reading

livros e leitura

Do you have …?	*Tem …?*	teng …
a book by	*algum livro*	ow·*goom* lee·vro
(Jorge	*do (Jorge*	do (*zhorzh*
Amado)	*Amado)*	aa·*maa*·do)
an entertain-	*um guia de*	oom *gee*·aa de
ment guide	*entretenimento*	eng·tre·te·nee·*meng*·to

---

listen for …

mais ow·*goo*·maa *koy*·zaa
Mais alguma coisa?   **Anything else?**

nowng nowng *te*·mos
Não, não temos.   **No, we don't have any.**

po·so aa·zhoo·*daarr*
Posso ajudar?   **Can I help you?**

I'd like a …	Gostaria de comprar um …	gos·taa·*ree*·aa de kong·*praarr* oom …
dictionary	dicionário	dee·see·o·*naa*·ryo
newspaper	jornal	zhorr·*now*
(in English)	(em inglês)	(eng eeng·*gles*)
notepad	bloco de notas	*blo*·ko de *no*·taas

Is there an English-language …?	Tem uma … de língua inglesa?	teng oo·maa … de leeng·gwaa eeng·*gle*·saa
bookshop	livraria	lee·vraa·*ree*·aa
section	seção	se·*sowng*

Can you recommend a book for me?

Você poderia me recomendar algum livro?

vo·*se* po·de·*ree*·aa me he·ko·meng·*daarr* ow·*goom* lee·vro

Do you have Lonely Planet guidebooks?

Vocês tem os guias de viagem do Lonely Planet?

vo·*ses* teng os *gee*·aas de vee·*aa*·zheng do *lo*·ne·lee *pla*·ne·tee

music

I'd like a …	Gostaria de comprar …	gos·taa·*ree*·aa de kong·*praarr* …
blank tape	uma fita virgem	oo·maa *fee*·taa veerr·zheng
CD	um CD	oom se·*de*

I'm looking for something by (Caetano Veloso).

Estou procurando por alguma coisa (do Caetano Veloso).

es·*to* pro·koo·*rang*·do porr ow·*goo*·maa *koy*·zaa (do kaa·e·*ta*·no ve·*lo*·zo)

What's his/her best recording?

Qual é o melhor disco dele/dela? m/f

kwow e o me·*lyorr* *dees*·ko de·le/de·laa

Can I listen to this?

Posso escutar?

po·so es·koo·*taarr*

Souvenir hunters will find music, local crafts and musical instruments worthy mementos of their trip. Artisan fairs (*feira de artesanato*) are common weekend events in larger cities and offer a good range of souvenirs.

regional souvenirs

Is there a souvenir typical of this region?

Tem algum lenbrança   teng al·*goom* leng·*braan*·sa
específico desta   es·pe·see·*fee*·ko *des*·ta
região ?   re·*zhowng*

artesanato indígena – Indian handicrafts, including wooden and woven items
artigos de couro – leather goods
bikini fio dental – 'dental floss' bikini – the original string bikini. The name says it all.
jóia – jewellery
pedras preciosas – gemstones
rede – cotton hammocks, usually dyed in bright colours

musical instruments

The instruments that feature in traditional Brazilian music make great souvenirs.

berimbau – a stringed instrument commonly used in *capoeira* performances. It consists of a bow with metal string attached to a dried gourd which acts as a resonating chamber. A rod and a ring or coin is struck against the string to produce sound.

pandeiro – originally from East Africa, the tambourine is considered an essential part of Brazilian rhythm and is common throughout the country

reco-reco – a grooved piece of bamboo or iron also used in *capoeira*. A rod is scraped against the grooves to produce the rasping sound.

photography

I need ... film for this camera.	Preciso de filme ... para esta câmera.	pre·see·zo de feel·me ... paa·raa es·taa ka·me·raa
APS	sistema APS	sees·te·maa aa pe e·se
B&W	Preto e Branco	pre·to e brang·ko
colour	colorido	ko·lo·ree·do
slide	de slide	de ees·lai·de
(200) speed	(duzentos) velocidade	(doo·zeng·tos) ve·lo·see·daa·de

Can you ...?	Você pode ...?	vo·se po·de ...
develop this film	revelar este filme	he·ve·laarr es·te feel·me
load my film	colocar o filme	ko·lo·kaarr o feel·me

I need a passport photo taken.
  Preciso tirar foto para passporte. pre·see·zo tee·raarr fo·to paa·raa paa·saa·porr·te

When will it be ready?
  Quando fica pronto? kwang·do fee·kaa prong·to

How much is it?
  Quanto custa? kwang·to koos·taa

I'm not happy with these photos.
  Não gostei destas fotos. nowng gos·tay des·taas fo·tos

post office

I want to send a ...	*Quero enviar ...*	*ke*·ro eng·*vee*·aarr ...
fax	*um fax*	oom faks
letter	*uma carta*	*oo*·maa *kaarr*·taa
parcel	*uma*	*oo*·maa
	encomenda	eng·ko·*meng*·daa
postcard	*um cartão*	oom kaarr·*towng*
	postal	pos·*tow*
I want to buy ...	*Quero comprar ...*	*ke*·ro kong·*praarr* ...
an aerogram	*um aerograma*	oom aa·e·ro·*gra*·maa
an envelope	*um envelope*	oom eng·ve·*lo*·pe
stamps	*selos*	*se*·los

airmail	*via aéreo/*	*vee*·aa aa·*e*·re·o/
	aérea m/f	aa·*e*·re·aa
customs	*declaração* f	de·klaa·raa·*sowng*
declaration	*da alfândega*	daa aal·*fang*·de·gaa
domestic	*doméstico*	do·*mes*·tee·ko
express	*rápido/*	*haa*·pee·do/
	rápida m/f	*haa*·pee·daa
fragile	*frágil*	*fraa*·zheel
international	*internacional*	eeng·ter·naa·syo·now
mail	*correspondência* f	ko·hes·pong·*deng*·syaa
mailbox	*caixa* f *postal*	*kai*·sha pos·*tow*
postcode	*CEP* m	*se*·pee
registered	*registrado/*	he·zhees·*traa*·do/
	registrada m/f	he·zhees·*traa*·daa
surface mail	*via terrestre*	*vee*·aa te·*hes*·tre

Please send it by air/surface mail to (Australia).
Por favor envie via aérea/terrestre para a (Austrália).
porr faa·*vorr* eng·*vee*·e *vee*·aa aa·e·re·aa/te·*hes*·tre *paa*·raa aa (ows·*traa*·lya)

It contains (souvenirs).
Contém (souvenirs).
kong·*teng* (soo·ve·*neers*)

Where's the poste restante section?
Onde fica a seção de Poste Restante?
ong·de *fee*·kaa a se·*sowng* de *pos*·te hes·*tang*·te

Is there any mail for me?
Tem alguma correspondência para mim?
teng ow·*goo*·maa ko·hes·pong·*deng*·syaa *paa*·raa meeng

phone

What's your phone number?
Qual é o número do teu telefone?
kwow e o *noo*·me·ro do te·oo te·le·*fo*·ne

Where's the nearest public phone?
Onde fica o telefône público mais perto?
ong·de *fee*·kaa o te·le·*fo*·ne *poo*·blee·ko mais *perr*·to

Do you have a phonebook I can look at?
Posso dar uma olhada no catálogo telefônico?
po·so daarr *oo*·maa o·*lyaa*·daa no kaa·*taa*·lo·go te·le·*fo*·nee·ko

How much does ... cost?	*Quanto custa ...?*	kwang·to koos·taa ...
a (three)-minute call	*uma ligação de (três) minutos*	*oo*·maa lee·gaa·*sowng* de (tres) mee·*noo*·tos
each extra minute	*cada minuto extra*	*kaa*·daa mee·*noo*·to *es*·traa

I want to …	Quero …	ke·ro …
buy a phone card	comprar um cartão telefônico	kong praarr oom kaar·towng te·le·fo·nee·ko
call (Singapore)	telefonar (para Cingapura)	te·le·fo·naarr (paa·raa seen·gaa·poo·raa)
make a local call	fazer uma chamada local	faa·zerr oo·maa shaa·maa·daa lo·kow
reverse the charges	fazer uma chamada a cobrar	faa·zerr oo·maa shaa·maa·daa aa ko·braarr
speak for (three) minutes	falar por (três) minutos	faa·laarr por (tres) mee·noo·tos

The number is …
O número é …   o noo·me·ro e …

What's the area code for (Recife)?
Qual é o código de discagem para (Recife)?   kwow e o ko·dee·go de dees·ka·zheng paa·raa (he·see·fe)

What's the country code for (New Zealand)?
Qual é o código de discagem para (Nova Zelândia)?   kwow e o ko·dee·go de dees·ka·zheng paa·raa (no·vaa ze·lang·dee·aa)

It's engaged.
Está ocupado.   es·taa o·koo·paa·do

I've been cut off.
A ligação caiu.   aa lee·gaa·sowng kaa·ee·oo

The connection's bad.
A conexão está ruim.   aa ko·nek·sowng es·taa hoo·eeng

Hello.	*Alô.*	aa·*lo*
Can I speak to ...?	*Posso falar com ...?*	*po*·so faa·*laarr* kong ...
It's ...	*Aqui é ...*	a·*kee* e ...
Is ... there?	*O/A ... está?* m/f	o/aa ... es·*taa*

listen for ...

e·le/e·laa nowng es·*taa*
Ele/Ela não está.

He/She is not here.

es·*pe*·raa oom mee·noo·*tee*·nyo
Espera um minutinho.

One moment.

keng es·*taa* faa·*lang*·do
Quem está falando?

Who's calling?

kong keng vo·*se* kerr faa·*laarr*
Com quem você quer falar?

Who do you want to speak to?

kwow o se·oo *noo*·me·ro *paa*·raa kong·*taa*·to
Qual o seu número para contato?

What's your contact number?

vo·*se* dees·*ko* o *noo*·me·ro e·*haa*·do
Você discou o número errado.

Wrong number.

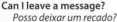

Can I leave a message?
Posso deixar um recado?

po·so day·*shaarr* oom he·*kaa*·do

Please tell him/her I called.
*Por favor diga a
ele/ela que eu liguei.*

por faa·*vorr* dee·gaa a
e·le/e·laa ke e·oo lee·*gay*

I'll call back later.
Eu vou ligar mais tarde.

e·oo vo lee·*gaarr* mais *taarr*·de

My number is ...
Meu telefone é ...

me·oo te·le·*fo*·ne e ...

mobile/cell phone

I'd like a …	*Eu gostaria de …*	e·oo gos·*taa·ree*·aa de …
charger for	*comprar uma*	kong·*praarr* oo·maa
my phone	*bateria para o*	baa·te·*ree*·aa *paa*·raa o
	meu telephone	*me*·oo te·le·*fo*·ne
mobile/cell	*alugar um*	aa·loo·*gaarr* oom
phone for hire	*cellular*	se·loo·*laarr*
prepaid mobile/	*comprar um*	kong *praarr* oom
cell phone	*cellular*	se·loo·*laarr*
	pré-pago	pre·*paa*·go
SIM card for	*comprar um*	kong·*praarr* oom
your network	*cartão SIM*	kaarr·*towng* seeng
	para sua rede	*paa*·raa soo·aa *he*·de

What are the rates?

Qual é o valor cobrado?   kwow e o vaa·*lorr* ko·*braa*·do

(30c) per (30) seconds.

(Trinta centavos) por   *(treeng*·taa seng·*taa*·vos) porr
(trinta) segundos.   *(treeng*·taa) se·*goong*·dos

Internetese

The word *Internetês* (Internetese) has been coined to describe the confusing mixture of English and Portuguese terms in Brazilian cyberspace. New words such as *surfar* (surf) and *scâner* (scanner) have been adapted from English but sometimes there are Portuguese alternatives for common internet terms:

bate-papo m	internet chat
ciberespaço m	cyberspace
endereço m *de email*	email address
hiperligação m	hyperlink
internauta f	net nerd
página f *inicial*	homepage
utilizador m&f	user

the internet

Where's the local Internet cafe?
Onde tem um internet   *ong*·de teng oom eeng·terr·*ne*·tee
café na redondeza?   kaa·*fe* naa he·dong·*de*·zaa

I'd like to ...	*Gostaria de ...*	gos·taa·*ree*·aa de ...
check my email	*checar meu*	she·*kaarr* me·oo
	e-mail	e·mail
get Internet	*ter acesso à*	terr aa·*se*·so aa
access	*internet*	eeng·terr·*ne*·tee
use a printer	*usar a*	oo·*zaarr* aa
	impressora	eeng·pre·*so*·raa
use a scanner	*usar o*	oo·*zaarr* o
	escaner	ees·*ka*·nerr

Do you have ...?	*Vocês tem ...?*	vo·*ses* teng ...
a Zip drive	*um zip drive*	oom zeep *drai*·vee
Macs	*Apple Mac*	e·pel mak
PCs	*PC*	pe·*se*

How much	*Quanto custa*	kwang·to koos·taa
per ...?	*por ...?*	por ...
hour	*hora*	*aw*·raa
(five) minutes	*(cinco) minutes*	(seeng·ko) mee·*noo*·tos
page	*página*	*paa*·zhee·naa

How do I log on?
Como é que eu entro?   *ko*·mo e ke *e*·oo *eng*·tro

Please change it to the English-language setting.
Troca para inglês,   *tro*·kaa *paa*·raa eeng·*gles*
por favor.   porr faa·*vorr*

It's crashed.
Deu crash.   *de*·o krash

Where can I ...?	*Onde posso ...?*	ong·de po·so ...
I'd like to ...	*Gostaria de ...*	gos·taa·ree·aa de ...
cash a cheque	*descontar um cheque*	des·kong·taarr oom she·kee
change a travellers cheque	*trocar traveller cheques*	tro·kaarr traa·ve·ler she·kes
change money	*trocar dinheiro*	tro·kaar dee·nyay·ro
get a cash advance	*fazer um saque adiantado*	fa·zerr oom saa·ke aa·dee·ang·taa·do
withdraw money	*retirar dinheiro*	he·tee·raarr dee·nyay·ro
Where's ...?	*Onde tem ...?*	ong·de teng ...
a foreign exchange office	*uma loja de câmbio*	oo·maa lo·zhaa de kang·byo
an automatic teller machine	*um caixa automático*	oom kai·shaa ow·to·maa·tee·ko

What time does the bank open?

A que horas abre o banco?	aa ke aw·raas aa·bre o bang·ko

Can I use my credit card to withdraw money?

Posso usar o meu cartão de crédito para retirar dinheiro?	po·so oo·zaarr o me·oo kaar·towng de kre·dee·to paa·raa he·tee·raarr dee·nyay·ro

What's the …? Qual …? kwow …
  exchange rate o câmbio do o *kang*·byo do
    dia *dee*·aa
  charge for a taxa aa *taa*·shaa
    that cobrada ko·*braa*·daa

Has my money arrived yet?
  O meu dinheiro já o *me*·oo dee·*nyay*·ro zhaa
  chegou? she·*go*

How long will it take to arrive?
  Quanto tempo vai levar *kwang*·to *teng*·po *vaa*·ee le·*vaarr*
  para chegar? *paa*·raa she·*gaarr*

The automatic teller machine took my card.
  O caixa eletrônico o *kai*·shaa e·le·*tro*·nee·ko
  engoliu meu cartão. eng·go·*lee*·oo *mee*·oo kaar·*towng*

I've forgotten my PIN.
  Esqueci a minha es·ke·*see* aa *mee*·nyaa
  senha. *se*·nyaa

---

listen for …

aa·*see*·ne aa·*kee*
  Assine aqui. **Sign here.**

nowng po·*de*·mos faa·*zerr ee*·so
  Não podemos fazer isso. **We can't do that.**

te·mos oom pro·*ble*·maa
  Temos um problema. **There's a problem.**

ee·deng·tee·*daa*·de *identidade* **identification**
paa·saa·*porr*·te *passaporte* **passport**

PRACTICAL

sightseeing

passeando

I'd like a/an ...	*Gostaria de um ...*	gos·taa·*ree*·aa de oom ...
audio set	*aparelho de audio*	aa·paa·*re*·lyo de *ow*·dee·o
catalogue	*catálogo*	kaa·*taa*·lo·go
guide (person)	*guia*	*gee*·aa
guidebook in English	*guia em Inglês*	*gee*·aa eng eeng·*gles*
(local) map	*mapa (local)*	*maa*·paa (lo·*kow*)

Do you have information on ... sights?	*Vocês tem informações sobre passeios ...?*	vo·*ses* teng eeng·forr·maa·*soyngs* *so*·bre paa·*se*·os ...
cultural	*culturais*	kool·too·*rais*
historical	*históricos*	ees·*to*·ree·kos
religious	*religiosos*	he·lee·zhee·o·zos

I'd like to see ...
Gostaria de ver ... — gos·ta·*ree*·a de ver ...

What's that?
O que é isso? — o ke e *ee*·so

Who made it?
Quem fez isso? — keng fes *ee*·so

How old is it?
Quantos anos tem? — *kwang*·tos *a*·nos teng

Could you take a photograph of me?
Você poderia tirar minha foto, por favor? — vo·*se* po·de·*ree*·aa tee·*raarr* *mee*·nyaa *fo*·to porr faa·*vor*

Can I take a photograph?
   Posso tirar uma foto?   po·so tee·*raarr* oo·ma fo·to

Can I take a photograph of you?
   Posso tirar uma foto   po·so tee·*raarr* oo·ma fo·to
   de você(s)? **sg/pl**   de vo·*se(s)*

I'll send you the photograph.
   Eu te envio a foto.   e·oo te eng·*vee*·o a fo·to

getting in

What time does it open/close?
   A que horas abre/fecha?   a ke *aw*·raas *aa*·bre/fe·shaa

What's the admission charge?
   Qual o preço da entrada?   kwow o *pre*·so daa eng·*traa*·daa

Is there a discount for …?	*Tem desconto para …?*	teng des·*kong*·to paa·raa …
children	*crianças*	kree·*ang*·saas
families	*famílias*	faa·*mee*·lyaas
groups	*grupos*	*groo*·pos
older people	*pessoas idosas*	pe·*so*·aas ee·*do*·zaas
pensioners	*pensionistas*	peng·see·o·*nees*·taas
students	*estudantes*	es·too·*dang*·tes

galleries & museums

When's the gallery open?
   Quando abre a galeria?   *kwang*·do *aa*·bre aa gaa·le·*ree*·aa

What kind of art are you interested in?
   Você se interessa por   vo·*se* se eeng·te·*re*·saa porr
   que tipo de arte?   ke *tee*·po de *aarr*·te

What's in the collection?
   O que tem na coleção?   o ke teng naa ko·le·*sowng*

What do you think of (Renaissance art)?
O que você acha (arte Renascença)?   o ke vo·se aa·shaa (aarr·te he·naas·seng·saa)

It's a (Volpi) exhibition.
É uma (Volpi) exposição.   e oo·maa (vol·pee) es·po·zee·sowng

I'm interested in …
Estou interessado/ interessada em … m/f   es·to eeng·te·re·saa·do/ eeng·te·re·saa·daa eng …

I like the works of …
Eu gosto do trabalho do/da … m/f   e·oo gos·to do traa·baa·lyo do/daa …

It reminds me of …
Lembra o/a … m/f   leng·braa o/aa …

… art	arte … f	aarr·te …
graphic	gráfica	graa·fee·kaa
impressionist	impressionista	eeng·pre·syo·nees·taa
indigenous	indígena	eeng·dee·zhe·naa
modern	moderna	mo·derr·naa
performance	performance	perr·forr·mang·se
popular	popular	aarr·te po·poo·laarr

sightseeing

81

tours

Can you recommend a ...?	Vocês podem recomendar um ...?	vo·ses po·deng he·ko·meng·daarr oom ...
When's the next ...?	Quando sai o próximo ...?	kwang·do sai o pro·see·mo ...
boat-trip	barco	baar·ko
day trip	passeio do dia	paa·se·yo do dee·aa
tour	tour	toor
Is ... included?	Inclui ...?	eeng·kloo·ee ...
accommodation	ospedagem	os·pe·daa·zheng
food	comida	ko·mee·daa
transport	transporte	trans·porr·te

The guide will pay.
O guia vai pagar.　　　　o gee·aa vai paa·gaarr

The guide has paid.
O guia pagou.　　　　o gee·aa paa·go

How long is the tour?
Quanto tempo dura o passeio?　　　　kwang·to teng·po doo·raa o paa·say·o

What time should we be back?
A que horas estaremos de volta?　　　　a ke aw·raas es·taa·re·mos de vol·taa

I'm with them.
Estou com eles.　　　　es·to kong e·les

I've lost my group.
Perdi o meu grupo.　　　　perr·dee o me·oo groo·po

I'm attending a ...	Estou participando de ...	es·*to* paar·tee·see·*pang*·do de ...
conference	uma conferência	*oo*·maa kong·fe·*reng*·syaa
course	um curso	oom *koor*·so
meeting	uma reunião	*oo*·maa he·oo·nee·*owng*
trade fair	uma feira de negócios	*oo*·maa *fay*·raa de ne·*go*·see·os
I'm with ...	Estou com ...	es·*to* kong ...
my colleagues	meus/minhas colegas de trabalho m/f	me·oos/mee·nyaas ko·*le*·gaas de traa·*baa*·lyo
(the UN)	(a ONU)	(aa o·noo)
(two) others	outros (dois)	o·tros (doys)

I'm alone.
Estou sozinho. es·*to* so·*zee*·nyo

I have an appointment with ...
Tenho uma hora marcada com ... *teng*·nyo oo·maa *aw*·raa maarr·*kaa*·daa kong ...

I'm staying at ..., room ...
Estou no ..., quarto ... es·*to* no ... *kwaarr*·to

I'm here for ...	Ficarei aqui por ...	fee·kaa·*ray* aa·*kee* porr ...
(two) days	(dois) dias	(doys) *dee*·aas
(two) weeks	(duas) semanas	(*doo*·aas) se·*ma*·naas

Here's my ...	Aqui está ...	a·kee es·taa ...
What's your ...?	Qual o seu ...?	kwow o se·oo ...
address	endereço	eng·de·re·so
business card	cartão de visitas	kaar·towng de vee·zee·taas
email address	endereço de e-mail	eng·de·re·so de e·mail
fax number	número de fax	noo·me·ro de faks
mobile number	número do celular	noo·me·ro do se·loo·laarr
pager number	número do pager	noo·me·ro do pa·zher
work number	telefone do trabalho	te·le·fo·ne do traa·baa·lyo

Where's the ...?	Onde é ...?	ong·de e ...
business centre	o centro de negócios	o seng·tro de ne·go·syos
conference	a conferência	aa kong·fe·reng·syaa
meeting	a reunião	a he·oo·nee·owng

I'd like to ...	Gostaria de ...	gos·taa·ree·aa de ...
check my email	checar meu e-mail	she·kaarr me·oo e·mail
send a fax	enviar um fax	eng·vee·aarr oom faks

That went very well.
Correu tudo muito bem.   ko·he·oo too·do mweeng·to beng

Thank you for your time.
Obrigado/Obrigada   o·bree·gaa·do/o·bree·gaa·daa
pela atenção. m/f   pe·laa aa·teng·sowng

Shall we go for a ...?	Vocês gostariam de ...?	vo·ses gos·taa·ree·ang de ...
drink	beber alguma coisa	be·berr ow·goo·maa koy·zaa
meal	jantar	zhang·taarr

It's on me.
Eu convido.   e·oo kong·vee·do

I have a disability.
   Eu tenho uma   e·oo te·nyo oo·ma
   deficiência física.   de·fee·see·eng·syaa *fee*·zee·kaa

I'm deaf.
   Sou surdo.   so *soorr*·do

I have a hearing aid.
   Uso aparelho para   oo·zo aa·paa·re·lyo *paa*·raa
   surdez.   soor·*des*

I need assistance.
   Preciso de ajuda.   pre·*see*·zo de a·*zhoo*·daa

What services do you have for people with a disability?
   Quais os serviços que   kwais os serr·*vee*·sos ke
   vocês oferecem para   vo·*ses* o·fe·*re*·seng *paa*·raa
   pessoas com   pe·*so*·aas kong
   deficiência física?   de·fee·see·*eng*·syaa *fee*·zee·kaa

Are there disabled toilets?
   Tem banheiro para   teng ba·*nyay*·ro *paa*·raa
   deficientes físicos?   de·fee·see·*eng*·tes *fee*·zee·kos

Are there rails in the bathroom?
   Tem corrimão no   teng ko·hee·*mowng* no
   banheiro?   ba·*nyay*·ro

Are there disabled parking spaces?
   Tem vaga para   teng *vaa*·gaa *paa*·raa
   deficientes físicos?   de·fee·see·*eng*·tes *fee*·zee·kos

Is there wheelchair access?

Tem acesso para cadeira de rodas?	teng aa·*se*·so *paa*·raa kaa·*day*·raa de *ho*·daas

How wide is the entrance?

Qual a largura da entrada?	kwow aa laarr·*goo*·raa daa eng·*traa*·daa

Is there a lift?

Tem elavador?	teng e·le·vaa·*dor*

How many steps are there?

Quantos degraus tem?	*kwang*·tos de·*grows* teng

Are guide dogs permitted?

É permitida a entrada de cães-guia?	e perr·mee·*tee*·daa aa eng·*traa*·daa de ka·*eengs*·*gee*·aa

Could you call me a disabled taxi?

Você poderia me chamar um taxi para deficientes físicos?	vo·*se* po·de·*ree*·aa me shaa·*maarr* oom *taak*·see *paa*·raa de·fee·see·*eng*·tes *fee*·zee·kos

Could you help me cross the street safely?

Você poderia me atravessar com segurança?	vo·*se* po·de·*ree*·aa me aa·traa·ve·*saarr* kong se·goo·*rang*·saa

Is there somewhere I can sit down?

Tem algum lugar onde eu posso sentar?	teng ow·*goom* loo·*gaarr* ong·de e·oo po·so seng·*taarr*

disabled person	*pessoa com deficiência física*	pe·*so*·aa kong de·fee·see·*eng*·syaa *fee*·zee·kaa
guide dog	*cães-guia* m	ka·*eengs*·*gee*·aa
older person	*pessoa idosa*	pe·*so*·aa ee·*do*·zaa
ramp	*rampa* f	*hang*·paa
walking frame	*andador* m	ang·daa·*dorr*
walking stick	*bengala* f	beng·*gaa*·laa
wheelchair	*cadeira* f *de rodas*	kaa·*day*·raa de *ho*·daas

travelling with children

viajando com crianças

Is there a ...?	Aqui tem ...?	aa·kee teng ...
baby change room	uma sala para trocar bebê	oo·maa saa·laa paa·raa tro·kaarr be·be
child discount	desconto para criança	des·kong·to paa·raa kree·ang·saa
child-minding service	serviço de babá	serr·vee·so de baa·baa
child-sized portion	porção para criança	porr·sowng paa·raa kree·ang·saa
children's menu	cardápio para criança	kaar·daa·pyo paa·raa kree·an·saa
creche	creche	kre·she
family ticket	passagem para familia	paa·saa·zheng paa·raa faa·mee·lyaa

Where's the nearest ...?	Qual ... mais perto?	kwow ... mais perr·to
drinking fountain	o bebedouro	o be·be·do·ro
park	o parque	o paarr·ke
playground	o playground	o play·grownd
swimming pool	a piscina	aa pee·see·naa
tap	a torneira	aa torr·nay·raa
theme park	o parque de diversões	o paarr·ke de dee·ver·soyngs
toyshop	a loja de brinquedos	aa lo·zhaa de breeng·ke·dos

I need a/an ...	Preciso de ...	pre·see·zo de ...
baby seat	um assento de criança	oom aa·seng·to de kree·ang·saa
(English-speaking) babysitter	uma babá (que fale ingles)	oo·maa baa·baa (ke faa·le eeng·gles)
booster seat	assento de elevação	aa·seng·to de e·le·vaa·sowng
highchair	uma cadeira de criança	oo·maa kaa·day·raa de kree·ang·saa
plastic sheet	um lençol plástico	oom leng·sol plaas·tee·ko
plastic bag	um saco plástico	oom saa·ko plaas·tee·ko
potty	um troninho	oom tro·nee·nyo
pram/pusher	carrinho de bebê	kaa·hee·nyo de be·be
sick bag	saco de vomito	saa·ko de vo·mee·to

Do you sell ...?	Vocês vendem ...?	vo·ses veng·deng ...
baby pain killers	analgésico para bebê	aa·naal·zhe·zee·ko paa·raa be·be
baby wipes	toalha molhada de bebê	to·aa·lyaa mo·lyaa·daa de be·be
disposable nappies	fraldas descartáveis	frow·daas des·kaarr·taa·vays
tissues	lencinhos de papel	leng·see·nyos de paa·pel

Do you hire prams?
Vocês alugam carrinho de bebê?
vo·ses aa·loo·gang kaa·hee·nyo de be·be

Are there any good places to take children around here?
Tem algum lugar agradável para levar as crianças por aqui perto?
teng ow·goom loo·gaarr aa·graa·daa·vel paa·raa le·vaarr aas kree·ang·saas porr aa·kee perr·to

Is there space for a pram?
   Tem espaço para o   teng es·*paa*·so *paa*·raa o
   carrinho de bebê?   kaa·*hee*·nyo de be·*be*

Are children allowed?
   É permitida a   e perr·mee·*tee*·daa aa
   entrada de crianças?   eng·*traa*·daa de kree·*ang*·saas

Where can I change a nappy?
   Onde posso trocar   *ong*·de *po*·so tro·*kaarr*
   a fralda?   aa *frow*·daa

Do you mind if I breast-feed here?
   Você se importa se   vo·*se* se eeng·*porr*·taa se
   eu amamentar aqui?   e·oo aa·maa·meng·*taarr* aa·*kee*

Could I have some paper and pencils, please?
   Pode me dar papel e   *po*·de me daarr paa·*pel* e
   lapis, por favor?   *laa*·pees porr faa·*vorr*

Is this suitable for (five-)year-old children?
   Isto é adequado para   *ees*·to e aa·de·*kwaa*·do *paa*·raa
   crianças de (cinco)   kree·*ang*·saas de (*seeng*·ko)
   anos de idade?   *a*·nos de ee·*daa*·de

Do you know a dentist/doctor who is good with children?
   Voce conhece algum   vo·*se* ko·*nye*·se ow·*goom*
   médico/dentista bom   me·dee·ko/deng·*tees*·taa bong
   para crianças?   *paa*·raa kree·*ang*·saas

For children's sicknesses, see **health**, page 177.

---

brazilian family tree

Ancient Celtic myths refer to the mist-shrouded island of Hy Brazil – a stormless haven somewhere in the Atlantic. The island appeared on charts in the 14th century and was to remain on British maps as late as the 1870s. Some scholars have suggested that Portuguese explorers were familiar with the Celtic stories and named the South American country after Hy Brazil. A more accepted theory is that Brazil is derived from the name of a dye-producing East Indian tree. When a similar tree was discovered in the new land it became Brazil's first successful export and lent the country its present name.

talking with children

Do you like …?	*Você gosta …?*	vo·*se gos*·taa …
school	*da escola*	daa es·*ko*·laa
sport	*de esporte*	de es·*porr*·te
your teacher	*do seu professor* m	do *se*·oo pro·fe·*sorr*
	da sua professora f	da *soo*·aa pro·fe·so·raa

When's your birthday?
Quando é o seu
aniversário?
kwang·do e o se·oo
aa·nee·ver·*saa*·ryo

Do you go to school?
Você vai para escola?
vo·*se* vai *paa*·raa es·*ko*·laa

What grade are you in?
Em que ano você está?
eng ke *a*·no vo·*se* es·*taa*

What do you do after school?
O que você faz depois da
escola?
o ke vo·*se* faaz de·*poys* daa
es·*ko*·laa

Do you learn English?
Você aprende ingles?
vo·*se* aa·*preng*·de eeng·*gles*

I come from very far away.
Eu venho de muito
longe.
e·oo *veng*·nyo de *mweeng*·to
long·zhe

Are you lost?
Você está perdido/
perdida? m/f
vo·*se* es·*taa* perr·*dee*·do/
perr·*dee*·daa

basics

conhecimentos básicos

Yes.	Sim.	seeng
No.	Não.	nowng
Please.	Por favor.	por faa vorr
Thank you	(Muito)	(mweeng·to)
(very much).	Obrigado/	o·bree·gaa·do/
	Obrigada. m/f	o·bree·gau·daa
You're welcome.	De nada.	de naa·daa
Excuse me.	Com licença.	kong lee·seng·saa
Sorry.	Desculpa.	des·kool·paa

greetings & goodbyes

saudações & despedidas

A greeting kiss on the cheek is quite common between women, and also between members of the opposite sex, even on first encounters. The number of kisses ranges from one to three, depending on the region. Shaking hands is the normal greeting between men, though a hug between friends is not uncommon.

| Hello. | Olá. | o·laa |
| Hi. | Oi. | oy |

Good ...		
afternoon	Boa tarde.	bo·aa taarr·de
day	Bom dia.	bong dee·aa
evening	Boa noite.	bo·aa noy·te
morning	Bom dia.	bong dee·aa

How are you?
Como vai? ko·mo vai

Fine, and you?
Bem, e você? beng e vo·*se*

What's your name?
Qual é o seu nome? kwow e o *se*·oo *no*·me

My name is …
Meu nome é … me·oo *no*·me e …

I'd like to introduce you to …
Eu gostaria de te e·oo gos·taa·*ree*·aa de te
apresentar ao/à … m/f aa·pre·zeng·*taarr aa*·o/aa …

I'm pleased to meet you.
Prazer em conhecê-lo/la. m/f praa·*zerr* eng ko·nye·*se*·lo/laa

This is my …	*Este é meu … m*	*es*·te e *me*·oo …
	Esta é minha … f	*es*·taa e *mee*·nyaa …
colleague	*colega m&f*	ko·*le*·gaa
daughter	*filha*	*fee*·lyaa
friend	*amigo/*	aa·*mee*·go/
	amiga m/f	aa·*mee*·gaa
husband	*marido*	maa·*ree*·do
partner	*companheiro/*	kong·pa·*nyay*·ro/
(intimate)	*companheira m/f*	kong·pa·*nyay*·raa
son	*filho*	*fee*·lyo
wife	*esposa*	es·*po*·zaa

For family members, see **family,** page 97.

| **See you later.** | *Até mais tarde.* | aa·*te* mais *taarr*·de |
| **Goodbye.** | *Tchau.* | tee·*show* |

---

many thanks

You'll notice that there are two words for 'thank you' in Brazilian Potuguese, *obrigado* and *obrigada*. Their use is determined by the gender of the person doing the thanking. A male uses *obrigado* and a female uses *obrigada*.

addressing people

It's always best to address older people using *Senhor* or *Senhora*. You'll notice that first names are used with titles, often more so than family names.

Mr/Sir	*Senhor*	se·*nyorr*
Mrs/Ms	*Senhora*	se·*nyo*·raa
Miss	*Senhorita*	se·nyo·*ree*·taa
Doctor	*Doutor/Doutora* m/f	do·*torr*/do·to·raa
Professor	*Professor/*	pro·fe·*sorr*/
	Professora m/f	pro·fe·*so*·raa
young man/woman	*moço/moça* m/f	*mo*·so/*mo*·sa
mate	*cara* m	*kaa*·raa

making conversation

How's everything?
Tudo bem? — *too*·do beng

Do you live here?
Você mora aqui? — vo·*se* mo·raa aa·*kee*

It's so hot/cold !
Que calor/frio ! — ke kaa·*lorr*/*free*·o

It's so quiet here.
Aqui é tão tranquilo. — a·*kee* e towng trang·*kwee*·lo

What a beautiful view.
Que vista linda. — ke *vees*·taa *leeng*·daa

This is great!
Isso é demais! — *ee*·so e de·*mais*

Where are you going?
Onde você está indo? — ong·de vo·*se* es·*taa* eeng·do

What are you doing?
O que você está fazendo? — o ke vo·*se* es·*taa* faa·*zeng*·do

Do you like it here?
    Você gosta daqui?   vo·*se gos*·taa daa·*kee*

I love it here.
    Eu adoro.   e·oo aa·*do*·ro

What's this called?
    Como se chama isto?   *ko*·mo se *sha*·maa *ees*·to

Can I take a photo (of you)?
    Posso tirar uma foto   *po*·so tee·*raarr oo*·maa *fo*·to
    (de você)?   (de vo·*se*)

That's (beautiful), isn't it!
    Isto é (lindo) você   *ees*·to e (*leeng*·do) vo·*se*
    não acha?   nowng *aa*·shaa

Just joking.
    Estou brincando.   es·to breeng·*kang*·do

Are you here on holiday?
    Você está aqui em férias?   vo·*se* es·*taa* a·*kee* eng *fe*·ree·aas

gringo

Chances are high that when travelling in Brazil, you'll hear or be addressed as *gringo* (or *gringa* for women). In Brazilian Portuguese, the term refers to almost anyone who is not Brazilian (including people from other countries in Latin America). It's generally not an insult (although if it's modified by *burro/burra* m/f, 'stupid', then it probably is!), so there's usually no need to take offence.

I'm here …	*Estou aqui …*	es·to a·kee …
for a holiday	*em férias*	eng *fe*·ree·aas
on business	*à negócios*	aa ne·*go*·syos
to study	*à estudos*	aa es·*too*·dos

How long are you here for?
    Quanto tempo você vai   *kwang*·to *teng*·po vo·*se* vai
    ficar aqui?   fee·*kaarr* aa·*kee*

I'm here for (four) weeks/days.
    Ficarei aqui (quatro)   fee·kaa·*ray* aa·*kee* (*kwaa*·tro)
    semanas/dias.   se·*ma*·naas/*dee*·aas

What a beautiful day!

Que lindo dia!   ke *leeng*·do *dee*·aa

Want to talk about the weather? See **outdoors**, page 138.

local talk		
Hey!	*Ei!*	ay
Great!	*Ótimo!*	o·*tee*·mo
Sure.	*É claro.*	e *klaa*·ro
Maybe.	*Talvez*	taal·*vez*
No way!	*De jeito nenhum!*	de *zhay*·to ne·*yoom*
Just a minute.	*Só um minuto.*	so oom mee·*noo*·to
It's OK.	*Está bom.*	es·*taa* bong
Good luck!	*Boa sorte!*	*bo*·aa sorr·te
No problem.	*Não tem problema.*	nowng teng pro·*ble*·maa

nationalities

nacionalidades

Where are you from?

De onde você é?   de *ong*·de vo·*se* e

I'm from …	*Eu sou …*	e·oo so …
Australia	*da Austrália*	daa ows·*traa*·lyaa
Canada	*do Canadá*	do kaa·naa·*daa*
Singapore	*de Cingapura*	de seeng·gaa·*poo*·raa

age

idade

How old …?	*Quantos anos …?*	*kwang*·tos *a*·nos …
are you	*você tem*	vo·*se* teng
is he/she	*ele/ela tem* m/f	e·le/e·laa teng

meeting people

95

I'm ... years old.
  Tenho ... anos. te·nyo ... *a*·nos

He/She is ... years old.
  Ele/Ela tem ... anos. m/f e·le/e·laa teng ... *a*·nos

Too old!
  Muito velho/velha! m/f mweeng·to ve·lyo/ve·lya

I'm younger than I look.
  Sou mais novo/nova do so mais *no*·vo/*no*·vaa do
  que aparento. m/f ke aa·paa·*reng*·to

For your age, see **numbers & amounts**, page 29.

occupations & studies

ocupação & educação

What's your occupation?
  Você trabalha em que? vo·se traa·*baa*·lyaa eng ke

I'm a ...	Eu sou ...	e·oo so ...
chef	*chefe* m&f *de cozinha*	*she*·fe de ko·zee·nyaa
computer programmer	*programador/ programadora de computação* m/f	pro·gra·maa·*dorr*/ pro·gra·maa·*do*·raa de kong·poo·ta·*sowng*
exporter	*exportador/ exportadora* m/f	es·porr·taa·*dorr*/ es·porr·taa·*do*·raa
journalist	*jornalista* m&f	zhor·naa·*lees*·taa
teacher	*professor/ professora* m/f	pro·fe·*sorr*/ pro·fe·*so*·raa

I work in ...	Trabalho na área de ...	traa·*baa*·lyo naa *aa*·re·aa de ...
administration	*administração*	aad·mee·nees· traa·*sowng*
health	*saúde*	saa·*oo*·de
sales & marketing	*vendas e marketing*	*veng*·daas e *maarr*·ke·teeng

I'm ...	Eu ...	e·oo ...
self-employed	sou autônomo/	so ow·to·no·mo/
	autônoma m/f	ow·to·no·maa
unemployed	estou	es·to
	desempregado/	de·zeng·pre·gaa·do/
	desempregada m/f	de·zeng·pre·gaa·daa

What are you studying?

O que você está estudando?	o ke vo·se es·taa es·too·dang·do

I'm studying ...	Estou estudando ...	es·to es·too·dang·do ...
humanities	ciências	see·eng·syaas
	humanas	oo·ma·naas
Portuguese	português	porr·too·ges
science	ciências	see·eng·syaas

For other occupations and areas of study, see the **dictionary**.

family

família

Do you have a ?	Você tem ...?	vo·se teng ...
I (don't) have a ...	Eu (não) tenho ...	e·oo (nowng) te·nyo ...
brother	irmão	eerr·mowng
daughter	filha	fee·lyaa
family	família	fa·mee·lyaa
father	pai	pai
grandfather	avô	aa·vo
grandmother	avó	aa·vaw
granddaughter	neta	ne·taa
grandson	neto	ne·to
husband	marido	maa·ree·do
mother	mãe	maing
partner	companheiro/	kong·pa·nyay·ro/
(intimate)	companheira m/f	kong·pa·nyay·raa
sister	irmã	eer·mang
son	filho	fee·lyo
wife	esposa	es·po·zaa

meeting people

Are you married?
    Você é casado/casada? m/f   vo·se e kaa·*zaa*·do/ kaa·*zaa*·daa

I live with someone.
    Moro com uma pessoa.   *mo*·ro kong *oo*·maa pe·*so*·aa

I'm …	*Eu sou …*	*e*·oo so …
married	*casado/*	kaa·*zaa*·do/
	casada m/f	kaa·*zaa*·daa
separated	*separado/*	se·paa·*raa*·daa
	separada m/f	se·paa·*raa*·do/
single	*solteiro/*	sol·*tay*·ro/
	solteira m/f	sol·*tay*·raa

farewells

Tomorrow is my last day here.
    Amanhã é o meu   a·ma·*nyang* e o *me*·oo
    ultimo dia aqui.   *ool*·tee·mo *dee*·aa aa·*kee*

Here's my …	*Aqui está meu …*	a·*kee* es·*taa me*·oo …
What's your …?	*Qual o seu …?*	kwow o *se*·oo …
address	*endereço*	eng·de·*re*·so
email address	*endereço de*	eng·de·*re*·so de
	e-mail	e·*mail*
phone number	*número de*	*noo*·me·ro de
	telephone	te·le·*fo*·ne

If you come to (Scotland), you can stay with me.
    Se você for à (Escócia)   se vo·*se* forr aa (es·*ko*·syaa)
    pode ficar na minha   *po*·de fee·*kaarr* naa *mee*·nyaa
    casa.   *kaa*·zaa

Keep in touch!
    Mantenha contato!   mang·*te*·nyaa kong·*taa*·to

It's been great meeting you.
    Foi ótimo te conhecer.   foy o·*tee*·mo te ko·nye·*serr*

common interests

What do you do in your spare time?
O que você gosta de fazer nas horas livres? — o ke vo·*se gos*·taa de faa·*zerr* naas *aw*·raas *lee*·vres

Do you like …?	*Você gosta de …?*	vo·*se gos*·taa de …
I (don't) like …	*Eu (não) gosto de …*	*e*·oo (nowng) *gos*·to de …

arts and crafts	*artesanato* m	aarr·te·zaa·*naa*·to
Brazilian music	*música* f *brasileira*	*moo*·zee·kaa braa·zee·*lay*·raa
capoeira	*capoeira* f	kaa·po·*ay*·raa
carnival	*carnaval* m	kaarr·naa·*vow*
cooking	*cozinhar*	ko·zee·*nyaarr*
dancing	*dançar*	dang·*saarr*
drawing	*desenhar*	de·ze·*nyaarr*
films	*cinema* f	see·ne·*maa*
gardening	*jardinagem* f	zhaarr·dee·*naa*·zheng
hiking	*fazer caminhadas*	faa·*zerr* kaa·mee·*nyaa*·daas
live shows	*show* m *ao vivo*	show ow *vee*·vo
music	*música* f	*moo*·zee·kaa
painting	*pintar*	peeng·*taarr*
photography	*fotografia* f	fo·to·graa·*fee*·aa
reading	*ler*	lerr
shopping	*fazer compras*	faa·*zerr kong*·praas
socialising	*socializar*	so·see·aa·lee·*zaarr*
sport	*esporte* m	es·*porr*·te
travelling	*viajar*	vee·aa·*zhaarr*

For sporting activities, see **sport**, page 125.

music

Do you ...?	Você ...?	vo·se ...
dance	dança	dang·saa
go to concerts	vai à shows	vai aa shows
listen to music	escuta música	es·koo·taa moo·zee·kaa
play an instrument	toca algum instrumento	to·kaa ow·goom eengs·troo·meng·to
sing	canta	kang·taa

What ... do you like?	De que ... você gosta?	de ke ... vo·se gos·taa
bands	bandas de música	bang·daas de moo·zee·kaa
music	música	moo·zee·kaa
singers	cantores	kang·to·res

kung fu dancing

Capoeira originated as an African martial art developed by slaves to fight their masters. It was disguised with the introduction of musical accompaniment to make it seem like dance. In its modern form, it combines elements of dance and fighting and is known for its fluid and circular movements.

classical music	música f clássica	moo·zee·kaa klaa·see·kaa
blues	blues m	blooz
electronic music	música f eletrônica	moo·zee·kaa e·le·tro·nee·kaa
jazz	jazz m	zhez
pop	pop m	po·pee
rock	rock m	ho·kee
traditional music	música f tradicional	moo·zee·kaa traa·dee·syo·now
world music	world music m	wol·dee mee·oo·zeek

Planning to go to a concert? See **tickets**, page 38 and **going out**, page 109.

cinema & theatre

I feel like going to a ...	Estou com vontade de ir ...	es·to kong vong·taa·de de eerr ...
Did you like the ...?	Você gostou ...?	vo·se gos·to ...
ballet	do balé	do baa·le
film	do filme	do feel·me
play	da peça	daa pe·saa
I thought it was ...	Eu achei ...	e·oo aa·shay ...
excellent	excelente	es·se·leng·te
long	longo	long·go
OK	bom	bong

What's showing at the cinema/theatre tonight?
O que está passando no cinema/teatro hoje à noite?
o ke es·taa paa·sang·do no see·ne·maa/te·aa·tro o·zhee aa noy·te

Is it in English?
É em ingles?
e eng eeng·gles

Does it have (English) subtitles?
Tem sub-título (em inglês?)
teng soo·bee·tee·too·lo (eng eeng·gles)

I want to sell this ticket.
Quero vender este ingresso.
ke·ro veng·derr es·te eeng·gre·so

Is this seat taken?
Este lugar está vago?
es·te loo·gaarr es·taa vaa·go

Have you seen ...?
Você viu ...?
vo·se vee·oo ...

Who's in it?
É com quem?
e kong keng

It stars ...
É com ...
e kong ...

I (don't)	Eu (não)	e·oo (nowng)
like ...	gosto de ...	gos·to de ...
action movies	filmes de ação	feel·mes de aa·sowng
animated films	filmes de animação	feel·mes de aa·nee·maa·sowng
Brazilian cinema	cinema (brasileiro)	see·ne·maa (braa·zee·lay·ro)
comedies	comédias	ko·me·dyaas
documentaries	documentários	do·koo·meng·taa·ree·os
drama	drama	dra·maa
film noir	filme noir	feel·me noir
horror movies	filme de terror	feel·me de te·horr
sci-fi	ficção científica	feek·sowng see·eng·tee·fee·kaa
thrillers	suspense	soos·peng·se
war movies	filme de guerra	feel·me de ge·haa

feelings

sentimentos

Some feelings (like those in the first list) are described using 'be', *estar*, while others (see the second list) use 'be with', *estar com*.

Are you ...?	Você está ...?	vo·*se* es·*taa* ...
I'm (not) ...	(Não) Estou ...	(nowng) es·*to* ...
annoyed	*irritado/*	ee·hee·*taa*·do/
	irritada m/f	ee·hee·*taa*·daa
happy	*feliz*	fe·*lees*
sad	*triste*	*trees*·te
surprised	*surpreso/*	soorr·*pre*·zo/
	supresa m/f	soorr·*pre*·zaa
tired	*cansado/*	kang·*saa*·do/
	cansada m/f	kang·*saa*·daa
worried	*preocupado/*	pre·o·koo·*paa*·do/
	preocupada m/f	pre·o·koo·*paa*·daa

Are you ...?	Você está com ...?	vo·*se* es·*taa* kong ...
I'm (not) ...	(Não) Estou com ...	(nowng) es·*to* kong...
cold	*frio*	*free*·o
embarrassed	*vergonha*	verr·*go*·nyaa
hot	*calor*	kaa·*lorr*
hungry	*fome*	*fo*·me
in a hurry	*pressa*	*pre*·saa
thirsty	*sede*	*se*·de

If feeling unwell, see **health**, page 177.

intense feelings		
a little	*um pouco*	oom *po*·ko
I'm a little sad.	*Estou um pouco triste.*	es·to oom po·ko *trees*·te
very	*muito/ muita* m/f	*mweeng*·to/ mweeng·taa
I feel very lucky.	*Estou com muita sorte.*	es·to kong mweeng·taa *sorr*·te
extremely	*super*	soo·*perr*
I'm extremely happy.	*Estou super feliz.*	es·to soo·perr fe·*lees*

opinions

Did you like it?
  Você gostou? vo·se gos·to

What do you think of it?
  O que você achou? o ke vo·se aa·*sho*·oo

I thought it was …	*Achei …*	aa·*shay* …
It's …	*É …*	e …
awful	*péssimo/ péssima* m/f	*pe*·see·mo/ *pe*·see·ma
beautiful	*lindo/ linda* m/f	*leeng*·do/ *leeng*·daa
boring	*chato*	*shaa*·to
great	*ótimo/ótima* m/f	*o*·tee·mo/*o*·tee·ma
interesting	*interessante*	eeng·te·re·*sang*·te
OK	*bom*	bong
too expensive	*muito caro/cara* m/f	*mweeng*·to *kaa*·ro/*kaa*·raa

SOCIAL

104

politics & social issues

Who do you vote for?
Em quem você vota?　　eng keng vo·se *vo*·taa

I support the … party.	*Eu voto para o partido …*	e·oo *vo*·to *paa*·raa o paarr·*tee*·do …
I'm a member of the … party.	*Eu sou membro do partido …*	e·oo so *meng*·bro do paarr·*tee*·do …
communist	*comunista*	ko·moo·*nees*·taa
conservative	*conservador*	kong·serr·vaa·*dorr*
democratic	*democrata*	de·mo·*kraa*·taa
green	*verde*	*verr*·de
liberal	*liberal*	lee·be·*row*
social democratic	*democrata-social*	de·mo·*kraa*·taa·so·*see*·ow
socialist	*socialista*	so·see·aa·*leeš*·taa
workers	*dos trabalhadores*	dos traa·baa·lyaa·*do*·res

Did you hear about …?
Você ouviu falar …?　　vo·se o·vee·oo faa·*laarr* …

Do you agree with it?
Você concorda com isto?　　vo·se kong·*korr*·daa kong *ees*·to

I (don't) agree with …
Eu (não) concordo com …　　e·oo (nowng) kong·*korr*·do kong …

How do people feel about …?
O que as pessoas acham …?　　o ke aas pe·*so*·aas *aa*·shang …

How can we protest against …?
Como podemos protestar contra …?　　*ko*·mo po·*de*·mos pro·tes·*taarr* kong·traa …

How can we support …?
Como podemos apoiar …?　　*ko*·mo po·*de*·mos aa·po·*yaarr* …

abortion	*aborto* m	aa·*borr*·to
animal rights	*direitos* m *dos*	dee·*ray*·tos dos
	animais	aa·nee·*mais*
crime	*crime* m	*kree*·me
discrimination	*descriminação* f	des·kree·mee·
		na·*sowng*
drugs	*drogas* f pl	*dro*·gaas
the economy	*a economia* f	aa e·ko·no·*mee*·aa
education	*educação* f	e·doo·kaa·*sowng*
the environment	*o meio*	o *may*·o
	ambiente m	ang·bee·*eng*·te
equal opportunity	*direitos* m pl *iguais*	dee·*ray*·tos ee·*gwais*
euthanasia	*euthanasia* f	e·oo·taa·*naa*·zyaa
globalisation	*globalização* f	glo·baa·lee·zaa·*sowng*
human rights	*direitos* m pl	dee·*ray*·tos
	humanos	oo·*ma*·nos
immigration	*imigração* f	ee·mee·graa·*sowng*
income	*distribuição* f	dees·tree·boo·ee·
distribution	*de renda*	*sowng* de *heng*·daa
inequality	*desigualdade* f	de·zee·gwow·*daa*·de
inflation	*inflação* f	eeng·flaa·*sowng*
party politics	*política* f	po·*lee*·tee·kaa
	partidária	paarr·tee·*daa*·ree·aa
privatisation	*privatização* f	pree·vaa·tee·
		zaa·*sowng*
racism	*racismo* m	haa·*sees*·mo
sexism	*machismo* m	maa·*shees*·mo
slums	*favelas* f pl	faa·*ve*·laas
social disparity	*disparidade* f	dees·paa·ree·*daa*·de
	social	so·see·*ow*
social welfare	*justiça* f *social*	zhoos·*tee*·sa so·see·*ow*
unemployment	*desemprego* m	de·*zeng*·pre·go
work safety	*segurança* f *no*	se·goo·*rang*·saa no
	trabalho	traa·*baa*·lyo
workers rights	*direitos* m *dos*	dee·*ray*·tos dos
	trabalhadores	traa·baa·lyaa·*do*·res

the environment

Is there a … problem here?
Aqui tem problema de …?   a·*kee* teng pro·*ble*·maa de …

What should be done about …?
O que deveria ser feito   o ke de·ve·*ree*·aa serr *fay*·to
sobre …?   *so*·bre …

conservation	*conservação* f	kong·ser·va·*sowng*
deforestation	*desflorestamento* m	des·flo·res·taa·*meng*·to
drought	*seca* f	*se*·kaa
ecosystem	*eco-sistema* f	e·ko·sees·te·maa
endangered species	*espécies* f pl *ameaçadas de extinção*	es·*pe*·syes aa·me·a·*saa*·daas de es·teeng·*sowng*
genetically modified food	*alimentos* m pl *geneticamente modificados*	aa·lee·*meng*·tos ge·ne·tee·kaa·*meng*·te mo·dee·fee·*kaa*·dos
hunting	*caça* f	*kaa*·saa
hydroelectricity	*energia* f *hidroelétrica*	e·nerr·*zhee*·aa ee·dro·e·*le*·tree·kaa
irrigation	*irrigação* f	ee·hee·gaa·*sowng*
nuclear energy	*energia* f *nuclear*	e·nerr·*zhee*·aa noo·kle·*aarr*
nuclear testing	*teste* m *nuclear*	*tes*·te noo·kle·*aarr*
ozone layer	*camada* f *de ozônio*	kaa·*maa*·daa de o·zo·nee·o
pesticides	*pesticidas* f pl	pes·tee·*see*·daas
pollution	*poluição* f	po·loo·ee·*sowng*
recycling programme	*programa* f *de reciclagem*	pro·*gra*·maa de he·see·*klaa*·zheng
toxic waste	*resíduos* m pl *tóxicos*	he·zee·dwos tok·see·kos
water supply	*abastecimento* m *de água*	aa·baas·te·see·*meng*·to de *aa*·gwaa

Is this a protected …?	Esta é …	es·taa e …
forest	uma floresta protegida	oo·maa flo·res·taa pro·te·zhee·daa
species	uma espécie protegida	oo·maa es·pe·sye pro·te·zhee·daa

indigenous languages

During the early days of colonisation, many Portuguese missionaries and colonists learnt how to speak *Tupinambá*, an indigenous language spoken along the Brazilian coast. Use of the language became so widespread within the colony that it became known as *Língua Brasilica* (Brazilian language) and later *Língua Geral* (general language). *Tupinambá* has since become extinct although *Nheengatu*, a derivation of the *Língua Geral*, is still spoken in the Negro River basin. It wasn't until the mid-eighteenth century that the Portuguese language truly began to predominate and hundreds of local languages were slowly wiped out by colonial expansion. Historians have estimated that, prior to the arrival of the Portuguese, there were probably 400 or 500 languages spoken within the present boundaries of Brazil. Today less than 200 remain. Most of these are facing extinction, although the *Guaraní* language, spoken by over 30,000 people, is showing little evidence of decline.

Indigenous languages, particularly *Tupinambá*, have had a significant influence on Brazilian Portuguese. The words *jabuti* (turtle), *jacaré* (alligator), *capim* (grass), *cipó* (vine) and *piranha* (piranha) all originate from *Tupinambá*. Other Brazilian Portuguese words derived from indigenous languages include *abacaxi* (pineapple), *mandioca* (manioc flour), *caju* (cashew) and *tatu* (armadillo).

where to go

para onde ir

What's there to do in the evenings?
O que se tem para fazer à noite? — o ke se teng *paa*·raa faa·*zerr* aa *noy*·te

What's on ...?	*O que está acontecendo ...?*	o ke es·*taa* aa·kong·te·*seng*·do ...
locally	*aqui perto*	aa·*kee perr*·to
this weekend	*neste final de semana*	*nes*·te fee·*now* de se·*ma*·naa
today	*hoje*	o·zhe
tonight	*à noite*	aa *noy*·te
Where can I find ...?	*Onde posso encontrar ...?*	ong·de po·so eng·kong·*traarr* ...
clubs	*um lugar para dançar*	oom loo·*gaarr* paa·raa dang·*saarr*
gay venues	*lugares gays*	loo·*gaa*·res gays
places to eat	*lugares para comer*	loo·*gaa*·res paa·raa ko·*merr*
pubs	*um bar*	oom baarr
Is there a local ... guide?	*Existe algum guia de ... dessa área?*	e·*zees*·te ow·*goom gee*·aa de ... *de*·saa *aa*·re·aa
entertainment	*entretenimento*	eng·tre·te·nee·*meng*·to
film	*cinema*	see·*ne*·maa
gay	*de lugares gays*	de loo·*gaa*·res gays
music	*música*	*moo*·zee·kaa

I feel like going to a ...	Estou com vontade de ir ...	es·to kong vong·taa·de de eerr ...
ballet	ao balé	ow baa·le
bar	a um bar	aa oom baarr
cafe	a um café	aa oom kaa·fe
concert	a um show	aa oom show
film	ao cinema	ow see·ne·maa
karaoke bar	a um karaoke	aa oom kaa·raa·o·ke
nightclub	a uma boate	aa oo·maa bo·aa·te
party	a uma festa	aa oo·maa fes·taa
performance	a uma performance	aa oo·maa perr·forr·mang·se
play	a uma obra	aa oo·maa o·braa
pub	a um bar	aa oom baarr
restaurant	a um restaurante	aa oom hes·tow·rang·te

For more on bars and drinks, see **eating out**, page 149.

invitations

convites

What are you doing ...?	O que você está fazendo ...?	o ke vo·se es·taa faa·zeng·do ...
now	agora	aa·go·raa
this weekend	neste final de semana	nes·te fee·now de se·ma·naa
tonight	hoje à noite	o·zhe aa noy·te

Would you like to go (for a) ...?	Você gostaria de ir ...?	vo·se gos·taa·ree·aa de irr ...
chat somewhere	bater um papo em algum lugar	baa·terr oom paa·po eng ow·goom loo·gaarr
coffee	tomar um café	to·maarr oom kaa·fe
drink	beber alguma coisa	be·berr ow·goo·maa koy·zaa
meal	jantar	zhang·taarr
walk	caminhar	kaa·mee·nyaarr

I feel like	Eu gostaria de	e·oo gos·taa·ree·aa de
going … dancing	dançar …	dang·saan …
samba	samba	sang·ba
forró	forró	fo·ho
gafieira	gafieira	gaa·fee·ay·raa
lambada	lambada	lang·baa·daa

My round.
Minha vez.   mee·nyaa vez

Do you know a good restaurant?
Você conhece um bom   vo·se ko·nye·se oom bom
restaurante?   hes·tow·rang·te

Do you want to come to the concert with me?
Você quer vir ao show   vo·se kerr veerr ow show
comigo?   ko·mee·go

We're having a party.
Estamos dando uma   es·ta·mos dang·do oo·maa
festa.   fes·taa

You should come.
Você deveria vir.   vo·se de·ve·ree·aa veer

responding to invitations

Sure!
Claro!   klaa·ro

Yes, I'd love to.
Sim, adoraria.   seeng aa·do·raa·ree·aa

That's very kind of you.
É muito gentil   e mweeng·to zheng·teel
de sua parte.   de soo·aa paarr·te

Where shall we go?
Onde podemos ir?   ong·de po·de·mos eer

No, I'm afraid I can't.
Não, infelizmente   nowng eeng·fe·lees·meng·te
não posso.   nowng po·so

going out

111

Sorry, I can't sing/dance.
*Desculpe, mas eu
não sei cantar/
dançar.*

des·*kool*·pe mas e·oo
nowng say kang·*taarr*/
dang·*saarr*

What about tomorrow?
Que tal amanhã?

ke tow aa·ma·*nyang*

arranging to meet

What time will we meet?
*A que horas nos
encontramos?*

aa ke *aw*·raas nos
eng·kong·*tra*·mos

Where will we meet?
*Onde vamos nos
encontrar?*

ong·de *va*·mos nos
eng·kong·*traarr*

Let's meet at ...	*Vamos nos encontrar ...*	*va*·mos nos eng·kong·*traarr* ...
(eight) o'clock	*às (oito) horas*	aas (*oy*·to) *aw*·raas
the (entrance)	*na (entrada)*	naa (eng·*traa*·daa)

I'll pick you up.
Eu te pego.

e·oo te *pe*·go

Are you ready?
*Você está pronto/
pronta?* m/f

vo·se es·*taa* prong·to/
prong·taa

I'm ready.
Estou pronto/pronta. m/f

es·to prong·to/*prong*·taa

I'll be coming later.
Eu vou mais tarde.

e·oo vo mais *taarr*·de

Where will you be?
   Onde você vai estar?   *ong*·de vo·*se* vai es·*taarr*

If I'm not there by (nine), don't wait for me.
   Se eu não chegar   se *e*·oo nowng she·*gaarr*
   até às (nove), não me   aa·*te* aas (*no*·ve) nowng me
   espere mais.   es·*pe*·re mais

OK!
   Tá bom!   taa bong

I'll see you then.
   Te vejo depois.   te *ve*·zho de·*poys*

See you later/tomorrow.
   Até mais tarde/   aa·*te* mais *taarr*·de/
   amanhã.   aa·ma·*nyang*

I'm looking forward to it.
   Vou aguardar   vo aa·gwaar·*daarr*
   ansiosamente.   ang·see·o·zaa·*meng*·te

Sorry I'm late.
   Desculpe o atraso.   des·*kool*·pe o aa·*traa*·zo

Never mind.
   Não tem problema.   nowng teng pro·*ble*·ma

samba jamming

From the religious dances of *Candomblé* to the martial arts movements of *capoeira*, dancing finds its way into almost all aspects of the Brazilian lifestyle. No dance has achieved the same popularity as *samba*, a composite of diverse indigenous, African and European dancing styles.

The origins of *samba* lie in a fusion between the indigenous *lundu* dance and the *batuque*, a circular dance practiced by African slaves. By the late-nineteenth century, these styles adopted European characteristics to become *mesemba* and eventually modern *samba*. The percussive music of *samba* is equally rich in its origins and influences.

Spontaneous *samba* jam sessions called *batucadas* erupt in the streets on occasions of national celebration.

drugs

I don't take drugs.
Eu não uso drogas. e·oo nowng oo·zo dro·gaas

I take ... occasionally.
Eu tomo ... de vez em e·oo to·mo ... de vez eng
quando. kwang·do

Do you want to have a smoke?
Você quer fumar um vo·se kerr foo·maarr oom
unzinho? oom·zee·nyo

Do you have a light?
Você tem isqueiro? vo·se teng ees·kay·ro

I'm high.
Estou doidão/ es·to doy·downg/
doidona. m/f doy·do·naa

asking someone out

Would you like to do something (tomorrow)?
*Você quer fazer alguma
coisa (amanhã)?*
vo·se kerr faa·*zerr* ow·*goo*·maa
koy·zaa (aa·ma·*nyang*)

Yes, I'd love to.
Sim, adoraria.
seeng aa·do·raa·*ree*·aa

No, I can't.
Não, não posso.
nowng nowng *po*·so

Where would you like to go (tonight)?
*Onde você quer ir
(hoje à noite)?*
ong·de vo·*se* kerr eerr
(o·zhe aa *noy* te)

pick-up lines

Would you like a drink?
*Você quer beber alguma
coisa?*
vo·se kerr be·*berr* ow·*goo*·maa
koy·zaa

You look like someone I know.
*Você parece com alguém
que eu conheço.*
vo·se paa·*re*·se kong ow·*geng*
ke e·oo ko·*nye*·so

You're a fantastic dancer.
Você dança super bem.
vo·se *dang*·saa soo·perr beng

You're so beautiful!
Você é lindo/linda! m/f
vo·se e *leeng*·do/*leeng*·daa

Can I ...?	*Posso ...?*	*po*·so ...
dance with you	*dançar com você*	dang·*saarr* kong vo·se
sit here	*sentar aqui*	seng·*taarr* aa·*kee*
take you home	*levar você em casa*	le·*vaarr* vo·se eng *kaa*·zaa

local talk

He/She is a …	*Ele/Ela é …*	e·le/e·laa e …
bastard	*um canalha* m	oom kaa·*naa*·lyaa
bitch	*uma cadela* f	oo·maa kaa·*de*·laa

He/She is …	*Ele/Ela é …*	e·le/e·laa e …
great	*demais*	de·*mais*
hot	*tesão*	te·*sowng*
very nice	*super legal*	soo·perr le·*gow*

What a babe!
Que gato/gata! m/f — ke *gaa*·to/*gaa*·taa

He/She gets around.
Ele/Ela dá suas — e·le/e·laa daa soo·aas
voltas. m/f — *vawl*·taas

rejections

I'm here with	*Estou com minha/*	es·to kong *mee*·nyaa
my …	*meu …* m/f	*me*·oo …
boyfriend	*namorado* m	naa·mo·*raa*·do
girlfriend	*namorada* f	naa·mo·*raa*·daa

Excuse me, I have to go now.
Me dá licença, eu — me daa lee·*seng*·saa e·oo
tenho que ir embora. — te·nyo ke eerr eng·*bo*·raa

I'd rather not.
Prefiro que não. — pre·*fee*·ro ke nowng

No, thank you.
Não, obrigado/ — nowng o·bree·*gaa*·do/
obrigada. m/f — o·bree·*gaa*·daa

getting closer

I like you very much.
Gostei muito de você.   gos·*tay* mweeng·to de vo·*se*

You're great.
Você é muito legal.   vo·se e mweeng·to le·*gow*

Can I kiss you?
Posso te dar um beijo?   *po·*so te daarr oom *bay*·zho

Do you want to come inside for a while?
Você quer entrar   vo·se kerr eng·*traarr*
um pouco?   oom *po*·ko

Do you want a massage?
Você quer uma   vo·se kerr *oo*·maa
massagem?   maa·*saa*·zheng

local talk

I'm not interested.
Nao estou   nowng es·*to*
interessado/   eeng·te·re·*saa*·do/
interessada. m/f   eeng·te·re·*saa*·daa

Leave me alone!
Me deixe em paz!   me *day*·she eng paas

Piss off!
Sai fora!   sai *fo*·raa

Give me a break!
Dá um tempo!   daa oom *teng*·po

romance

sex

Kiss me.
Me beija.   me *bay*·zhaa

I want you.
Eu quero você.   e·oo *ke*·ro vo·*se*

I want to make love to you.
Eu quero fazer amor   e·oo *ke*·ro faa·*zerr* aa·*morr*
com você.   kong vo·*se*

Let's go to bed.
Vamos para a cama.   va·mos *paa*·raa aa *ka*·maa

Do you have a (condom)?
Você tem (camisinha)?   vo·*se* teng (kaa·mee·*zee*·nyaa)

Let's use a (condom).
Vamos usar (camisinha).   va·mos oo·*zaarr* (kaa·mee·*zee*·nyaa)

I won't do it without protection.
Não faço sem proteção.   nowng *faa*·so seng pro·te·*sowng*

Touch me here.
Me toca aqui.   me *to*·kaa aa·*kee*

Do you like this?
Você gosta disso?   vo·*se gos*·taa *dee*·so

I (don't) like that.
Eu (não) gosto disso.   e·oo (nowng) *gos*·to *dee*·so

I think we should stop now.
Acho que devemos parar   *aa*·sho ke de·*ve*·mos paa·*raarr*
agora.   aa·*go*·raa

Oh yeah!	*Uau!*	oo·*ow*
Oh my god!	*Ai meu Deus!*	ai *me*·oo de·oos
That's great.	*Que delícia.*	ke de·*lee*·syaa
Easy tiger!	*Calma!*	*kaal*·maa

faster	*mais rápido*	mais *haa*·pee·do
harder	*mais forte*	mais *forr*·te
slower	*mais devagar*	mais de·vaa·*gaarr*
softer	*mais suave*	mais soo·*aa*·ve

It's my first time.
É a minha primeira vez.   e aa *mee*·nyaa pree·*may*·raa vez

It helps to have a sense of humour.
É bom ter senso de humor.   e bong terr *seng*·so de oo·*morr*

Don't worry, I'll do it myself.
Não se preocupe, eu   nowng se pre·o·*koo*·pe e·oo
mesmo/mesma faço. m/f   *mes*·mo/*mes*·maa *faa*·so

That was …	Foi …	foy …
amazing	incrível	eeng·*kree*·vel
weird	estranho	es·*tra*·nyo
wild	uma loucura	oo·maa lo·*koo*·raa

Can I …?	Posso …?	*po*·so …
call you	te ligar	te lee·*gaarr*
meet you	te encontrar	te eng·kong·*traarr*
tomorrow	amanhã	aa·ma·*nyang*
stay over	dormir aqui	dorr·*meerr* aa·*kee*

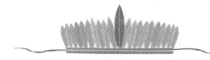

love

I love you.
Eu te amo.   e·oo te *a*·mo

I think we're good together.
Eu acho que nós somos   e·oo *aa*·sho ke nos *so*·mos
ótimos juntos.   *o*·tee·mos zhoong·tos

Will you …?	Você quer …	vo·*se* kerr …
	comigo?	ko·*mee*·go
go out with me	sair	saa·*eerr*
live with me	morar	mo·*raarr*
marry me	casar	kaa·*zaarr*

problems

Are you seeing someone else?
Você está saindo com — vo·*se* es·*taa* saa·*eeng*·do kong
outra pessoa? — o·traa pe·*so*·aa

We're just friends.
Somos só amigos. — so·mos so aa·*mee*·gos

You're just using me for sex.
Você está só me usando — vo·*se* es·ta so me oo·*zang*·do
para sexo. — *paa*·raa sek·so

I don't think it's working out.
Acho que não está — *aa*·sho ke nowng es·*taa*
dando certo. — dang·do serr·to

We'll work it out.
Vamos tentar resolver. — va·mos teng·*taarr* he·sol·*verr*

leaving

I have to leave tomorrow.
Eu tenho que ir — e·oo *te*·nyo ke eerr
embora amanhã. — eng·*bo*·raa aa·ma·*nyang*

I'll … | *Eu vou …* | e·oo vo …
  keep in touch | *manter* | vo mang·*terr*
   | *contato* | kong·*taa*·to
  miss you | *sentir* | seng·*teerr*
   | *sua falta* | soo·aa *fow*·taa

terms of endearment		
amorzão	aa·morr·*zowng*	big love
coração	ko·raa·*sowng*	heart
meu bem	me·oo beng	my good
meu amor	me·oo aa·*morr*	my love
querido/	ke·*ree*·do/	dear
querida m/f	ke·*ree*·daa	

SOCIAL

120

religion

religião

What's your religion?
Qual é a sua religião?
kwow e aa soo·aa he·lee·zhee·owng

I'm not religious.
Não sou religioso/ religiosa. m/f
nowng so he·lee·zhee·o·zo/ he·lee·zhee·o·zaa

I'm ...	Sou ...	so ...
agnostic	agnóstico/ agnóstica m/f	aag·nos·tee·ko/ aaq·nos·tee·kaa
Buddhist	Budista	boo·dees·taa
Catholic	Católico/ Católica m/f	kaa·to·lee·ko/ kaa·to·lee·kaa
Christian	Cristão/ Cristã m/f	krees·towng/ krees·tang
Hindu	Hindu	eeng·doo
Jewish	Judeu/ Judia m/f	zhoo·de·oo/ zhoo·dee·aa
Muslim	Muçulmano/ Muçulmana m/f	moo·sool·ma·no/ moo·sool·ma·naa
spiritist	Espírita	es·pee·ree·taa

gender bending

Remember, gender is indicated on nouns and adjectives. A useful and almost guaranteed way to tell the gender: if it ends in -a, it's femine, in -o, it's masculine.

out of africa

In addition to being home to various world religions, Brazil accommodates a number of unique faiths, often blends of indigenous beliefs, African cults, and mainstream religions that have been introduced to the country. Two of the more common cults that you might come across are *Candomblé* and *Umbanda*.

Candomblé, an African word denoting a dance in honour of the gods, is a general term for the cult in Bahia, and was brought by the Nago, Yoruba, and Jeje peoples. Elsewhere in Brazil the cult is known by different names and it has been adapted to include elements from other belief systems, from christiananity to indigenous faiths: in Rio it's *Macumba*; in Amazonas and Pará it's *Babassuê*; in Pernambuco and Alagoas it's *Xangô*; in Rio Grande do Sul it's either *Pará* or *Batuque*; and the term *Tambor* is used in Maranhão.

Umbanda, or white magic, is a mixture of *Candomblé* and spiritism. It traces its origins from various sources, including Bantu culture.

I (don't) believe in ...	Eu (não) acredito em ...	e·oo (nowng) aa·kre·dee·to eng ...
astrology	astrologia	aas·tro·lo·zhee·aa
fate	destino	des·tee·no
God	Deus	de·oos

Can I ... here?	Posso ... aqui?	po·so ... aa·kee
Where can I ...?	Onde posso ...?	ong·de po·so ...
attend	assistir	aa·sees·teerr
mass	uma missa	oo·maa mee·saa
pray	rezar	he·zaarr
worship	venerar	ve·ne·haarr

cultural differences

Is this a local or national custom?
Este é um costume es·te e oom kos·*too*·me
local ou nacional? lo·*kow* o·oo naa·see·o·*now*

I don't want to offend you.
Não quero ofendê-lo/ nowng *ke*·ro o·feng·*de*·lo/
ofendê-la. m/f o·feng·*de*·laa

I'm not used to this.
Não estou nowng es·*to*
acostumado/ aa·kos·too·*maa*·do/
acostumada com isso. m/f aa·kos·too·*maa*·daa kong *ee*·so

I'd rather not join in.
Prefiro não fazer parte.   pre·*fee*·ro nowng faa·*zerr* *paarr*·te

I'll try it.
Vou experimentar.   vo es·pe·ree·meng·*taarr*

I didn't mean to do/say anything wrong.
Não tive intenção de fazer/dizer qualquer coisa errada.   nowng *tee*·ve eeng·teng·*sowng* de faa·*zerr*/dee·*zerr* kwow·*kerr* *koy*·zaa e·*haa*·daa

I'm sorry, it's against my ...	*Me desculpe, mas é contra minha ...*	me des·*kool*·pe maas e *kong*·traa *mee*·nyaa ...
beliefs	*crença*	*kreng*·saa
religion	*religião*	he·lee·zhee·*owng*
This is ...	*Isto é ...*	*ees*·to e ...
different	*diferente*	dee·fe·*reng*·te
fun	*divertido*	dee·verr·*tee*·do
interesting	*interessante*	eeng·te·re·*sang*·te

sporting interests

interesses esportivos

What sport do you ...?	*Que esporte você ...?*	ke es·*porr*·te vo·*se* ...
follow	*acompanha*	aa·kong·*pa*·nyaa
play	*pratica*	praa·*tee*·kaa
I play ...	*Eu jogo ...*	e·oo *zho*·go ...
basketball	*basquete*	baas·*ke*·te
tennis	*tênis*	*te*·nees
volleyball	*vôlei*	vo·lay
I do ...	*Eu faço ...*	e·oo *faa*·so ...
athletics	*atletismo*	aat·le·*tees*·mo
karate	*karatê*	kaa·raa·*te*
scuba diving	*mergulho*	merr·*goo*·lyo

I follow ...	*Eu acompanho ...*	e·oo aa·kong·*pa*·nyo ...
football (soccer)	*futebol de campo*	foo·te·*bol* de *kang*·po
motor racing	*corrida de carros*	ko·*hee*·daa de *kaa*·hos
surfing	*surfe*	*soorr*·fe
I ...	*Eu ...*	e·oo ...
cycle	*ando de bicicleta*	*ang*·do de bee·see·*kle*·taa
run	*corro*	*ko*·ho
walk	*caminho*	ka·*mee*·nyo

For more sports, see the **dictionary**.

Do you like (cricket)?
Você gosta (de cricket)?   vo·*se gos*·taa (de *kree*·ke·tee)

Yes, very much.
Sim, gosto muito.   seeng *gos*·to *mweeng*·to

Not really.
Não muito.   nowng *mweeng*·to

I like watching it.
Eu gosto de assistir.   e·oo *gos*·to de aa·sees·*teerr*

Who's your	*Qual é o seu …*	kwow e o *se*·oo …
favourite …?	*favorito?*	faa·vo·*ree*·to
sportsperson	*esportista*	es·*porr*·tees·taa
team	*time*	*tee*·me

scoring

What's the score?
Quanto está o jogo?   *kwang*·to es·*taa* o *zho*·go

draw/even	*empate*	eng·*paa*·te
love	*zero*	*ze*·ro
match-point	*match point*	*me*·tee po·eeng·tee
nil	*zero*	*ze*·ro

going to a game

indo a um jogo

Would you like to go to a game?
Você gostaria de ir   vo·*se* gos·taa·*ree*·aa de eerr
a um jogo?   aa oom *zho*·go

Who are you supporting?
Para quem você torce?   *paa*·raa keng vo·*se torr*·se

Who's ...?	Quem está ...?	keng es·taa ...
playing	jogando	zho·gang·do
winning	ganhando	ga·nyang·do

That was a ... game!	Foi um jogo ...!	foy oom zho·go ...
bad	ruim	hoo·eeng
boring	chato	shaa·to
great	ótimo	o·tee·mo

playing sport

Do you want to play?
Você quer jogar?
vo·se kerr zho·gaarr

Can I join in?
Posso jogar com vocês?
po·so zho·gaarr kong vo·ses

That would be great.
Seria ótimo.
se·ree·aa o·tee·mo

I can't.
Não posso.
nowng po·so

I have an injury.
*Estou machucado/
machucado.* m/f
es·to maa·shoo·kaa·do
maa·shoo·kaa·daa

Your/My point.
Teu/Meu ponto.
te·oo/me·oo pong·to

Kick/Pass it to me!
*Chuta/Passa para
mim!*
shoo·taa/paa·saa paa·raa
meeng

You're a good player.
Você é um bom jogador.
vo·se e oom bong zho·gaa·dorr

Thanks for the game.
*Obrigado/obrigada
pelo jogo.* m/f
o·bree·gaa·do/o·bree·gaa·daa
pe·lo zho·go

Where's a good place to ...?	Onde tem um bom lugar para ...?	ong·de teng oom bong loo·gaarr paa·raa ...
fish	pescar	pes·kaarr
go horse riding	andar à cavalo	ang·daar aa kaa·vaa·lo
run	correr	ko·herr
ski	esquiar	es·kee·aarr
snorkel	fazer snorkel	faa·zerr ees·norr·kel
surf	surfar	soor·faarr

Where's the nearest ...?	Onde fica ... mais perto?	ong·de fee·kaa ... mais perr·to
golf course	o campo de golfe	o kang·po de gol·fe
gym	a ginástica	aa zhee·naas·tee·kaa
swimming pool	a piscina	aa pee·see·naa
tennis court	a quadra de tênis	aa kwaa·draa de te·nees

What's the charge per ...?	Quanto custa por ...?	kwang·to koos·taa porr ...
day	dia	dee·aa
game	jogo	zho·go
hour	hora	aw·raa
visit	visita	vee·zee·taa

Can I hire a ...?	Posso alugar uma ...?	po·so aa·loo·gaarr oo·maa ...
ball	bola	bo·laa
bicycle	bicicleta	bee·see·kle·taa
court	quadra	kwaa·draa
racquet	raquete	haa·ke·te

Do I have to be a member to attend?
Tem que ser membro — têng ke ser *meng*·bro
para entrar? — paa·raa eng·*traarr*

Is there a women-only session?
Tem uma seção só — teng oo·maa se·*sowng* so
para mulheres? — paa·raa moo·*lye*·res

Where are the changing rooms?
Onde ficam os — ong·de fee·kang os
vestiários? — ves·tee·*aa*·ree·os

diving

Where's a good diving site?
Onde tem um lugar — ong·de teng oom loo·*gaarr*
bom para mergulho? — bong *puu·raa* merr·*goo*·lyo

Is the visibility good?
A visibilidade é boa? — aa vee·zee·bee·lee·*daa*·de e bo·aa

How deep is the dive?
Qual a profundidade? — kwow aa pro·foong·dee·*daa*·de

I need an air fill.
Preciso encher o — pre·*see*·zo eng·sherr o
tanque de ar. — tang·ke de aarr

Is it a …	Este é um	es·te e oom
dive?	mergulho …?	merr·*goo*·lyo …
boat	a partir de	aa paarr·*teerr* de
	um barco	oom *baar*·ko
shore	litorâneo	lee·to·*ra*·ne·o

Are there …?	Tem …?	teng …
currents	corrente	ko·*heng*·te
sharks	tubarão	too·ba·*rowng*
whales	baleia	baa·*le*·yaa

I want to hire (a) …	Quero alugar …	ke·ro aa·loo·gaarr …
buoyancy vest	colete	ko·le·te
diving equipment	equipamento de mergulho	e·kee·paa·meng·to de merr·goo·lyo
flippers	nadadeiras	na·da·dei·ras
mask	máscara	maas·kaa·raa
regulator	regulador	he·goo·laa·dorr
snorkel	snorkel	ees·norr·kel
tank	tanque	tang·ke
weight belt	cinto com peso	seeng·to kong pe·zo
wetsuit	roupa de borracha	ho·paa de bo·haa·shaa

I'd like to …	Gostaria de …	gos·taa·ree·aa de …
explore caves	explorar cavernas	es·plo·raar kaa·verr·naas
explore wrecks	explorar navios naufragados	es·plo·raar naa·vee·os now·fraa·gaa·dos
go night diving	fazer um mergulho noturno	faa·zerr oom merr·goo·lyo no·toor·no
go scuba diving	mergulhar com tanque	merr·goo·lyaarr kong tang·ke
go snorkelling	fazer snorkel	faa·zerr ees·norr·kel
join a diving tour	fazer parte de um grupo de mergulho	faa·zerr paarr·te de oom groo·po de merr·goo·lyo
learn to dive	aprender a mergulhar	aa·preng·derr aa merr·goo·lyaarr

buddy	companheiro m	kong·pa·*nyay*·ro
cave	caverna f	kaa·*verr*·naa
a dive	mergulho m	merr·*goo*·lyo
to dive	mergulhar	merr·goo·*lyaarr*
diving boat	barco m para	*baar*·ko paa·raa
	mergulho	merr·*goo*·lyo
diving course	curso m de	*koor*·so de
	mergulho	merr·*goo*·lyo
night dive	mergulho m	merr·*goo*·lyo
	noturno	no·*toorr*·no
wreck	navio m	naa·*vee*·o
	naufragado	now·fraa·*gaa*·do

See also **watersports**, page 134.

extreme sports

I'd like to go ...	Eu queria	e·oo ke·*ree*·aa
	fazer ...	faa·*zerr* ...
abseiling	rapel	haa·*pel*
caving	exploração de	es·plo·raa·*sowng* de
	cavernas	kaa·*verr*·naas
canyoning	canyoning	*kang*·nyo·neeng
hang-gliding	vôo livre	*vo*·o *lee*·vre
mountain	mountain	*maa*·oong·tayng
biking	bike	*bai*·kee
paragliding	parapente	paa·raa·*peng*·te
parasailing	parasailing	paa·raa·*say*·leeng
rock-climbing	escalada	es·kaa·*laa*·daa
skydiving	skydiving	ees·kai·*dai*·veeng
white-water	rafting	*haa*·fee·teeng
rafting		

Is the equipment secure?
Este equipamento é — es·te e·kee·paa·*meng*·to e
seguro? — se·*goo*·ro

This is insane.
Isto é loucura. — *ees*·to e lo·*koo*·raa

horse riding

How much is a (one) hour ride?
> Quanto é o passeio de
> (uma) hora?

> kwang·to e o paa·se·yo de
> (oo·maa) aw·raa

How long is the ride?
> Quanto tempo é
> o passeio?

> kwang·to teng·po e
> o paa·se·yo

I'm (not) an experienced rider.
> Eu (não) sou experiente.

> e·oo (nowng) so es·pe·ree·eng·te

Can I rent a hat and boots?
> Posso alugar um
> chapéu e botas?

> po·so aa·loo·gaarr oom
> shaa·pe·oo e bo·taas

bit	freio m	fre·yo
bridle	rédea f	he·dyaa
canter	galope m	gaa·lo·pe
crop	chicote m	shee·ko·te
gallop	galope m	gaa·lo·pe
groom	tratar	tra·taarr
horse	cavalo m	kaa·vaa·lo
pony	pônei m	po·nay
reins	rédeas f pl	he·dyaas
saddle	sela f	se·laa
stable	estábulo m	es·taa·boo·lo
stirrup	estribo m	es·tree·bo
trot	trote m	tro·te
walk	andar	ang·daarr

soccer

Who plays for (Flamengo)?
Quem joga no (Flamengo)? — keng *zho*·gaa no (flaa·*meng*·go)

He's a great (player).
Ele é um ótimo (jogador). — e·le e oom o·tee·mo (zho·gaa·*dorr*)

He played brilliantly in the match against (Argentina).
Ele jogou muito bem no jogo contra (a Argentina). — e·le zho·goo mweeng·to beng no *zho*·go *kong*·traa (aa aarr·zheng·*tee*·naa)

Which team is at the top of the league?
Que time está na frente da liga? — ke *tee*·me es·*taa* naa *freng*·te daa *lee*·qaa

What a great/terrible team!
Que time ótimo/horrível! — ke *tee*·me o·tee·mo/o·*hee*·vel

ball	*bola* f	*bo*·laa
coach	*técnico* m	*tek*·nee·ko
corner (kick)	*escanteio* m	es·kang·*te*·yo
fan	*fã* m&f	fang
foul	*falta* f	*fow*·taa
free kick	*bater a falta*	baa·*terr* aa *fow*·taa
goal	*gol* m	gol
goal (place)	*trave* f	*tra*·ve
goalkeeper	*goleiro* m	go·*lay*·ro
offside	*lateral*	laa·te·*row*
penalty	*pênalti* m	*pe*·now·tee
player	*jogador* m	zho·gaa·*dorr*
red card	*cartão* m *vermelho*	kaarr·*towng* verr·*me*·lyo
referee	*juiz* m	joo·*ees*
striker	*atacante* m	aa·taa·*kang*·te
team	*time* m	*tee*·me
throw in	*bater a lateral*	baa·*terr* aa laa·te·*row*
yellow card	*cartão* m *amarelo*	kaarr·*towng* aa·maa·*re*·lo

water sports

Can I book a lesson?
Posso marcar uma   po·so maarr·*kaarr* oo·maa
aula?   ow·laa

Can I hire (a) ...	*Posso alugar ...*	po·so aa·loo·*gaarr* ...
boat	*um barco*	oom *baar*·ko
canoe	*uma canoa*	oo·maa ka·*no*·aa
kayak	*um caiaque*	oom kai·*aa*·ke
life jacket	*um colete*	oom ko·*le*·te
	salva-vidas	sow·vaa·*vee*·daas
snorkelling	*equipamento*	e·kee·paa·*meng*·to
gear	*para fazer*	paa·raa faa·*zerr*
	snorkel	ees·*norr*·kel
water-skis	*esqui*	es·*kee*
	aquático	aa·*kwaa*·tee·ko
wetsuit	*roupa de*	ho·paa de
	borracha	bo·*haa*·shaa

Are there any ...?	*Tem ...?*	teng ...
reefs	*recifes*	he·*see*·fes
rips	*corredeira*	ko·he·*day*·raa
water hazards	*algum risco*	ow·*goom* hees·ko
	na água	naa *aa*·gwaa
waves	*ondas*	ong·daas

boogie board	*morey* m *boogie*	mo·ray boo·gee
motorboat	*barco* m *a motor*	baarr·ko aa mo·*torr*
oars	*remos* m pl	he·mos
sailing boat	*barco* m *a vela*	baarr·ko aa ve·laa
surfboard	*prancha* f *de surfe*	prang·shaa de soor·fee
surfing	*surfe* m	soorr·fee
wave	*onda* f	ong·daa
wind	*vento* f	veng·to
windsurfing	*windsurf* m	weeng·dee·soor·fee

See also **diving,** page 129.

hiking

caminhada

Where can I ...?	*Onde posso ...?*	ong·de po·so ...
buy supplies	*comprar*	kong·*praarr*
	mantimentos	mang·tee·*meng*·tos
find someone	*encontrar*	eng·kong·*traarr*
who knows	*alguém que*	ow·*geng* ke
this area	*conheça esta*	ko·*nye*·saa es·taa
	area	*aa*·re·aa
get a map	*pegar um*	pe·*gaarr* oom
	mapa	*maa*·paa
hire hiking gear	*alugar*	aa·loo·*gaarr*
	equipamento	e·kee·paa·*meng*·to
	de caminhada	de kaa·mee·*nyaa*·daa
How ...?	*Qual é a ...?*	kwow e aa ...
high is the	*altura*	ow·*too*·raa
climb	*da subida?*	daa soo·*bee*·daa
long is the trail	*distância*	dees·*tang*·syaa
	do caminho	do ka·*mee*·nyo

Do we need a guide?
Precisamos de um guia? pre·see·*za*·mos de oom *gee*·aa

Are there guided treks?
Tem caminhadas teng ka·mee·*nyaa*·daas
com guia? kong *gee*·aa

Is it safe?
É seguro? e se·*goo*·ro

Is there a hut?
Tem abrigo? teng aa·*bree*·go

When does it get dark?
Quando escurece? *kwang*·do es·koo·*re*·se

Do we need to take …?	Precisamos levar …?	pre·see·za·mos le·vaarr …
bedding	roupa de cama	ho·paa de ka·maa
food	comida	ko·mee·daa
water	água	aa·gwaa

Is the track …?	O caminho …?	o ka·mee·nyo …
(well-)marked	é (bem) marcado	e (beng) maarr·kaa·do
open	esta aberto	es·taa aa·berr·to
scenic	é pitoresco	e pee·to·res·ko

Which is the … route?	Qual é a rota mais …?	kwow e aa ho·taa mais …
easiest	fácil	faa·seel
most interesting	interessante	eeng·te·re·sang·te
shortest	curta	koorr·taa

Where can I find a/the …?	Onde posso encontrar …?	ong·de po·so eng·kong·traarr …
camping ground	a área de camping	aa aa·re·aa de kang·peeng
nearest village	cidade mais perto	see·daa·de mais perr·to
showers	um chuveiro	oom shoo·vay·ro
toilets	um banheiro	oom ba·nyay·ro

Where have you come from?
De onde você veio?   de ong·de vo·se vay·o

How long did it take?
Quanto tempo leva?   kwang·to teng·po le·vaa

Does this path go to ...?
Este caminho   es te ka·mee·nyo
leva para ...?   le·vaa paa·raa ...

Can I go through here?
Posso ir por aqui?   po·so eerr porr aa·kee

Is the water OK to drink?
A água é boa para   a aa·gwaa e bo·aa paa·raa
beber?   be·berr

I'm lost.
Estou perdido/perdida. m/f   es·to perr·dee·do/perr·dee·daa

listen for ...

e pe·ree·go·zo
É perigoso.   **It's dangerous.**

koo·ee·daa·do kom a he·saa·kaa
Cuidado com a ressaca!   **Be careful of the undertow!**

beach

a praia

Where's the ... beach?	Onde fica a ...?	ong·de fee·kaa aa ...
best	melhor praia	me·lyorr prai·aa
nearest	praia	praa·yaa
	mais perto	mais perr·to
nudist	praia de	praa·yaa de
	nudismo	noo·dees·mo
public	praia	praa·yaa
	pública	poo·blee·kaa

outdoors

137

Proibido Mergulhar	pro·ee·*bee*·do mer·goo·*lyaarr*	**No Diving**
Proibido Nadar	pro·ee·*bee*·do naa·*daarr*	**No Swimming**

How much for a/an ...?	*Quanto custa ...?*	kwang·to koos·taa ...
chair	*uma cadeira*	*oo*·maa kaa·*day*·raa
hut	*um abrigo*	oom aa·*bree*·go
umbrella	*um guarda sol*	oom *gwaarr*·daa sol

weather

tempo

What's the weather like?
Como está o tempo?   ko·mo es·*taa* o teng·po

What will the weather be like tomorrow?
Como estará o tempo amanhã?   ko·mo es·taa·*raa* o teng·po aa·ma·*nyang*

It's ...	*Está ...*	es·taa ...
cloudy	*nublado*	noo·*blaa*·do
cold	*frio*	*free*·o
fine	*bom*	bong
freezing	*um gelo*	oom *zhe*·lo
hot	*quente*	*keng*·te
raining	*chovendo*	sho·*veng*·do
snowing	*nevando*	ne·*vang*·do
sunny	*ensolarado*	eng·so·laa·*raa*·do
warm	*ameno*	aa·*me*·no
windy	*ventando*	veng·*tang*·do

Where can I buy ...?	Onde posso comprar um ...?	ong·de po·so kong·praarr oom
a rain jacket	casaco de chuva	kaa·zaa·ko de shoo·vaa
an umbrella	guarda-chuva	gwaarr·daa·shoo·vaa
dry season	época f de seca	e·po·kaa de se·kaa
wet season	época f de chuvas	e·po·kaa de shoo·vaas

flora & fauna

What ... is that?	O que é ...?	o ke e ...
animal	aquele animal	aa·ke·le aa·nee·mow
flower	aquela flor	aa·ke·laa florr
plant	aquela planta	aa·ke·laa plang·taa
tree	aquela árvore	aa·ke·laa aarr·vo·re

local plants & animals

arara (macaw)	arara f	aa·raa·raa
golden lion	mico leão m	mee·ko le·owng
parrot	papagaio m	paa·paa·gaa·yo
toucan	tucano m	too·ka·no

jacaranda (flowering Brazilian tree)
jacarandá f zhaa·kaa·rang·daa

Victoria Amazonica (the national flower, a water lily)
vitória-régia f vee·to·ree·a·he·gee·aa

outdoors

What's it used for?
 Para que serve? — paa·raa ke serr·ve

Can you eat the fruit?
 Pode-se comer a fruta? — po·de·se ko·merr aa froo·taa

Is it ...?	*Isto ...?*	ees·to ...
common	*é comum*	e ko·moom
dangerous	*é perigoso*	e pe·ree·go·zo
endangered	*está ameaçado/ ameaçada de extinção* m/f	es·taa aa·me·aa·saa·do/ aa·me·aa·saa·daa de es·teeng·sowng
poisonous	*é venenoso*	e ve·ne·no·zo
protected	*está protegido/ protegida* m/f	es·taa pro·te·zhee·do/ pro·te·zhee·daa

A typical breakfast consists of coffee, milk, juice, bread, jam, cheese, ham and fruit. Lunch is usually rice, beans (black or white depending on the region), vegetables and meat of some kind. Dinner is similar to lunch, though a lighter style of dinner, more akin to breakfast, is increasing in popularity.

key language

linguagem chave

breakfast	café m da manhã	kaa·fe daa ma·nyang
lunch	almoço m	ow·mo·so
dinner	jantar m	zhang·taarr
snack	lanche m	lang·she
eat	comer	ko·merr
drink	beber	be·berr
I'd like …	Gostaria de …	gos·taa·ree·aa de …
Please.	Por favor.	porr faa·vorr
Thank you.	Obrigado/ Obrigada. m/f	o·bree·gaa·do/ o·bree·gaa·daa
I'm starving!	Estou faminto/ faminta! m/f	es·to faa·meeng·to/ faa·meeng·taa

finding a place to eat

encontrando um lugar para comer

Can you recommend a …	Você pode recomendar um …	vo·se po·de he·ko·meng·daarr oom …
bar	bar	baarr
cafe	café	kaa·fe
restaurant	restaurante	hes·tow·rang·te

Where would you go for …?	Onde você iria para …?	ong·de vo·se ee·ree·aa paa·raa …
a celebration	uma comemoração	oo·maa ko·me·mo·ra·sowng
a cheap meal	uma refeição barata	oo·maa he·fay·sowng baa·raa·taa
local specialities	especialidades locais	es·pe·see·aa·lee·daa·des lo·kais

I'd like to reserve a table for …	Eu gostaria de reservar uma mesa para …	e·oo gos·taa·ree·aa de he·zer·vaarr oo·maa me·zaa paa·raa …
(two) people	(duas) pessoas	(doo·aas) pe·so·aas
(eight) o'clock	(às oito) horas	(aas oy·to) aw·raas

I'd like …, please.	Eu queria …, por favor.	e·oo ke·ree·aa … porr faa·vorr
a children's menu	o cardápio de crianças	o kaar·da·pyo de kree·ang·saas
a half portion	meia porção	me·yaa porr·sowng
a menu in English	o cardápio em inglês	o kaar·daa·pyo eng eeng·gles
a table for (five)	uma mesa para (cinco)	oo·maa me·zaa paa·raa (seeng·ko)
the drink list	a lista de bebidas	aa lees·taa de be·bee·daas
the menu	o cardápio	o kaar·daa·pyo
the (non-) smoking section	(não-) fumantes	(nowng·) foo·mang·tes

Are you still serving food?

Vocês ainda estão
servindo comida?

vo·ses aa·eeng·daa es·towng
serr·veeng·do ko·mee·daa

How long is the wait?

A espera é de quanto tempo?   aa es·pe·raa e de kwang·to teng·po

going nuts

There's no single word to translate 'nuts'. You have to say which kind of nut you mean, for example *noz* (walnut), *amendoin* (peanut), and *amêndoas* (almond).

listen for ...

aa·*kee* es·*taa*
Aqui está!   **Here you go!**

es·*ta*·mos fe·*shaa*·dos
Estamos fechados.   **We're closed.**

es·*ta*·mos lo·*taa*·dos
Estamos lotados.   **We're full.**

o ke *po*·so serr·*vee*·los
O que posso serví-los?   **What can I get for you?**

ong·de vo·*ses* gos·*taa·ree*·ang de seng·*taarr*
Onde vocês gostariam   **Where would you**
de sentar?   **like to sit?**

oom mo·*meng*·to
Um momento.   **One moment.**

restaurant

restaurante

At a restaurant, use *senhor* or *senhora* when addressing the
waiter or waitress.

What would you recommend?
O que você recomenda?   o ke vo·*se* he·ko·*meng*·daa

What's in that dish?
O que tem neste prato?   o ke teng *nes*·te *praa*·to

I'll have that.
Eu quero isto.   *e*·oo *ke*·ro *ees*·to

Does it take long to prepare?
Leva muito tempo   *le*·vaa *mweeng*·to *teng*·po
para preparar?   *paa*·raa pre·paa·*raar*

Is it self-serve?
Nós mesmos nos servimos?   nos *mes*·mos nos serr·*vee*·mos

Is service included in the bill?
O serviço está   o serr·*vee*·so es·*taa*
incluído na conta?   eeng·kloo·*ee*·do naa *kong*·taa

Are these complimentary?
É cortesia da casa?   e kor·te·*zee*·aa daa *kaa*·zaa

eating out

143

I'd like ...	Eu quero ...	e·oo ke·ro ...
a local speciality	a especialidade local	aa es·pe·see·aa·lee·*daa*·de lo·*kow*
a meal fit for a king	uma refeição suntuosa	oo·maa he·fay·*sowng* soom·too·o·zaa
the chicken	o frango	o *frang*·go

I'd like it with/ without ...	Eu queria com/ sem ...	e·oo ke·*ree*·aa kong/ seng ...
chilli	pimenta	pee·*meng*·taa
garlic	alho	*aa*·lyo
oil	óleo	o·lyo

listen for ...

e·oo soo·*zhee*·ro ...
Eu sugiro ...   I suggest ...

ko·mo vo·*se* gos·taa·*ree*·aa ke fo·se ko·*zee*·do
Como você gostaria que   How would you like
fosse cozido?   that cooked?

vo·*se* gos·taa de ...
Você gosta de ...?   Do you like ...?

at the table

à mesa

Please bring ...	Por favor traga ...	porr faa·*vorr* traa·gaa ...
a cloth	uma toalha	oo·maa to·*aa*·lyaa
a serviette	um guardanapo	oom gwaar·daa·*naa*·po
a wineglass	uma taça de vinho	oo·maa *taa*·saa de *vee*·nyo
the bill	a conta	aa *kong*·taa

talking food

I love this dish.
Adorei este prato.
aa·do·*ray* es·te *praa*·to

I love the local cuisine.
Adorei a cozinha local.
aa·do·*ray* aa ko·*zee*·nyaa lo·*kow*

That was delicious!
Estava delicioso!
es·*taa*·vaa de·lee·see·o·zo

My compliments to the chef.
Meus cumprimentos ao chefe.
me·oos koom·pree·*meng*·tos ow *she*·fe

I'm full.
Estou satisfeito/ satisfeita. m/f
es·*to* saa·tees·*fay*·to/ saa·tees·*fay*·taa

This is …	Está …	es·*taa* …
(too) cold	(demais) frio	(*zhee*·mais) *free*·o
spicy	apimentado	aa·pee·meng·*taa*·do
superb	excelente	e·se·*leng*·te

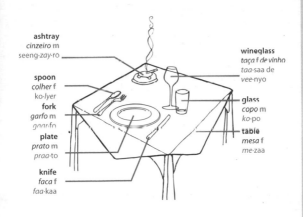

ashtray
cinzeiro m
seeng·*zay*·ro

spoon
colher f
ko·*lyer*

fork
garfo m
gaar·fo

plate
prato m
praa·to

knife
faca f
faa·kaa

wineglass
taça f *de vinho*
taa·saa de *vee*·nyo

glass
copo m
ko·po

table
mesa f
me·zaa

look for ...		
aperitivos	aa·pe·ree·*tee*·vos	appetisers
sopas	*so*·paas	soups
entradas	eng·*traa*·daas	entrees
saladas	saa·*laa*·daas	salads
pratos	*praa*·tos	main courses
principais	preeng·see·*pais*	
sobremesas	so·bre·*me*·zaas	desserts
aperitivos	aa·pe·ree·*tee*·vos	aperitifs
refrigerantes	he·free·zhe·*rang*·tes	soft drinks
bebidas	be·*bee*·daas	spirits
destiladas	des·tee·*laa*·daas	
cervejas	serr·*ve*·zhaas	beers
vinhos	*vee*·nyos	sparkling wines
espumantes	es·poo·*mang*·tes	
vinhos brancos	*vee*·nyos *brang*·kos	white wines
vinhos tintos	*vee*·nyos *teeng*·tos	red wines
vinhos de	*vee*·nyos de	dessert wines
sobremesa	so·bre·*me*·zaa	
digestivos	dee·zhes·*tee*·vos	digestifs

breakfast

café da manhã

What's a typical breakfast?

Como é um típico	ko·mo e oom *tee*·pee·ko
café da manhã?	kaa·*fe* daa ma·*nyang*

bacon	*bacon* m	*bay*·kon
bread	*pão* m	powng
butter	*manteiga* f	mang·*tay*·gaa
cake	*bolo* m	*bo*·lo
cereal	*cereal* m	se·re·*ow*
cheese bread	*pão* m *de queijo*	powng de *kay*·zho
cold cuts	*frios* m	*free*·os
corn bread	*broa* f *de milho*	*bro*·aa de *mee*·lyo

... eggs	ovos ... m	o·vos ...
boiled	quentes	keng·tes
fried	fritos	free·tos
hard-boiled	cozidos duros	ko·zee·dos doo·ros
poached	pochés	po·shes
scrambled	mexidos	me·shee·dos

fruit juice	suco m de frutas	soo·ko de froo·taas
jam	geléia f	zhe·le·yaa
milk	leite m	lay·te
muesli	muesli m	moos·lee
omelette	omelete f	o·me·le·te
(oat/maize)	mingau m	meeng·gow
porridge	(de aveia/maizena)	(de aa·ve·yaa/mai·ze·naa)
toast	torrada f	to·haa·daa

For other breakfast items and related language, see **self-catering**, page 153, and the **culinary reader**, page 159.

light meals

refeições leves

What's that called?

Como se chama isso?   ko·mo se sha·maa ee·so

I'd like ...,	Eu queria ....,	e·oo ke·ree·aa ...
please.	por favor.	porr faa·vorr
a piece	um pedaço	oom pe·daa·so
a sandwich	um sanduíche	oom sang·doo·ee·she
one slice	uma fatia	oo·maa faa·tee·aa
that one	aquele	aa·ke·le
two	dois	doys

condiments

Do you have ...?	Tem ...?	teng ...
chilli sauce	molho de pimenta	mo·lyo de pee·meng·taa
ketchup	ketchup	ket·shoo·pee
pepper	pimenta	pee·meng·taa
salt	sal	sow
tomato sauce	molho de tomate	mo·lyo de to·maa·te
vinegar	vinagre	vee·naa·gre

For additional items, see the **culinary reader**, page 159.

methods of preparation

métodos de preparo

I'd like it ...	Eu queria ...	e·oo ke·ree·aa ...
I don't want it ...	Eu não queria ...	e·oo nowng ke·ree·aa ...
boiled	cozido/ cozido m/f	ko·zee·do/ ko·zee·daa
broiled	na brasa	naa braa·zaa
deep-fried	frito/frita em recipiente m/f	free·to/free·taa eng he·see·pyeng·te
fried	frito/frita m/f	free·to/free·taa
grilled	grelhado/ grelhada m/f	gre·lyaa·do/ gre·lyaa·daa
medium	ao ponto	ow pong·to
rare	mal passado/ passada m/f	mow paa·saa·do/ paa·saa·daa
re-heated	requentado/ requentada m/f	he·keng·taa·do/ he·keng·taa·daa
steamed	ao vapor	ow vaa·porr
well-done	bem passado/ passado m/f	beng paa·saa·do/ paa·saa·daa
with the dressing on the side	com o molho separado	kong o mo·lyo se·paa·raa·do
without ...	sem ...	seng ...

Everywhere you go, you'll find places selling the famous *pastel* and *caldo de cana*, a must. The *pastel* is a deep-fried pastry with chicken, mince or cheese filling. Don't be intimidated by their size (usually huge!) – there's a lot of air inside the pastry. It's generally washed down with *caldo de cana*, sugar cane juice. Other local snacks include:

coxinha f *de galinha*	ko·*shee*·nyaa de gaa·*lee*·nyaa	chicken-filled croquette
empada f *de frango/camarão*	eng·paá·*daa* de fran·go/kaa·maa·*rowng*	chicken/prawn pastry
quibe m	*kee*·be	deep-fried meatballs

in the bar

Excuse me!
  Com licença!   kong lee·*seng*·saa

I'll have …
  Eu queria …   e·oo ke·*ree*·aa …

I'm next.
  Eu sou o próximo/ próxima. m/f   e·oo so o pro·*see*·mo/ pro·*see*·maa

Same again, please.
  O mesmo, por favor.   o *mes*·mo porr faa·*vorr*

No ice, thanks.
  Sem gelo, obrigado/ obrigada. m/f   seng *zhe*·lo o·bree·*gaa*·do/ o bree·*gaa*·daa

I'll buy you a drink.
  Eu te pago uma bebida.   e·oo te *paa*·go *oo*·maa be·*bee*·daa

What would you like?
  O que você quer?   o ke vo·*se* kerr

It's my round.
É minha vez. e *mee*·nyaa ves

How much is that?
Quanto é? *kwang*·to e

Do you serve meals here?
Vocês servem refeições vo·ses serr·*veng* he·fay·*soyngs*
aqui? aa·kee

listen for ...

a·sho ke ja *she*·gaa *paa*·raa vo·*se*
Acho que já chega para **I think you've had**
você. **enough.**

o ke vo·*se* es·*taa* be·*bang*·do
O que você está bebendo? **What are you having?**

ool·tee·mos pe·*dee*·dos
Últimos pedidos. **Last orders.**

nonalcoholic drinks

bebidas sem álcool

... mineral water	*água mineral ...*	aa·gwaa mee·ne·*row* ...
sparkling	*com gás*	kong gaas
still	*sem gás*	seng gaas
orange juice	*suco de laranja*	soo·ko de laa·*rang*·zhaa
soft drink	*refrigerante*	he·*free*·zhe·*rang*·te
(hot) water	*água (quente)*	aa·gwaa (*keng*·te)
(cup of) tea	*(xícara) de chá*	(*shee*·kaa·raa) de shaa
(cup of) coffee	*(xícara) de café*	(*shee*·kaa·raa) de kaa·*fe*
... with (milk)	*... com (leite)*	... kong (*lay*·te)
... without (sugar)	*... sem (açúcar)*	... seng (aa·*soo*·kaarr)

alcoholic drinks

beer	*cerveja* f	serr·*ve*·zhaa
brandy	*brandy* m	*brang*·dee
champagne	*champagne* f	shang·*pa*·nye
cocktail	*coquetel* m	ko·ke·*tel*

a shot of ...	*uma dose de ...*	oo·maa *do*·ze de ...
gin	*gin*	zheeng
rum	*rum*	hoom
tequila	*tequila*	te·*kee*·laa
vodka	*vodka*	*vo*·dee·kaa
whisky	*whisky*	oo·*ees*·kee
cachaça	*cachaça*	kaa·*shaa*·saa
a bottle/glass of ... wine	*uma garrafa/ taça de vinho ...*	oo·maa gaa·*haa*·faa/ *taa*·saa de *vee*·nyo ...
dessert	*de sobremesa*	de so·bre·*me*·zaa
red	*tinto*	*teeng*·to
rosé	*rosé*	ho·*ze*
sparkling	*espumante*	es·poo·*mang*·te
white	*branco*	*brang*·ko
a ... of beer	*... de cerveja*	... de serr·*ve*·jaa
glass	*um copo*	oom *ko*·po
jug	*uma jarra*	oo·maa *zhaa*·haa
large bottle	*uma garrafa grande*	oo·maa gaa·*haa*·faa *grang*·de
pint	*um choppe*	oom *sho*·pee
small bottle	*uma garrafa pequena*	oo·maa gaa·*haa*·faa pe·*ke*·naa

drinking up

Cheers!
Saúde!
sa·*oo*·de

This is hitting the spot.
Caiu bem.
kaa·*ee*·oo beng

Pull my finger!
Puxe meu dedo!
poo·*she* me·oo *de*·do

I think I've had one too many.
Acho que bebi mais do que deveria.
a·sho ke be·*bee* mais do ke de·ve·*ree*·aa

I'm feeling drunk.
Estou me sentindo bêbado/bêbada. m/f
es·*to* me seng·*teeng*·do be·baa·do/be·baa·daa

I feel ill.
Estou me sentindo mal.
es·*to* me seng·*teeng*·do mow

Where's the toilet?
Onde é o banheiro?
ong·de e o ba·*nyay*·ro

Can you call a taxi for me?
Você pode chamar um táxi para mim?
vo·*se po*·de shaa·*maarr* oom taak·see *paa*·raa meeng

local drinks

água f **de côco**	aa·gwaa de *ko*·ko	coconut water
batida f	baa·*tee*·daa	pureed fruit and *cachaça* cocktail
cachaça f	kaa·*shaa*·saa	white spirit made from sugar cane
caipirinha f	kai·pee·*ree*·nyaa	lime and *cachaça* cocktail
caldo m **de cana**	kow·do de ka·naa	sugar cane juice
mate m	maa·te	iced tea

buying food

comprando alimentos

What's the local speciality?
Qual é a especialidade local?
kwow e a es·pe·see·aa·lee·*daa*·de lo·*kow*

What's that?
O que é aquilo?
o ke e aa·*kee*·lo

Can I taste it?
Posso experimentar?
po·so es·pe·ree·meng·*taarr*

Can I have a bag, please?
Pode me dar uma bolsa, por favor?
po·de me daarr oo·ma *bol*·sa porr ʃaa·vorr

How much is (a kilo of cheese)?
Quanto é (o kilo do queijo)?
kwung·to e (o *kee*·lo do *kay*·zho)

How much is it?
Quanto custa?
kwang·to koos·taa

food stuff		
cooked	cozido/cozida m/f	ko·zee·do/ko·zee·daa
cured	curado/curada m/f	koo·raa·do/koo·raa·daa
dried	seco/seca m/f	se·ko
fresh	fresco/fresca m/f	fres·ko/fres·kaa
frozen	congelado/ congelada m/f	kong·zhe·laa·do kong·zhe·laa·daa
smoked	defumado/ defumada m/f	de·foo·maa·do de·foo·maa·daa
raw	cru/crua m/f	kroo/kroo·a

I'd like …	Eu gostaria de …	e·oo gos·taa·ree·aa de …
(200) grams	(duzentas) gramas	(doo·zeng·taas) gra·maas
half a kilo	meio kilo	me·yo kee·lo
a kilo	um kilo	oom kee·lo
(two) kilos	(dois) kilos	(doys) kee·los
a bottle	uma garrafa	oo·maa gaa·haa·faa
a dozen	uma dúzia	oo·maa doo·zyaa
half a dozen	meia dúzia	me·yaa doo·zee·aa
a jar	um vidro	oom vee·dro
a packet	um pacote	oom paa·ko·te
a piece	um pedaço	oom pe·daa·so
(three) pieces	(três) pedaços	(tres) pe·daa·sos
a slice	uma fatia	oo·maa faa·tee·aa
(six) slices	(seis) fatias	(says) faa·tee·aas
a tin	uma lata	oo·maa laa·taa
(just) a little	(só) um pouco	(so) oom po·ko
more	mais	mais
some …	um pouco …	oom po·ko …
that one	aquele	aa·ke·le
this one	este	es·te

Less.	*Menos.*	*me·nos*
A bit more.	*Um pouco mais.*	*oom po·ko mais*
Enough.	*Chega.*	*she·gaa*
Do you have ...?	*Vocês tem ...?*	*vo·ses teng ...*
anything	*algo mais*	*ow·go mais*
cheaper	*barato*	*baa·raa·to*
other kinds	*outros tipos*	*o·tros tee·pos*
Where can I	*Onde posso*	*ong·de po·so*
find the ...	*encontrar a*	*eng·kong·traarr aa*
section?	*seção de ...?*	*se·sowng de ...*
dairy	*laticínios*	*laa·tee·see·nyos*
fish	*peixe*	*pay·she*
frozen goods	*congelados*	*kong·zhe·laa·dos*
fruit and	*frutas e*	*froo·taas e*
vegetable	*legumes*	*le·goo·mes*
meat	*carne*	*kaar·ne*
poultry	*frango*	*frang·go*

cooking utensils

Could I please borrow a/an ...?
Posso pegar um/uma ...   po·so pe·*gaarr* oom/*oo*·maa ...
emprestado/   eng·pres·*taa*·do/
emprestada? m/f   eng·pres·*taa*·daa

I need a/an ...
Preciso de um/uma ... m/f   pre·*see*·zo de oom/*oo*·maa ...

bottle opener	*abridor* m	aa·bree·*dor*
	de garrafas	de gaa·*haa*·faas
bowl	*tigela* f	tee·*zhe*·laa
can opener	*abridor* m	aa·bree·*dorr*
	de latas	de *laa*·taas
chopping board	*tábua* f *de*	*taa*·bwaa de
	cortar	korr·*taarr*
corkscrew	*abridor* m	aa·bree·*dorr*
cup	*xícara* f	shee·*kaa*·raa
fork	*garfo* m	*gaarr*·fo
fridge	*geladeira* f	zhe·laa·*day*·raa
frying pan	*frigideira* f	free·zhee·*day*·raa
glass	*copo* m	*ko*·po
knife	*faca* f	*faa*·kaa
microwave	*microondas* m	mee·kro·*ong*·daas
oven	*forno* m	*forr*·no
plate	*prato* m	*praa*·to
saucepan	*panela* f	paa·*ne*·laa
spoon	*colher* f	ko·*lyerr*
toaster	*torradeira* f	to·haa·*day*·raa

vegetarian & special meals

comida vegetariana & especial

ordering food

Is there a (vegetarian) restaurant near here?
Tem um restaurante (vegetariana) aqui por perto?
teng oom hes·tow·*rang*·te (ve·zhe·taa·ree·*a*·naa) aa·*kee* porr *perr*·to

Do you have ... food?
Você tem comida ...?
vo·*se* teng ko·*mee*·daa ...

halal	halal	a·*low*
kosher	kosher	ko·sherr
vegetarian	vegetariana	ve·zhe·taa·ree·*a*·naa

I don't eat ...
Eu não como ...
e·oo nowng ko·mo ...

fish	peixe	*pay*·she
poultry	franqo	*franq*·qo
(red) meat	carne (vermelha)	*kaar*·ne (verr·*me*·lyaa)

Is it cooked in/with ...?
Isto é feito em/ com ...?
ees·to e *fay*·to eng/ kong ...

butter	manteiga	mang·*te*·gaa
fish stock	caldo de peixe	*kow*·do de *pay*·she
meat stock	caldo de carne	*kow*·do de *kaarr*·ne

Could you prepare a meal without ...?
Você poderia preparar uma refeição sem ...?
vo·*se* po·de·*ree*·aa pre·paa·*raarr* oo·maa he·fay·*sowng* seng ...

eggs	ovos	*o*·vos
pork	porco	*porr*·ko
seafood	frutos do mar	*froo*·tos do maarr

Is this ...?
Isto é ...?
ees·to ee ...

free of animal produce	sem derivados de animais	seng de·ree·*vaa*·dos de aa·nee·*mais*
free-range	de caipira	kai·pee·raa
genetically modified	transgênico	trans·*zhe*·nee·ko

decaffeinated	*descafeinado*	des·kaa·fe·ee·*naa*·do
gluten-free	*sem glúten*	seng *gloo*·teng
halal	*halal*	a·*low*
kosher	*kosher*	*ko*·sherr
low-fat	*de baixo teor*	de *bai*·sho te·*orr*
	de gordura	de gorr·*doo*·raa
low in sugar	*de baixo teor*	de *bai*·sho te·*orr*
	de açúcar	de aa·*soo*·kaarr
organic	*orgânico*	orr·*ga*·nee·ko
salt-free	*sem sal*	seng sow

special diets & allergies

dietas especiais & alergias

I'm on a special diet.
  Estou numa dieta es·to *noo*·maa dee·*e*·taa
  especial. es·pe·see·*ow*

I'm (a) ...	*Eu sou ...*	e·oo so ...
Buddhist	*Budista*	boo·*dees*·taa
Hindu	*Hindu*	*eeng*·doo
Jewish	*Judeu/Judia* m/f	zhoo·*de*·o/zhoo·*dee*·aa
Muslim	*Muçulmano/*	moo·sool·*ma*·no/
	Muçulmana m/f	moo·sool·*ma*·naa
vegan	*vegitalista* m&f	ve·zhe·ta·*lees*·taa
vegetarian	*vegetariano/*	ve·zhe·taa·ree·*a*·no/
	vegetariana m/f	ve·zhe·taa·ree·*a*·naa

I'm allergic to ...	*Eu sou alérgico/*	e·oo so aa·*lerr*·zhee·ko/
	alérgica à ... m/f	aa·*lerr*·zhee·kaa aa ...
dairy produce	*laticínios*	laa·tee·*see*·nyos
eggs	*ovos*	*o*·vos
gelatin	*gelatina*	zhe·laa·*tee*·naa
gluten	*glúten*	*gloo*·teng
honey	*mel*	mel
MSG	*monoglutamato*	mo·no·gloo·taa·*maa*·to
	de sódio	de *so*·dyo
peanuts	*amendoims*	aa·meng·do·*eengs*
seafood	*frutos do mar*	*froo*·tos do maarr

A

abacate ⓜ a·ba·*kaa*·te avocado

abacaxí ⓜ aa·baa·kaa·*shee* pineapple

abóbora ⓕ aa·bo·bo·raa pumpkin

açafrão ⓜ aa·saa·*frowng* saffron

açaí ⓜ aa·saa·*ee* deep purple fruit of a palm tree – it has a gritty taste

acarajé ⓜ aa·kaa·raa·*zhe* a Bahian street food made from mashed brown beans formed into balls & stuffed with **vatapá**, then fried in **dendê** oil

acebolado/acebolada ⓜ/ⓕ aa·se·bo·*laa*·do/aa·se·bo·*laa*·daa saute of onion, garlic, olive oil & sometimes a bay leaf served with steak

acompanhamento ⓜ aa·kong·pa·nyaa·*meng*·to accompaniment

açúcar ⓜ aa·*soo*·kaarr sugar
— **mascavo** maas·*kaa*·vo brown sugar
— **refinado** he·fee·*naa*·do/ he·fee·*naa*·daa refined sugar

adoçante ⓜ aa·do·*sang*·te sugar substitute

agrião ⓜ aa·gree·*owng* watercress

água ⓕ aa·*gwaa* water
— **da nascente** daa naa·*seng*·te spring water
— **da torneira** daa torr·*nay*·raa tap water
— **mineral (com/sem gás)** mee·ne·*row* (kong/seng gas) mineral water (still/sparkling)

aguardente ⓜ aa·gwaarr·*deng*·te strong sugar cane alcohol drunk throughout the country, also known as **cachaça**

aipo ⓜ *aí*·po celery

alcachofra ⓕ ow·kaa·*sho*·fraa artichoke

alecrim ⓜ aa·le·*kreeng* rosemary

alface ⓜ ow·*faa*·se lettuce

alho ⓜ **porro** aa·lyo po·ho garlic leek

almoço ⓜ ow·*mo*·so lunch

almôndegas ⓕ pl ow·*mong*·de·gaas meatballs, usually beef or pork, served in a tomato-based sauce

ambrosia ⓕ ang·bro·*zee*·aa sweetened egg yolks thickened to a soft creamy texture, eaten as a dessert

amêijoa ⓕ aa·*may*·zho·aa cockle

ameixa ⓕ aa·*may*·shaa plum

amêndoa ⓕ aa·*meng*·dwaa almond

amendoim ⓜ aa·meng·doo·*eeng* peanut

amora ⓕ aa·*mo*·raa blackberry

angú ⓜ ang·*goo* runny polenta (corn meal porridge)

cordeiro ⓜ korr·*day*·ro lamb

arroz ⓜ aa·*hoz* rice
— **cozido** ko·zee·do cooked rice
— **de carreteiro** de kaa·he·*tay*·ro rice mixed with fried salted beef, served with fried manioc
— **de marisco** de maa·*rees*·ko casserole of seafood & rice in tomato sauce
— **integral** eeng·te·*grow* brown rice

asa ⓕ *aa·zaa* wing

— **assada** *aa·saa·daa* roasted wing

— **de frango** de *fraung·*go
chicken wing

— **frita** *free·*taa fried wing

asparago ⓜ *aas·paar·*go asparagus

atum ⓜ *aa·toong* tuna

avelã ⓕ *aa·ve·lang* hazelnut

aves ⓕ pl *aa·*ves poultry

avestruz ⓜ *aa·ves·troos* ostrich

azeite ⓜ *aa·zay·*te olive oil

azeitonas ⓕ pl *aa·zay·to·*naas olives

— **pretas** *pre·*taas black olives

— **recheadas** *re·she·aa·*daas
stuffed olives

— **sem caroço** seng *kaa·ro·*so
pitted olives

— **verdes** *verr·*des green olives

B

bacaba ⓕ *baa·kaa·*baa Amazonian
fruit used in wines & syrups

bacalhau ⓜ *baa·kaa·lyow*
dried salted cod

banha ⓕ *ba·*nyaa lard

batata ⓕ **doce** *baa·taa·*taa *do·*se
sweet potato

batatas ⓕ pl *baa·taa·*taas potatoes

— **cozidas** *ko·zee·*daas
boiled potatoes

— **fritas** *free·*taas potato chips
or crisps

baunilha ⓕ *bow·nee·lyaa* vanilla

bavaroise ⓕ *baa·vaa·hoo·waa·*ze
whipped gelatinous dessert made
with cream & pieces of fruit such as
strawberries or pineapple

bebida ⓕ *be·bee·*daa beverage

— **(sem) álcool** (seng) *ow·*kol
(non)alcoholic beverage

— **destilada** *des·tee·laa·*daa spirits

— **gelada** *zhe·laa·*daa cold beverage

— **quente** *keng·*te hot beverage

beringela ⓕ *be·reeng·zhe·*laa
aubergine • eggplant

beterraba ⓕ *be·te·haa·*baa beetroot

bicarbonato ⓜ **de sódio**
*bee·kaa·borr·naa·*to de *so·*dyo
baking soda • bicarbonate of soda

bife ⓜ *bee·*fe steak of beef, other meats,
poultry or fish • fillet

— **ao ponto** ow *pong·*to steak that's
medium cooked

— **bem passado** beng *paa·saa·*do
well-done steak

— **de alcatra** de *ow·kaa·*traa
rump steak

— **de atum** de *aa·toong* tuna steak

— **de filé** de *fee·le* sirloin steak

— **de lombinho** de *long·bee·*nyo
pork fillet steak

— **de vaca** de *vaa·*kaa beef steak

biscoitos ⓜ pl *bees·koy·*tos
biscuits • cookies

bobó ⓜ **de camarão** *bo·bo* de
kaa·maa·rowng thick stew of fresh
prawns, coconut milk, **dendê** oil,
coriander & pureed manioc

bolachas ⓕ pl as *bo·laa·*shaas
crackers • biscuits

bolo ⓜ *bo·*lo cake

— **de aniversário**
de *aa·nee·verr·saa·*ryo birthday cake

— **de carne** de *kaar·*ne meatloaf

— **de casamento**
de *kaa·zaa·meng·*to wedding cake

— **de chocolate** de *sho·ko·laa·*te
chocolate cake

— **de laranja** de *laa·rang·*zhaa
orange cake

— **de nozes** de *no·*zes walnut cake

— **rei** hay a Christmas bread in the
shape of a large ring, studded with
walnuts, pine nuts, almonds & raisins &
decorated with glazed fruit

bombons ⓜ pl *bong·bongs* bonbons

brasa *braa·*zaa see **na brasa**

brócolis ⓜ pl *bro·ko·*lees broccoli

bucho ⓜ boo·sho tripe

bufet ⓜ **de saladas frias** boo·fe de saa·*laa*·daas free·aas cold salad buffet with vegetable, pasta & bean salads

buriti ⓜ boo·ree·tee a palm-tree fruit with a mealy texture & a hint of peach

C

cabidela, à kaa·bee·*de*·la, aa any dish made with blood & giblets of poultry

cabrito ⓜ kaa·*bree*·to kid (goat)

cacau ⓜ ka·kow cocoa • pulp from cocoa pod

— **chocolate quente** sho·ko·*laa*·te *keng*·te hot çocoa (beverage)

caça ⓕ kaa·saa game

cação ⓜ kaa·sowng shark meat

cachaça ⓕ kaa·*shaa*·saa strong sugar cane spirit produced & drunk throughout the country

café ⓜ kaa·fe coffee • cafe

— **com leite** kong *lay*·te medium-sized cup of half milk & half filter coffee

— **descafeinado** des·kaa·fe·ee·*naa*·do decaffeinated coffee

— **em grão** eng growng coffee beans

— **instantâneo** eengs·tang·*ta*·nyo instant coffee

— **moído** mo·ee·do ground coffee

— **pingado** peen·*gaa*·do short black • espresso with a dash of cold milk

cafeteria ⓕ kaa·fe·te·*ree*·aa coffee shop or cafeteria

cafezinho kaa·fe·*zee*·nyo short black • espresso topped with hot water

caipirinha ⓕ kai·pee·*ree*·nyaa cocktail of lime, sugar & **cachaça** on ice

cajú ⓜ kaa·zhoo cashew • tart fruit of cashew (the nut is enclosed in the fruit), usually used in juices

caldeirada ⓕ kow·day·*raa*·daa soup-like stew, usually made with fish

caldo ⓜ kow·do soup • broth

— **de galinha** de gaa·*lee*·nyaa chicken broth

— **verde** *verr*·de potato-based soup with **couve** & **paio**

camarão ⓜ kaa·maa·*rowng* prawn

— **á paulista** aa pow·*lees*·taa unshelled fresh prawn fried in olive oil with garlic & salt

canela ⓕ kaa·ne·la cinnamon

canja ⓕ *kang*·zhaa soup made with chicken broth, often a meal in itself

— **de galinha** de gaa·*lee*·nyaa chicken soup

carambola ⓕ kaa·rang·*bo*·laa starfruit

caramelo ⓜ kaa·raa·*me*·lo caramel • hard candy

carangueijada ⓕ kaa·rang·ge·*zhaa*·daa a feast of crab cooked whole on salt, accompanied by chilli & **farofa**

camarão ⓜ ka·ma·*rowng* prawns

— **frito com alho** *free*·to kong *aa*·lyo prawns sautéed in garlic, sometimes with chilli

carne ⓕ *kaar*·ne meat

— **assada** aa·*saa*·daa roast meat

— **de porco** de *porr*·ko pork

— **de sol** de sol a tasty, salted meat, fried in oil

— **de vaca** de vaa·kaa beef

— **picada** pee·*kaa*·daa chopped meat

carneiro ⓜ kaarr·*nay*·ro mutton

cardápio ⓜ kaar·*daa*·pyo menu

— **de vinhos** de vee·nyos wine list

carvão, no ⓜ&ⓕ kaar·*vowng*, no char-grilled

caruru ⓜ kaa·roo·*roo* one of the most popular Brazilian dishes of African origin, made with okra, onions, salt, dried shrimp & **dendê** oil. Traditionally, a sea fish such as grouper is added.

casa, à moda da ⓜ&ⓕ *kaa-zaa, aa mo-daa daa* house-style
casa ⓕ **de chá** *kaa-zaa de shaa* teahouse selling pastries, sweets, coffee as well as herbal & black teas
caseira/caseiro ⓜ/ⓕ *kaa-zay-raa/ kaa-zay-ro* home-style cooking
castanhas ⓕ pl **de cajú** *kas-ta-nyaas de kaa-zhoo* chestnuts
castanhas ⓕ pl **portuguesas** *kas-ta-nyaas porr-too-ge-zaas* chestnuts
cavalas ⓕ pl *kaa-vaa-laas* mackerel
casquinha ⓕ **de siri** *kaas-kee-nyaa de see-ree* stuffed crab
cebola ⓕ *se-bo-la* onion
cenoura ⓕ *se-no-raa* carrot
cereal ⓜ *se-re-ow* cereal, grains or breakfast cereal
cereja ⓕ *se-re-zhaa* (sweet) cherry
cerveja ⓕ *serr-ve-zhaa* beer
cervejaria ⓕ *serr-ve-zhaa-ree-aa* beer house (also serves food)
chá ⓜ *shaa* tea
— **com limão** *kong lee-mowng* black tea with thick strip of lemon peel
— **de ervas** *de err-vaas* herb tea
— **de erva doce** *de err-vaa do-se* aniseed tea (very commonly given to children)
— **de limão** *de lee-mowng* glass or cup of hot water with a twist of lemon rind
— **preto** *pre-to* black tea
— **verde** *verr-de* green tea
champanhe ⓜ *shang-pa-nye* champagne
chef ⓜ&ⓕ *she-fe* chef
chocolate ⓜ *sho-ko-laa-te* chocolate
— **ao leite** *ow lay-te* milk chocolate
— **branco** *brang-ko* white chocolate
— **preto** *pre-to* dark chocolate
choppe ⓜ *sho-pee* large glass of draught beer
— **preto** *pre-to* dark beer • stout

chouriço ⓜ *sho-ree-so* garlicky pork sausage flavoured with red pepper paste
— **de sangue** *de sang-ge* blood sausage
churrasco ⓜ *shoo-haas-ko* barbecue
claras ⓕ pl **de ovos** *klaa-raas de o-vos* egg whites
côco ⓜ *ko-ko* coconut
codorna ⓕ *ko-dorr-na* quail
coelho ⓜ *ko-e-lyo* rabbit
— **à caçador** *aa kaa-saa-dorr* 'hunter's style rabbit' – rabbit stewed with red & white wine & tomato
— **ao vinha d'alho** *ow vee-nyaa daa-lyo* baked rabbit set atop slices of fried bread, covered with onion slices & drizzled with port or white wine
coentro ⓜ *ko-eng-tro* coriander
cogumelos ⓜ pl *ko-goo-me-los* mushrooms
colorau ⓜ *ko-lo-row* sweet paprika
com tudo *kong too-do* 'with everything' – a dish with the lot
compota ⓕ *kong-po-taa* fruit preserve
confeitaria ⓕ *kong-fay-taa-ree-aa* patisserie
congelado/congelada ⓜ/ⓕ *kong-zhe-laa-do/kong-zhe-laa-daa* frozen
conserva ⓕ *kong-serr-vaa* tinned/ canned goods
consomé ⓜ *kong-so-me* consomme
corante ⓜ *ko-rang-te* food colouring
cordeiro ⓜ *korr-day-ro* mutton
costeleta ⓕ **de porco** *kos-te-le-taa de porr-ko* pork chop
couve ⓕ *ko-ve* green edible leaf
— **de Bruxelas** *de broo-she-laas* Brussels sprout
— **flor** *florr* cauliflower
coxinha ⓕ **de galinha** *ko-shee-nyaa de gaa-lee-nyaa* fried, savoury chicken mixture in the form of a drumstick

cozido ⓜ **(à brasileira)** ko·zee·do (aa braa·see·le·raa) *Brazilian stew, full of meat, vegetables, beans & rice*

cozido/cozida ⓜ/ⓕ ko·zee·do/ ko·zee·daa *cooked*

cozinha ⓕ ko·zee·nyaa *kitchen*
  — **tradicional** traa·dee·syo·now *traditional cooking*

cravo ⓜ kraa·vo *cloves*

creme ⓜ kre·me *whipped cream*
  — **chantilly** shang·tee·lee *whipped cream*
  — **de legumes** de le·goo·mes *cream of vegetable soup*
  — **pasteleiro** paas·te·lay·ro *egg-based cream filling used in pastries*

croissant ⓜ krwaa·sang *croissant*
  — **com chocolate** kong sho·ko·laa·te *chocolate-filled croissant*
  — **com creme** kong kre·me *custard-filled croissant*
  — **com presunto** kong pre·zoong·to *croissant with ham*
  — **com queijo** kong kay·zho *croissant with cheese*
  — **misto** mees·to *croissant with ham & cheese*

croquete ⓜ kro·ke·te *meat croquette*

cru/crua m/f kroo/kroo·a *raw*

curado/curada m/f koo·raa·do/ koo·raa·daa *cured*

D

damasco ⓜ daa·maas·ko *apricot*

defumado/defumada ⓜ/ⓕ de·foo·maa·do/de·foo·maa·daa *smoked*

dendê ⓜ deng·de *palm oil*

desossado/desossada ⓜ/ⓕ de·zo·saa·do/de·zo·saa·daa *boned*

digestivo ⓜ dee·zhes·tee·vo *after-dinner drink, usually a liqueur, brandy or port*

dobradinha ⓕ do·braa·dee·nyaa *tripe with white beans & rice*

doce ⓜ do·se *sweet · dessert · jam*
  — **de abóbora com requeijão** de aa·bo·bo·raa kong he·kay·zhowng *pumpkin jam*
  — **de goiaba** de go·yaa·baa *guava jam*
  — **de ovos** de o·vos *egg yolk sweets*

doces ⓜ pl **regionais** do·ses he·zhyo·nais *regional sweets*

dourado ⓜ do·raa·do *freshwater fish found throughout Brazil*

E

empada ⓕ eng·paa·daa *miniature pot pie*
  — **de carne** de kaarr·ne *with meat filling*
  — **de camarão** dekaa·maa·rowng *with prawn filling*
  — **de frango** de fran·go *with chicken filling*
  — **de galinha** de gaa·lee·nyaa *with chicken filling*
  — **de legumes** de le·goo·mes *with vegetable filling*

empadão ⓜ eng·paa·downg *a big empada*

enguia ⓕ eng·gee·aa *eel*

entrada ⓕ eng·traa·daa *entree*

erva-doce ⓕ err·vaa·do·se *aniseed*

ervas ⓕ pl err·vaas *herbs*
  — **aromáticas** aa·ro·maa·tee·kaas *mixture of cooking herbs*

ervilhas ⓕ pl err·vee·lyaas *peas*

escabeche ⓜ es·kaa·be·she *tomato, onion, parsley & garlic fried with a dash of vinegar & poured over fried fish*

escalopinho ⓜ es·kaa·lo·pee·nyo *medallion-shaped, high quality cuts of boneless meat*

espada ⓕ es·paa·daa *swordfish*

espanhola, à es·pa·nyo·laa, aa *dish in tomato & onion sauce*

espaguete ⓜ es·paa·ge·te *spaghetti*

especialidade ⓕ **da casa**
es·pe·syaa·lee·*daa*·de daa *kaa*·zaa
house speciality

especiarias ⓕ pl es·pe·syaa·*ree*·aas
spices

espeto ⓜ es·*pe*·to *on a skewer*
— **de camarão** de kaa·maa·*rowng*
skewered prawn
— **de carne** de *kaar*·ne *skewered beef*
— **de lula** de *loo*·laa *skewered squid*
— **misto** *mees*·to *mixed grill ·
skewered chunks of veal and/or pork,
separated by bacon or sausage slices,
green capsicum & onion*

espinafre ⓜ es·pee·*naa*·fre *spinach*

espumante ⓜ&ⓕ es·poo·*mang*·te
sparkling wine

F

faisão ⓜ fai·*sowng* *pheasant*

farinha ⓕ **de trigo** fa·*ree*·nyaa de
tree·go *wheat flour*

farinha ⓕ **de mandioca** faa·*ree*·nyaa
de mang·dee·o·kaa *manioc flour*

farofa ⓕ faa·ro·faa *manioc flour fried
with oil, garlic, salt & sometimes
sausage & eggs*

favas ⓕ pl *faa*·vaas *broad beans*

feijão ⓜ fay·*zhowng* *bean*
— **branco** *brang*·ko *white bean*
— **fradinho** fraa·dee·nyo
black-eyed pea
— **manteiga** mang·*tay*·gaa
butter bean
— **preto** *pre*·to *black bean*

feijoada ⓕ fay·zho·aa·daa *the national
dish of Brazil – pork & black bean stew
served with rice*

fígado ⓜ *fee*·gaa·do *liver*

figo ⓜ *fee*·go *fig*

filé ⓜ fee·*le* *fish fillet*
— **de pescada** de pes·*kaa*·daa
breaded & fried whiting fillet

folhado ⓜ **de carne** fo·*lyaa*·do de
kaarr·ne *puff pastry with meat filling*

folhado ⓜ **de salsicha** fo·*lyaa*·do de
sow·*see*·shaa *puff pastry with sausage
filling*

forno, ao forr·no, ow *oven baked*

framboesa ⓕ frang·bo·e·zaa *raspberry*

frango ⓜ *frang*·go *chicken*
— **assado** aa·*saa*·do *roast chicken*
— **na brasa** naa *braa*·zaa *char-grilled
chicken seasoned with garlic, bay leaf,
paprika & olive oil*

fresco/fresca ⓜ/ⓕ fres·ko/fres·kaa
fresh · cool · cold

frigideira ⓕ free·zhee·*day*·raa *frying
pan or skillet*

frio/fria ⓜ/ⓕ free·o/free·aa *cold*

frito/frita ⓜ/ⓕ free·to/free·taa *fried*

frios ⓜ pl free·os *cold cuts of meat*

fruta ⓕ *froo*·taa *fruit*
— **cristalizada** krees·taa·lee·*zaa*·daa
candied/glazed fruit
— **da época** daa e·po·kaa
seasonal fruit

fruta-do-conde ⓕ froo·taa·do·kong·de
custard apple

frutas secas ⓕ pl froo·taas se·kaas
dried fruit & nuts

folha ⓜ **do funcho** fo·lyaa do
foong·sho *dill*

G

galinha ⓕ gaa·*lee*·nyaa *chicken*
— **caipira** kai·pee·raa *free-range
chicken*

garrafa ⓕ gaa·*haa*·faa *bottle*
— **de meio litro** de me·yo lee·tro
half-litre bottle
— **de um litro** de oom lee·tro
litre bottle
— **pequena** pe·ke·naa *small bottle*

gelatina ⓕ zhe·laa·*tee*·naa *gelatin*

geléia ⓕ zhe·*le*·yaa *jelly*

gelo ⓜ *zhe*·lo *ice*

gemas ⓕ pl *zhe*·maas *egg yolks*

gengibre ⓜ zheng-*zhee*-bre *ginger*

goiaba ⓕ go-*yaa*-baa *guava*

goiabada ⓕ go-yaa-*baa*-daa *guava jam*

grão (de bico) ⓜ growng (de *bee*-ko)
chickpeas • garbanzo beans

gratinado/gratinada ⓜ/ⓕ
graa-tee-*naa*-do/graa-tee-*naa*-daa
*au gratin – topped with breadcrumbs &
browned*

graviola ⓕ graa-vee-o-laa
custard apple

grelhado/grelhada ⓜ/ⓕ
gre-*lyaa*-do/gre-*lyaa*-daa *grilled*

groselha ⓕ gro-*ze*-lyaa *gooseberry •
gooseberry syrup*

guarnecido/guarnecida ⓜ/ⓕ
gwaar-ne-*see*-do/gwaar-ne-*see*-daa
*garnished with pickled cauliflower,
carrots, onion & sometimes olives*

guisado/guisada ⓜ/ⓕ
gee-*zaa*-do/gee-*zaa*-daa *braised*

H

hortaliça ⓕ or-taa-*lee*-saa *green leafy
vegetables*
— **cozida** ko-*zee*-daa *boiled green
leafy vegetables*
— **refogada** he-fo-*gaa*-daa
sauteed green leafy vegetables

hortelã ⓕ or-te-*lang* *mint*

I

inhame ⓜ ee-*nyaa*-me *yam*

iogurte ⓕ ee-o-*goorr*-te *yogurt*
— **líquido** *lee*-kee-do *liquid yogurt*

iscas ⓕ pl **de fígado** *ees*-kaas de
fee-gaa-do *chopped liver*

J

jaca ⓕ *zhaa*-kaa *jackfruit*

jambu ⓜ zham-*boo* *a Brazilian herb*

jantar ⓜ zhang-*taarr* *dinner*

jardineira ⓕ zhaar-dee-*nay*-raa *hearty
beef & vegetable stew*

javali ⓜ zhaa-vaa-*lee* *wild boar*

L

lagosta ⓕ laa-*gos*-taa *lobster*

lagostim ⓜ laa-gos-*teeng* *crayfish*

lanche ⓜ *lang*-she *afternoon snack*

laranja ⓕ laa-*rang*-zhaa *orange*

lata ⓕ *laa*-taa *can*

lebre ⓕ *le*-bre *hare*

legumes ⓜ pl le-*goo*-mes *vegetables*

leitão ⓜ lay-*towng* *suckling pig roasted
in a wood-fired oven*

leite ⓜ *lay*-te *milk*
— **condensado** kong-deng-*saa*-do
condensed milk
— **gordo** *gorr*-do *full cream milk*
— **desnatado** des-naa-*taa*-do
skim milk

lesma ⓕ *les*-maa *snails*

licor ⓜ lee-*korr* *liqueur*

limão ⓜ lee-*mowng* *lime*
— **galego** gaa-*le*-go *lemon*

língua ⓕ *leeng*-gwaa *tongue*

linguado ⓜ leeng-*gwaa*-do *sole*
— **à (la) Meunière** aa (laa)
mo-nee-*err* *lightly pan-fried sole
sprinkled with parsley & lemon juice*

linguiça ⓕ leen-*gwee*-saa *thin, long
garlicky pork sausage*

lombinho ⓜ **de porco** long-*bee*-nyo
de *porr*-ko *thinly sliced pork
tenderloin*

lombo ⓜ **de porco assado** *long*-bo de
porr-ko aa-*saa*-do *roast pork loin*

louro ⓜ *lo*-ro *bay leaf*

lula ⓕ *loo*-laa *squid*
— **à Sevilhana** aa se-vee-*lya*-naa
*fried squid rings served with
mayonnaise*
— **recheada** he-she-*aa*-daa *small
squid stuffed with rice, tomatoes &
parsley*

M

maçã ① maa·*sang* apple
— **assada** a·*saa*·daa baked apple

maduro/madura ⑩/①
maa·*doo*·ro/maa·*doo*·raa
ripe (fruit) • mature (wine)

maionese ① maa·yo·*ne*·ze mayonnaise

mamão ⑩ maa·*mowng* papaya

mandioca ① mang·dee·o·kaa manioc •
cassava
— **frita** *free*·taa deep-fried cassava –
a common bar snack

moda, à mo·daa, aa in the manner of

manga ① *mang*·gaa mango

manjerona ① mang·zhe·*ro*·naa
marjoram

manteiga ① mang·*tay*·gaa butter

maracujá ① maa·raa·koo·*zhaa*
passionfruit

margarina ① maarr·gaa·*ree*·naa
margarine

marisco ⑩ maa·*rees*·ko shellfish

marmelada ① maarr·me·*laa*·daa
firm quince paste

marisqueira ① maa·rees·*kay*·raa
seafood restaurant

massa ① *maa*·saa pasta • dough
— **folhada** fo·*lyaa*·daa flaky pastry

medalhão ⑩ me·daa·*lyowng*
medallion of meat or fish

mel ⑩ mel honey

melaço ⑩ me·*laa*·so molasses

melancia ① me·lang·*see*·aa
watermelon

melão ⑩ me·*lowng* melon
— **com presunto** kong pre·*zoong*·to
slices of honeydew melon topped with
thin slices of ham

mercado ⑩ merr·*kaa*·do market

merenda ① me·*reng*·daa snack •
light lunch • picnic lunch

merengue ⑩ me·*reng*·ge meringue

mexilhões ⑩ pl me·shee·*lyoyngs*
mussels

mil folhas ⑩ pl meel fo·*lyaas* layers of
flaky pastry with custard filling

milho ⑩ **doce** *mee*·lyo *do*·se sweet corn

minimercado ⑩ mee·nee·merr·*kaa*·do
small convenience store

mini-prato ⑩ mee·nee·*praa*·to
very small serving

miolos ⑩ pl mee·o·los brains

miudos ⑩ pl mee·oo·dos giblets

moda ① **da casa** mo·daa daa *kaa*·zaa
house-style – usually describes a meat
dish accompanied by rice, chips,
salad & a fried egg

moelas ① pl as mo·e·laas
chicken gizzards

molho ⑩ *mo*·lyo sauce • gravy • dressing
— **branco** *brang*·ko white sauce
— **de caramelo** de kaa·raa·*me*·lo
caramel sauce
— **de cocktail** de ko·kee·*tel* sauce
made from mayonnaise, tomato
sauce & a dash of whisky
— **de manteiga** de mang·*tay*·gaa
butter sauce
— **verde** *verr*·de sauce for fish or
octopus made with chopped onion,
garlic, red capsicum, parsley, vinegar
& lots of olive oil

molusco ⑩ mo·*loos*·ko clam

moqueca ① mo·*ke*·kaa style of cooking
from Bahia • a kind of sauce or stew
made from **dendê** oil & coconut milk,
cooked in a covered clay pot

moqueca ① **(de peixe) capixaba**
mo·*ke*·kaa (de *pay*·she)
kaa·pee·*shaa*·baa fish stew
traditionally made in a clay pot

morangos ⑩ pl mo·*rang*·gos
strawberries

morcela ① morr·se·laa blood sausage

moscatel ⑩ mos·kaa·*tel* sweet dessert
wine

mostarda ① mos·*taarr*·daa mustard

N

na brasa naa *braa-zaa*
char-grilled

na chapa naa *shaa-paa* cooked on
a hot steel plate

na pedra naa *pe-draa* meat or fish
grilled on a hot stone at the table

nabo ⓜ *naa-bo* turnip

nêspera ⓕ *nes-pe-raa* loquat

novilho ⓜ *no-vee-lyo* veal

noz ⓕ *noz* walnut

O

óleo ⓜ *o-lyo* oil
— **de amendoim** de
aa-meng-do-*eeng* peanut oil
— **de cozinha** de ko-*zee*-nyaa
cooking oil
— **de girassol** de zhee-raa-*sol*
sunflower seed oil
— **de milho** de *mee*-lyo corn oil
— **de soja** de so-*zhaa* soybean oil
— **vegetal** ve-zhe-*tow* vegetable oil

omelete ⓜ o-me-*le*-te omelette

orégano ⓜ o-*re*-ga-no oregano

ostra ⓕ *os*-traa oyster

ovas ⓕ pl **(de pescada)** o-*vaas* (de
pes-*kaa*-daa) fish eggs, usually hake

ovo ⓜ o-vo egg
— **cozido** ko-*zee*-do boiled egg
— **frito** *free*-to fried egg
— **mexido** me-*shee*-do
scrambled egg
— **poché** po-*she* poached egg

P

pá ⓕ paa beef cut

padaria ⓕ paa-daa-*ree*-aa bakery

paio ⓜ *paa*-yo smoked pork tenderloin
sausage

palmier ⓜ pow-mee-*err* flat, palm-
shaped puff pastry

panqueca ⓕ pang-*ke*-kaa crepe
— **de galinha** de gaa-*lee*-nyaa
chicken crepe
— **de legumes** de le-*goo*-mes
vegetable crepe

pão ⓜ powng bread
— **com linguiça**
kong leeng-*gwee*-saa
bread roll with sausage
— **da casa** daa *kaa*-zaa 'house bread'
— **de centeio** de seng-*te*-yo
light rye bread
— **de forma** de *forr*-maa
loaf of bread
— **de-ló** de *lo* collapsed sponge cake
— **de milho** de *mee*-lyo corn bread
— **de trigo integral** de *tree*-go
eeng-te-*grow* wheat-flour bread
— **doce** *do*-se sweetened bread roll
with cream, icing or sugar
— **integral** eeng-te-*grow* wholegrain
bread

papa ⓕ **de milho** *paa*-paa de *mee*-lyo
cornmeal porridge

papos-de-anjo ⓜ pl *paa*-pos-de-*ang*-zho
little egg-based puffs in a sugar syrup

passas ⓕ pl *paa*-saas raisins

pastéis ⓜ pl pas-*tays* pastries • small
savoury fritters or something that
looks more like a pie
— **de bacalhau** de baa-kaa-*lyow*
deep-fried, oval-shaped savouries
made from mashed potato, onion,
parsley & salt cod

pastel ⓜ paas-*tel* pastry

pastelaria ⓕ paas-te-laa-*ree*-aa
pastry shop • coffee shop • pastries

pato ⓜ *paa*-to duck
— **no tucupi** no too-koo-*pee*
roast duck flavoured with garlic &
cooked in **tucupi**

pé ⓜ **de porco com feijão branco** pe
de *porr*-ko kong fay-*zowng* brang-ko
stew made from pig's feet and white
beans

peito ⊚ **de frango** pay·to de frang·go
chicken breast

peixada ① pay·shaa·daa fish cooked in
broth with vegetables & tomatoes

peixe ⊚ pay·she fish
— **assado no forno** aa·saa·do no
forr·no baked fish
— **frito** free·to fried fish

pepino ⊚ pe·pee·no cucumber

pêra ① pe·raa pear

peru ⊚ pe·roo turkey

pescada ① pes·kaa·daa whiting

pescadinhas ① pl pes·kaa·dee·nyaas
fried small whiting

pêssego ⊚ pe·se·go peach

petiscos ⊚ pl pe·tees·kos appetisers
including sausages, cheese & olives,
fried manioc, French fries

picanha ① pee·ka·nyaa thin cut of
rump steak

picante pee·kang·te describes any spicy
or hot sauce

pimenta ① pee·meng·taa pepper
— **branca** brang·kaa white pepper
— **do reino** do hay·no black pepper

pimentão ⊚ pee·meng·towng
(sweet) pepper • capsicum
— **assado** aa·saa·do roast capsicum
— **verde** verr·de green capsicum
— **vermelho** verr·me·lyo red
capsicum

pinhão ⊚ pee·nyowng pine nut

pirarucu ⊚ pee·raa·hoo·koo common
Amazonian river fish
— **ao forno** ow forr·no oven-
cooked **pirarucu** with lemon & other
seasonings

poché ⊚ po·she poached

polpa ① pol·paa fruit or vegetable pulp
— **de fruta** de froo·taa fruit pulp
— **de tomate** de to·maa·te
tomato pulp

polvo ⊚ pol·vo octopus

porco ⊚ porr·ko pork

posta ① pos·taa fish steak

prato ⊚ praa·to dish
— **de verão** de ve·rowng fruit salad
common in Rio de Janeiro
— **do dia** do dee·aa the daily special
— **feito (PF)** fay·to (pe·e·fe) set meal
— **principal** preeng·seee·pow
main dish

presunto ⊚ pre·zoong·to smoked ham

pudim ⊚ poo·deeng pudding
— **de leite condensado** de lay·te
kong·deng·saa·do a desert similar to
creme caramel
— **de ovos** de o·vos baked egg-
custard pudding

pupunha ① poo·poo·nyaa a fatty,
vitamin-rich Amazonian fruit eaten
with coffee

Q

queijo ⊚ kay·zho cheese
— **de cabra** de kaa·braa
goat's milk cheese
— **de ovelha** de o·ve·lyaa
sheep's milk cheese
— **de vaca** de vaa·kaa
cow's milk cheese
— **quente** keng·te cheese melt

quibe ⊚ kee·be deep-fried meatballs

R

recheado/recheada ⊚/①
he·she·aa·do/he·she·aa·daa stuffed

recheio ⊚ he·shay·o stuffing or filling

refeição ① he·fay·sowng meal
— **rápida** haa·pee·daa quick meal •
fast food

refogado ⊚ he·fo·gaa·do quick fry

refrigerante ⊚ he·free·zhe·rang·te
soft drink

repolho ⊚ he·po·lyo variety of cabbage
with crinkly leaves
— **roxo** ho·sho purple cabbage

rim ⊚ heeng kidney

FOOD

risole ⊚ hee·zo·le *rissole • fried pasty*
— **de camarão** de kaa·maa·*rowng* *pasty or rissole with prawn filling*
— **de carne** de *kaarr*·ne *pasty or rissole with meat filling*
— **de frango** de *frang*·go *pasty or rissole with chicken filling*
rodízio ⊚ ho·*dee*·zyo *Brazilian barbecue featuring various grilled meats on skewers and a cold salad buffet*
rosbife ⊚ hos·*bee*·fe *roast beef*

S

sal ⊚ sow *salt*
salada ① saa·*laa*·daa *salad*
— **de alface** de ow·*faa*·se *lettuce salad*
— **de atum** de aa·*toong* *salad of tuna, potato, peas, carrots, boiled eggs with an olive oil & vinegar dressing*
— **de bacalhau com feijao fradinho** de baa·kaa·*lyow* kong fay·*zhowng* fraa·dee·nyo *salad of shredded, uncooked salt cod & black-eyed peas with olive oil & vinegar dressing*
— **de feijão fradinho** de fay·*zhowng* fraa·dee·nyo *black-eyed pea salad flavoured with onion, garlic, olive oil & vinegar, sprinkled with chopped boiled egg & parsley*
— **de tomate** de to·*maa*·te *tomato & onion salad, often flavoured with oregano*
— **mista** *mees*·taa *tomato, lettuce & onion salad*
— **palmito** pow·*mee*·to *palm heart salad*
— **russa** *hoo*·saa *potato salad with peas, carrots mayonnaise*
salgadinho ⊚ sow·gaa·*dee*·nyos *small savoury pastry*

salgado/salgada ⊚/① sow·*gaa*·do/ sow·*gaa*·daa *small savoury pastry*
salmão ⊚ sow·*mowng* *salmon*
— **defumado** de·foo·*maa*·do *smoked salmon*
salpicão ⊚ sow·pee·*kowng* *smoked pork sausage flavoured with garlic, bay leaf & sometimes wine*
salsa ① sow·*saa* *parsley*
salsicha ① sow·*see*·shaa *sausage*
sálvia ① sow·*vyaa* *sage*
sanduíche ⊚ sang·doo·ee·she *sandwich*
sardinha ① saarr·*dee*·nyaa *sardine*
seco/seca ⊚/① se·ko/se·kaa *dry • dried*
sobremesa ① so·bre·*me*·zaa *sweet • dessert • jam*
sonhos ⊚ pl so·nyos *doughnut-like pastry sprinkled with sugar & cinnamon*
sopa ① so·paa *soup*
— **de feijão** de fay·*zhowng* *soup made from dried pulses or beans*
— **de feijão fradinho** de fay·*zwong* fraa·dee·nyo *black-eyed pea soup flavoured with sausages*
— **de legumes** de le·*goo*·mes *vegetable soup*
— **de peixe** de *pay*·she *fish in a tomato & onion broth, served over chunks of bread*
— **do dia** do *dee*·aa *soup of the day*
— **juliana** zhoo·lee·*a*·naa *soup made with mixed, julienned vegetables*
sorvete ⊚ sorr·*ve*·te *ice cream*
suco ⊚ *soo*·ko *juice*
— **de laranja natural** de laa·rang·zhaa naa·too·row *freshly squeezed orange juice*

T

tacacá ① taa·kaa·*kaa* *an Indian dish of dried shrimp cooked with pepper,* **jambu** *& manioc*

tamboril ⑩ tang·bo·*reel monkfish*

tamarindo ⑩ taa·maa·*reeng*·do *tamarind*

torta ① **de amêndoaa** torr·taa de aa·*meng*·dwaa *almond tart*

torta ① **de maçã** torr·taa de maa·*sang apple tart*

tomate ⑩ to·*maa*·te *tomato*

tomilho ⑩ to·*mee*·lyo *thyme*

torrada ① to·*haa*·daa *toast*

torresmo ⑩ to·*hes*·mo *pork cracklings served hot or cold as a snack*

toucinho ⑩ too·*see*·nyo *bacon*
  — **defumado** de·foo·*maa*·do *smoked bacon*
  — **salgado** sow·*gaa*·do *salt-cured bacon*

trança ① trang·saa *pastry topped with coconut mixture & chopped nuts*

tremoços ⑩ pl tre·mo·sos *salted, preserved yellow beans eaten as a snack*

tripa ① tree·pa *tripe*

truta ① troo·taa *trout*

tucupi ⑩ too·koo·*pee* *sauce made from the juice of the manioc plant &* **jambu**

tutu ⑩ **á mineira** too·*too* aa mee·*nay*·raa *a bean paste with toasted bacon & manioc flour, often served with cooked cabbage*

U

uvas ① pl *oo*·vaas *grapes*

V

vatapá ⑩ vaa·taa·*paa* *dried shrimp, cashew, fish, pepper & tomato sauce*

veado ⑩ ve·*aa*·do *venison*

vinagre ⑩ vee·*naa*·gre *vinegar*

vinha ① **d'alho** vee·nyaa *daa*·lyo *meat marinated in wine or vinegar, olive oil, garlic & bay leaf*

vinho ⑩ vee·nyo *wine*
  — **branco** brang·ko *white wine*
  — **da casa** daa *kaa*·zaa *house wine*
  — **da região** daa he·zhee·*owng* *local wine*
  — **quente** keng·te *mulled wine*
  — **rosé** ho·ze *rosé wine*
  — **tinto** teeng·to *red wine*
  — **verde** verr·de *'green wine' – light sparkling red, white or rosé wine*

vitamina ① vee·taa·*mee*·naa *milk & fruit shake*

vitela ① vee·*te*·laa *veal*

X

xerém chouriço ⑩ she·*reng* sho·*ree*·so *cornmeal porridge served with shellfish, pork or other meat*

xinxim de galinha ⑩ sheeng·*sheeng* de gaa·*lee*·nyaa *chicken pieces flavoured with garlic, salt & lemon*

emergencies

emergências

Help, I'm being robbed!
*Socorro, estou sendo
assaltado/assaltada!* m/f
so·ko·ho es·to seng·do
aa·sow·taa·do/aa·sow·taa·daa

Stop, thief!
Pega ladrão!
pe·gaa la·drowng

Can I use your phone?
Posso usar seu telefone?
po·so oo·zaarr se·oo te·le·fo·ne

It's an emergency.
É uma emergência.
e oo·maa e·merr·zheng·see·aa

Call the police!
Chame a polícia!
sha·me aa po·lee·syaa

Call a doctor!
Chame um médico!
sha·me oom me·dee·ko

Call an ambulance!
*Chame uma
ambulância!*
sha·me oo·maa
am·boo·lang·see·aa

Could you please help?
*Você pode ajudar,
por favor?*
vo·se po·de aa·zhoo·daarr
porr faa·vorr

I'm lost.
*Estou perdido/
perdida.* m/f
es·to perr·dee·do/
perr·dee·daa

Is it dangerous here?
Aqui é perigoso?
a·kee e pe·ree·go·zo

Where are the toilets?
Onde tem um banheiro?
on·de teng oom ba·nyay·ro

I'm ill.
Estou doente. es·to do·*eng*·te

She's having a baby.
Ela está tendo um bebê e·laa es·*taa teng*·do oom be·*be*

My … is ill.	… está doente.	… es·*taa* do·*eng*·te
daughter	*Minha filha*	mee·nyaa *fee*·lyaa
friend (female)	*Minha amiga*	mee·nyaa aa·*mee*·gaa
friend (male)	*Meu amigo*	me·oo aa·*mee*·go
son	*Meu filho*	me·oo *fee*·lyo

He/She is having a/an …	Ele/Ela está tendo …	e·le/e·laa es·*taa teng*·do …
allergic reaction	*uma reação alérgica*	oo·maa he·aa·*sowng* aa·*lerr*·zhee·kaa
asthma attack	*um ataque de asma*	oom aa·*taa*·ke de *aas*·maa
epileptic fit	*um ataque epilético*	oom aa·*taa*·ke e·pee·*le*·tee·ko
heart attack	*um ataque cardíaco*	oom aa·*taa*·ke kaarr·*dee*·aa·ko

signs

Delegacia de Polícia	de·le·gaa·*see*·aa de po·*lee*·syaa	Police Station
Hospital	os·pee·*tow*	Hospital
Polícia	po·*lee*·syaa	Police
Pronto Socorro	*prong*·to so·*ko*·ho	Emergency Department

SAFE TRAVEL

police

Where's the police station?
Onde é a delegacia   ong·de e aa de·le·gaa·*see*·aa
de polícia?   de po·*lee*·syaa

Please telephone the Tourist Police.
Por favor telefone para   porr faa·*vorr* te·le·*fo*·ne *paa*·raa
a Polícia de Turistas.   aa po·*lee*·syaa de too·*rees*·taas

I want to report an offence.
Eu quero fazer uma   e·oo *ke*·ro faa·*zerr* oo·maa
queixa.   *kay*·shaa

He/She tried	Ele/Ela tentou	e·le/e·laa teng·to
to … me.	me …	me …
rape	estrupar	es·troo·*paarr*
rob	roubar	ho·*baarr*
I've been …	Eu fui …	e·oo *foo*·ee …
He/She has been …	Ele/Ela foi …	e·le/e·laa foy …
assaulted	agredido/	aa·gre·*dee*·do/
	agredida m/f	aa·gre·*dee*·daa
raped	estrupado/	es·troo·*paa*·do/
	estrupada m/f	es·troo·*paa*·daa
robbed	assaltado/	aa·sow·*taa*·do/
	assaltada m/f	aa·sow·*taa*·daa
My … was stolen.	… foi roubado/	… foy ho·*baa*·do/
	roubada. m/f	ho·*baa*·daa
credit card	Meu cartão m	me·oo kaarr·*towng*
	de crédito	de *kre*·dee·to
money	Meu dinheiro m	me·oo dee·*nyay*·ro
wallet	Minha	*mee*·nyaa
	carteira f	kaar·*tay*·raa

My ... were stolen.	... foram roubados/ roubadas. m/f pl	... fo·rang ho·baa·dos/ ho·baa·daas
bags	Minhas bolsas f pl	mee·nyaas bol·saas
papers	Meus papéis m pl	me·oos paa·peys
travellers cheques	Meus travellers cheques m pl	me·oos traa·ve·ler she·kes

You're charged with ...
Você está sendo   vo·se es·taa seng·do
acusado/   aa·koo·zaa·do/
acusada de ... m/f   aa·koo·zaa·daa de ...

He/She is charged with ...
Ele/Ela está sendo   e·le/e·laa es·taa seng·do
acusado/   aa·koo·zaa·do/
acusada de ... m/f   aa·koo·zaa·daa de ...

assault	agressão	aa·gre·sowng
disturbing the peace	perturbar a paz	perr·toor·baarr aa pas
not having a visa	não ter visto	nowng terr vees·to
overstaying your visa	ter ultrapassado o seu visto	terr ool·traa·paa·saa·do o se·oo vees·to
possession (of illegal substances)	posse (de substâncias ilegais)	po·se (de soo·bees·tang·syaas ee·le·gais)
shoplifting	furto	foor·to
theft	roubo	ho·bo

It's a ... fine.	É uma multa de ...	e oo·maa mool·taa de ...
parking	estacionamento	es·taa·see·o·naa·meng·to
speeding	velocidade	ve·lo·see·daa·de

I've lost my ...	*Perdi ...*	perr·dee ...
backpack	*minha mochila*	mee·nyaa mo·shee·laa
handbag	*minha bolsa de mão*	mee·nyaa bol·saa de mowng
passport	*meu passaporte*	me·oo paa·saa·porr·te

It was him/her.
Foi ele/ela.　　　　　foy e·le/e·laa

I have insurance.
Eu tenho seguro.　　　e·oo te·nyo se·goo·ro

What am I accused of?
Do que estou sendo　　do ke es·to seng·do
acusado/acusada? m/f　aa·koo·zaa·do/aa·koo·zaa·daa

I'm sorry.
Desculpe.　　　　　　des·kool·pe

I didn't realise I was doing anything wrong.
Eu não sabia que　　　e·oo nowng saa·bee·aa ke
estava fazendo algo　　es·taa·vaa faa·zeng·do ow·go
errado.　　　　　　　e·haa·do

I didn't do it.
Eu não fiz isso.　　　　e·oo nowng fees ee·so

Can I pay an on-the-spot fine?
Posso pagar a multa　　po·so paa·gaarr aa mool·taa
na hora?　　　　　　naa aw·raa

Can I make a phone call?
Posso fazer uma　　　po·so faa·zerr oo·maa
ligação?　　　　　　lee·gaa·sowng

Can I have a lawyer (who speaks English?)
Posso ter um advogado　po·so terr oom ad·vo·gaa·do
(que fale inglês?)　　　(ke faa·le eeng·gles)

This medication is for personal use.

Esta medicação é   *es*·taa me·dee·ka·*sowng* e
para uso pessoal.   *paa*·raa oo·zo pe·so·*ow*

I have a prescription for this drug.

Eu tenho receita médica   e·oo te·nyo he·*say*·taa me·dee·kaa
para esta droga.   *paa*·raa *es*·taa *dro*·gaa

I (don't) understand.

Eu (não) entendo.   e·oo (nowng) eng·*teng*·do

I want to	*Eu quero entrar em*	e·oo *ke*·ro eng·*traarr* eng
contact my ...	*contato com a ...*	kong·*taa*·to kong aa ...
consulate	*meu*	*me*·oo
	consulado	kong·soo·*laa*·do
embassy	*minha*	*mee*·nyaa
	embaixada	eng·bai·*shaa*·daa

---

as the saying goes ...

A mentira tem pernas curtas.
    aa meng·*tee*·ra *perr*·naas   A lie has short legs.
    koor·taas

Mais vale um pássaro na mâo que dois voando.
    mais *vaa*·le oom *paa*·saa·ro na   A bird in the hand
    mowng ke doys *vwang*·do   is worth two in the bush.

doctor

o médico

Where's the nearest ...?	*Onde fica ... mais perto?*	ong·de fee·kaa ... mais perr·to
(night) chemist	*a farmácia (noturna)*	aa faarr·*maa*·syaa (no·*toor*·naa)
dentist	*o dentista*	o deng·*tees*·taa
doctor	*o médico*	o *me*·dee·ko
emergency department	*o pronto socorro*	o *prong*·to so·*ko*·ho
hospital	*o hospital*	o os·pee·*tow*
medical centre	*a clínica médica*	aa *klee*·nee·kaa *me*·dee·kaa
optometrist	*o optometrista*	o op·to·me·*trees*·taa

I need a doctor (who speaks English).
Eu preciso de um médico (que fale inglês). — e·oo pre·*see*·zo de oom *me*·dee·ko (ke *faa*·le eeng·*gles*)

Could I see a female doctor?
Posso ver uma médica? — *po*·so verr oo·maa *me*·dee·kaa

Could the doctor come here?
O médico pode vir aqui? — o *me*·dee·ko *po*·de veerr aa·*kee*

Is there an after-hours emergency number?
Tem um número para emergência? — teng oom *noo*·me·ro *paa*·raa e·merr·*zheng*·syaa

the doctor may say ...

What's the problem?
Qual é o problema?   kwow e o pro·*ble*·maa

Where does it hurt?
Onde dói?   ong·de doy

Do you have a temperature?
Você tem febre?   vo·*se* teng *fe*·bre

How long have you been like this?
Há quanto tempo você   aa *kwang*·to *teng*·po vo·*se*
está assim?   es·*taa* aa·*seeng*

Have you had this before?
Você já teve isso antes?   vo·*se* jaa *te*·ve *ee*·so ang·*tes*

Are you sexually active?
Você está sexualmente   vo·*se* es·*taa* sek·soo·ow·*meng*·te
ativo/ativa? m/f   aa·*tee*·vo/aa·*tee*·vaa

Have you had unprotected sex?
Você fez sexo sem   vo·*se* fes *sek*·so seng
proteção?   pro·te·*sowng*

Do you ...?	*Você ...?*	vo·*se* ...
drink	*bebe*	*be*·be
smoke	*fuma*	*foo*·maa
take drugs	*usa drogas*	oo·zaa *dro*·gaas

Are you ...?	*Você ...?*	vo·*se* ...
allergic to	*é alérgico/*	e aa·*lerr*·zhee·ko/
anything	*alérgica*	aa·*lerr*·zhee·kaa
	à alguma	aa ow·*goo*·maa
	coisa m/f	*koy*·zaa
on medication	*está tomando*	es·*taa* to·*mang*·do
	remédio	he·*me*·dyo

How long are you travelling for?
Quanto tempo você   *kwang*·to *teng*·po vo·*se*
vai viajar?   vai vee·aa·*zhaarr*

You need to be admitted to hospital.
Você precisa ser   vo·*se* pre·*see*·zaa serr
internado/internada   eeng·terr·*naa*·do/eeng·terr·*naa*·daa
num hospital. m/f   noom os·pee·*tow*

You should have it checked when you go home.

Você deverá checar — vo·*se* de·ve·*raa* she·*kaarr*
isto quando voltar — ees·to kwang·do vol·*taarr*
para casa. — paa·raa kaa·zaa

You should return home for treatment.

Você deveria voltar — vo·*se* de·ve·*ree*·aa vol·*taarr*
para casa para — paa·raa kaa·zaa paa·raa
tratamento. — traa·taa·*meng*·to

You're a hypochondriac.

Você é hipocondríaco/ — vo·*se* e ee·po·kong·*dree*·aa·ko/
hipocondríaca. m/f — ee·po·kong·*dree*·aa·kaa

I've run out of my medication.

Estou sem remédio. — es·to seng he·*me*·dee·yo

This is my usual medicine.

Este é meu remédio — es·te e me·oo he·*me*·dyo
habitual. — aa·bee·too·*ow*

My son weighs (20 kilos).

Meu filho pesa — me·oo fee·lyo pe·zaa
(vinte kilos). — (veeng·te kee·los)

My daughter weighs (20 kilos).

Minha filha pesa — mee·nyaa fee·lyaa pe·zaa
(vinte kilos). — (veeng·te kee·los)

What's the correct dosage?

Qual é a dosagem — kwow e aa do·zaa·*zheng*
correta? — ko·*he*·taa

I don't want a blood transfusion.

Eu não quero uma — e·oo nowng *ke*·ro oo·maa
transfusão de sangue. — trans·foo·*zowng* de *sang*·ge

Please use a new syringe.

Por favor use uma — porr faa·*vorr* oo·ze oo·maa
seringa nova. — se·*reeng*·gaa *no*·vaa

I have my own syringe.

Eu tenho minha — e·oo te·nyo mee·nyaa
própria seringa. — pro·pree·ya se·*reeng*·gaa

I've been vaccinated against …	Eu fui vacinado/ vacinada contra … m/f	e·oo foo·ee vaa·see·naa·do/ vaa·see·naa·daa kong·traa …
hepatitis A/B/C	hepatite A/B/C	e·paa·tee·te aa/be/se
yellow fever	febre amarela	fe·bre aa·maa·re·laa
He/She has been vaccinated against …	Ele/Ela foi vacinado/ vacinada contra …	e·le/e·laa foy vaa·see·naa·do/ vaa·see·naa·daa kong·traa …
tetanus	tétano	te·ta·no
typhoid	tifo	tee·fo
I need new …	Eu preciso de …	e·oo pre·see·zo de …
contact lenses	novas lentes de contato	no·vaas leng·tes de kong·taa·to
glasses	novos óculos	no·vos o·koo·los

My prescription is …
> Minha receita médica é …
> mee·nyaa he·say·taa me·dee·kaa e …

How much will it cost?
> Quanto vai custar?
> kwang·to vai koos·tarr

Can I have a receipt for my insurance?
> Posso pegar um recibo para meu seguro?
> po·so pe·gaarr oom he·see·bo paa·raa me·oo se·goo·ro

symptoms & conditions

I'm ill.
Estou doente.   es·*to* do·*eng*·te

My friend is ill.
Meu amigo está   me·oo aa·*mee*·go es·*taa*
doente. m   do·*eng*·te
Minha amiga está   mee·nyaa aa·*mee*·gaa es·*taa*
doente. f   do·*eng*·te

My son is ill.
Meu filho está doente.   me·oo *fee*·lyo es·*taa* do·*eng*·te

My daughter is ill.
Minha filha está   mee·nyaa *fee*·lyaa es·*taa*
doente.   do·*eng*·te

It hurts here.
Aqui dói.   aa·*kee* doy

I'm dehydrated.
Estou desidratado/   es·*to* de·zee·draa·*taa*·do/
desidratada. m/f   de·zee·draa·*taa*·daa

I can't sleep.
Eu não consigo   e·oo nowng kong·*see*·go
dormir.   dorr·*meerr*

I've been ...	*Fui ...*	*foo*·ee ...
He/She has been ...	*Ele/Ela está ...*	*e*·le/*e*·laa es·*taa* ...
injured	*machucado/*	maa·shoo·*kaa*·do/
	machucada m/f	maa·shoo·*kaa*·daa
vomiting	*vomitando*	vo·mee·*tang*·do

I feel ...	Estou me sentindo ...	es·to me seng·teeng·do ...
anxious	ansioso/ ansiosa m/f	ang·see·o·zo/ ang·see·o·zaa
better	melhor	me·lyorr
depressed	deprimido/ deprimida m/f	de·pree·mee·do/ de·pree·mee·daa
dizzy	tonto/tonta m/f	tong·to/tong·taa
hot and cold	com calor e com frio	kong kaa·lorr e kong free·o
nauseous	enjoado/ enjoada m/f	eng·zho·aa·do/ en·zho·aa·daa
shivery	com tremedeira	kong tre·me·day·raa
strange	estranho/ estranha m/f	es·tra·nyo/ es·tra·nyaa
weak	fraco/fraca m/f	fraa·ko/fraa·kaa
worse	pior	pee·orr

I think it's the medication I'm on.
Acho que é este remédio que estou tomando.
a·sho ke e es·te he·me·dyo ke es·to to·mang·do

I'm on medication for ...
Estou tomando remédio para ...
es·to to·mang·do he·me·dyo paa·raa ...

He/She is on medication for ...
Ele/Ela está tomando remédio para ...
e·le/e·laa es·taa to·mang·do he·me·dyo paa·raa ...

I have ...
Tenho ...
te·nyo ...

He/She has ...
Ele/Ela tem ...
e·le/e·laa teng ...

I've (recently) had ...
(Recentemente) Tive ...
(he·seng·te·meng·te) tee·ve ...

He/She has (recently) had ...
Ele/Ela (recentemente) teve ...
e·le/e·laa (he·seng·te·meng·te) te·ve ...

asthma	*asma* f	*aas*·maa
cold	*resfriado* f	hes·free·*aa*·do
headache	*dor* f *de cabeça*	dorr de kaa·*be*·saa
diabetes	*diabete* f	dee·aa·*be*·te
diarrhoea	*diarréia* f	dee·aa·*he*·yaa
fever	*febre* f	*fe*·bre
nausea	*náusea* f	*now*·ze·aa
pain	*dor* f	dorr
sore throat	*dor* f *de garganta*	dorr de gaar·*gang*·taa

women's health

(I think) I'm pregnant.
(Acho que) Estou grávida. (aa·sho ke) es·*to* graa·vee·daa

I'm on the Pill.
Estou tomando a pílula. es·*to* to·*mang*·do a *pee*·loo·laa

I haven't had my period for (six) days/weeks.
Não fico menstruada nowng *fee*·ko mengs·troo·*aa*·daa
há (seis) dias/semanas. aa (says) *dee*·aas/se·*ma*·naas

I've noticed a lump here.
Notei um caroço aqui. no·*tay* oom kaa·ro·so aa·*kee*

the doctor may say ...

Are you using contraception?
Você está usando vo·*se* es·*taa* oo·*zang*·do
algum método ow·*goom* me·to·do
anticoncepcional? an·tee·kong·*sep*·syo·now

Are you menstruating?
Você está vo·*se* es·*taa*
menstruando? mengs·troo·*ang*·do

Are you pregnant?
Voce esta gravida? vo·*se* es·*taa* graa·vee·daa

When did you last have your period?
Quando foi sua *kwang*·do foy soo·aa
última menstruação? ool·tee·maa mengs·troo·aa·*sowng*

You're pregnant.
Você está grávida. vo·*se* es·*taa* graa·vee·daa

183

I need ...	Eu preciso ...	e·oo pre·see·zo ...
a pregnancy test	fazer um teste de gravidez	faa·zerr oom tes·te de graa·vee·dez
contraception	de anticoncepcional	de ang·tee·kong·sep·syo·now
the morning-after pill	a pílula do dia seguinte	aa pee·loo·laa do dee·aa se·geeng·te

allergies

For food-related allergies, see **vegetarian & special meals**, page 158.

I have a skin allergy.
  Eu tenho alergia de pele.   e·oo te·nyo aa·lerr·zhee·aa de pe·le

I'm allergic to ...	Tenho alergia à ...	te·nyo aa·lerr·zhee·aa aa ...
He/She is allergic to ...	Ele/Ela é alérgico/ alérgica à ... m/f	e·le/e·laa e aa·lerr·zhee·ko/ aa·lerr·zhee·kaa aa ...
antibiotics	antibióticos	ang·tee·bee·o·tee·kos
anti-inflammatories	anti-inflamatórios	ang·tee· eeng·fla·ma·to·ree·os
aspirin	aspirina	aas·pee·ree·naa
bees	abelhas	aa·be·lyaas
codeine	codeína	ko·de·ee·naa
penicillin	penicilina	pe·nee·see·lee·naa
pollen	pólem	po·leng
sulphur-based drugs	drogas à base de súlfura	dro·gaas aa baa·ze de sool·foo·raa
inhaler	respirador m	hes·pee·raa·dorr
injection	injeção f	eeng·zhe·sowng
antihistamines	antiestamínico m	ang·tee·es·ta·mee·nee·ko

parts of the body

My ... hurts.
Meu/Minha ... dói. m/f — me·oo/mee·nyaa ... doy

I can't move my ...
Não consigo mover
meu/minha ... m/f — nowng kong·see·go mo·verr
me·oo/mee·nyaa ...

My ... is swollen.
Meu ... está inchado. m — me·oo ... es·taa eeng·shaa·do
Minha ... está inchada. f — mee·nyaa ... es·taa eeng·shaa·daa

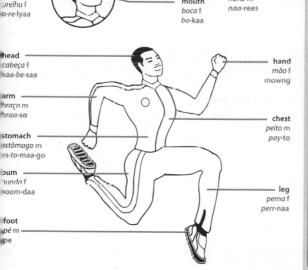

ear
orelha f
o·re·lyaa

nose
nariz m
naa·rees

mouth
boca f
bo·kaa

eye
olho m
o·lyo

head
cabeça f
kaa·be·saa

arm
braço m
braa·so

stomach
estômago m
es·to·maa·go

bum
bunda f
boom·daa

foot
pé m
pe

hand
mão f
mowng

chest
peito m
pay·to

leg
perna f
perr·naa

alternative treatments

tratamentos alternativos

I don't use (Western medicine).
Eu não uso   e·oo nowng oo·zo
(medicina ocidental).   (me·dee·see·naa o·see·deng·tow)

I prefer …	*Eu prefiro …*	e·oo pre·fee·ro …
Can I see	*Posso ver alguém*	po·so verr ow·geng
someone who	*que pratica …*	ke pra·tee·kaa …
practices …?		
acupuncture	*acupuntura*	aa·koo·poom·too·raa
naturopathy	*naturapatia*	naa·too·ro·paa·tee·aa
reflexology	*reflexologia*	he·flek·so·lo·zhee·aa

chemist

farmácia

I need something for …
Preciso de alguma   pre·see·zo de ow·goo·maa
coisa para …   koy·zaa paa·raa …

Do I need a prescription for …?
Preciso de receita   pre·see·zo de he·say·taa
médica para …?   me·dee·kaa paa·raa …

I have a prescription.
Eu tenho receita médica.   e·oo te·nyo he·say·taa me·dee·kaa

How many times a day?
Quantas vezes ao dia?   kwang·taas ve·zes ow dee·aa

Will it make me drowsy?
Isto vai me deixar   ees·to vai me day·shaarr
tonto/tonta? m/f   tong·to/tong·taa

186

antiseptic	*anti-séptico* m	ang·tee·*sep*·tee·ko
contraceptive	*anti-concepcional* m	ang·tee·kong·*sep*·syo·now
painkillers	*analgésicos* m pl	aa·now·*zhe*·zee·kos
thermometer	*termômetro* m	terr·*mo*·me·tro
rehydration salts	*sais* m pl *de hidratação*	sais de ee·draa·taa·*sowng*

listen for ...

*doo·*aas ve·zes porr *dee·*aa (aas he·fay·*soyngs*)
  Duas vezes por dia   **Twice a day**
  (às refeições).   **(with food).**

vo·*se* zhàa to·*mo* ee·so ang·tes
  Você já tomou isso antes?   **Have you taken this before?**

vo·*se* teng ke to·*maarr* too·do
  Você tem que tomar tudo.   **You must complete the course.**

dentist

dentista

I have a ...	*Eu tenho ...*	e·oo te·nyo ...
broken tooth	*um dente quebrado*	oom deng·te ke·*braa*·do
cavity	*uma cárie*	oo·maa *kaa*·ree·e
toothache	*dor de dente*	dorr de deng·te

I've lost a filling.
  Perdi uma obturação.   perr·*dee* oo·maa ob·too·raa·*sowng*

My dentures are broken.
  Minha dentadura   mee·nyaa deng·taa·*doo*·raa
  está quebrada.   es·taa ke·*braa*·daa

health

187

My gums hurt.
Minha gengivas dói.   mee·nyaa zheng·*zhee*·vaas doy

I don't want it extracted.
Eu não quero extrair.   e·oo nowng *ke*·ro es·traa·*eerr*

Ouch!
Au!   ow

I need ...	*Preciso ...*	pre·*see*·zo ...
an anaesthetic	*de analgésico*	de aa·now·*zhe*·zee·ko
a filling	*de uma*	de *oo*·maa
	obturação	ob·too·ra·*sowng*

---

listen for ...

aa·bre beng
Abra bem.   **Open wide.**

eng·*shaa*·gwe
Enxágue.   **Rinse.**

morr·de
Morde.   **Bite down on this.**

nowng se *me*·shaa
Não se mexa.   **Don't move.**

nowng vai do·*err naa*·daa
Não vai doer nada.   **This won't hurt a bit.**

Nouns in the dictionary have their gender indicated by ⓜ or ⓕ. If it's a plural noun, you'll also see pl. Where a word that could be either a noun or a verb has no gender indicated, it's the verb. For all words relating to local food, see the **culinary reader**, page 159.

A

aboard *a bordo* aa borr-do
abortion *aborto* ⓜ aa-borr-to
about *sobre* so-bre
above *sobre* so-bre
abroad *exterior* es-te-ree-orr
accident *acidente* ⓜ aa-see-deng-te
accommodation *hospedagem* ⓕ
  os-pe-daa-zheng
across *através* aa-traa-ves
activist *ativista* ⓜ&ⓕ aa-tee-vees-taa
acupuncture *acupuntura* ⓕ
  aa-koo-poom-too-raa
adaptor *adaptador* ⓜ aa-daa-pee-taa-dorr
addiction *vício* ⓜ vee-syo
address *endereço* ⓜ eng-de-re-so
administration *administração* ⓕ aa-dee-
  mee-nees-traa-sowng
admission price *preço* ⓜ *da entrada*
  pre-so daa eng-traa-daa
admit (acknowledge) *admitir*
  aa-dee-mee-teerr
adult *adulto/adulta* ⓜ/ⓕ
  aa-dool-to/aa-dool-taa
advertisement *anúncio* ⓜ aa-noom-see-o
advice *conselho* ⓜ kong-se-lyo
aerobics *aeróbica* ⓕ aa-e-ro-bee-kaa
aeroplane *aeroplano* ⓜ aa-e-ro-pla-no
Africa *África* ⓕ aa-free-kaa
after *depois de* poys
(this) afternoon *(esta) tarde* ⓕ
  (es-)taa) taarr-de
aftershave *pós barba* ⓜ pos baarr-baa
again *novamente* no-vaa-meng-te
age *idade* ⓕ ee-daa-de
(three days) ago *há (três dias)*
  aa (tres dee-aas)
agree *concordar* kong-korr-daarr

agriculture *agricultura* ⓕ
  aa-gree-kool-too-raa
ahead *em frente* eng freng-te
AIDS *Aids* ⓕ ai-dees
air *ar* ⓜ aarr
air-conditioning *ar* ⓜ *condicionado*
  aarr kong-dee-syo-naa-do
airline *linha aérea* ⓕ pl lee-nyaa aa-e-re-aa
airmail *via* ⓕ *aérea* vee-aa aa-e-re-aa
airplane *avião* ⓜ aa-vee-owng
airport *aeroporto* ⓜ aa-e-ro-porr-to
airport tax *taxa* ⓕ *de aeroporto*
  taa-shaa de aa-e-ro-porr-to
aisle *corredor* ⓜ ko-he-dorr
alarm clock *despertador* ⓜ
  des-perr-taa-dorr
alcohol *álcool* ⓜ ow-kol
all *tudo/tuda* ⓜ/ⓕ too-do/too-daa
allergy *alergia* ⓕ aa-lerr-zhee-aa
almond *amêndoa* ⓕ aa-meng-dwaa
almost *quase* kwaa-ze
alone *sozinho/sozinha* ⓜ/ⓕ so-zee-nyo/
  so-zee-nyaa
already *já* zhaa
also *também* tang-beng
altar *altar* ⓜ ow-taarr
altitude *altitude* ⓕ ow-tee-too-de
always *sempre* seng-pre
ambassador *embaixador/*
  embaixadora ⓜ/ⓕ
  eng-bai-shaa-dorr/eng-bai-shaa-do-raa
American football *futebol* ⓜ *americano*
  foo-te-bol aa-me-ree-ka-no
anaemia *anemia* ⓕ aa-ne-mee-aa
anarchist *anarquista* ⓜ&ⓕ
  aa-naarr-kees-taa
ancient *ancião/anciã* ⓜ/ⓕ
  ang-see-owng/ang-see-ang
and *e* e

angry *zangado/zangada* ⓜ/ⓕ
zang-*gaa*-do/zang-*gaa*-daa
animal *animal* ⓜ&ⓕ aa-nee-*mow*
ankle *tornozelo* ⓜ torr-no-*ze*-lo
answer *resposta* ⓕ hes-*pos*-taa
ant *formiga* ⓕ forr-*mee*-gaa
antibiotics *antibióticos* ⓜ pl
ang-tee-bee-o-*tee*-kos
antinuclear *antinuclear*
ang-tee-noo-kle-*aarr*
antique *antigo/antiga* ⓜ/ⓕ ang-*tee*-go/
ang-*tee*-gaa
antiseptic *anti-séptico* ⓜ
ang-tee-*sep*-tee-ko
any *qualquer* kwow-*kerr*
apartment *apartamento* ⓜ
aa-paarr-taa-*meng*-to
appendix (body) *apêndice* ⓜ
aa-*peng*-dee-se
apple *maçã* ⓕ maa-*sang*
appointment *consulta* ⓕ kong-*sool*-taa
apricot *damasco* ⓜ daa-*maas*-ko
April *abril* aa-*breel*
archaeological *arqueológico/*
arqueológica ⓜ/ⓕ aarr-ke-o-*lo*-zhee-ko/
aarr-ke-o-lo-zhee-kaa
architect *arquiteto/arquiteta* ⓜ/ⓕ
aarr-kee-te-to/aarr-kee-te-taa
architecture *arquitetura* ⓕ
aarr-kee-te-*too*-raa
argue *discutir* dees-koo-*teerr*
arm *braço* ⓜ *braa*-so
aromatherapy *aromaterapia* ⓕ aa
aa-ro-maa-te-raa-*pee*-aa
arrest *prender* preng-*derr*
arrival *chegada* ⓕ she-*gaa*-daa
arrivals *chegadas* ⓕ pl she-*gaa*-daas
arrive *chegar* she-*gaarr*
art *arte* ⓕ *aarr*-te
art gallery *galeria* ⓕ *de arte* gaa-le-*ree*-aa
de *aarr*-te
artist *artista* ⓜ&ⓕ aar-*tees*-taa
Asia *Ásia* ⓕ *aa*-zyaa
ask (a question) *perguntar*
perr-goong-*taarr*
ask (for something) *pedir* pe-*deerr*
asparagus *aspargo* ⓜ aas-*paarr*-go
aspirin *aspirina* ⓕ aas-pee-*ree*-naa

asthma *asma* ⓕ *aas*-maa
athletics *atletismo* ⓜ aat-le-*tees*-mo
atmosphere *atmosfera* ⓕ
aa-tee-mos-*fe*-raa
aubergine *beringela* ⓕ be-reeng-*zhe*-la
August *agosto* aa-*gos*-to
aunt *tia* ⓕ *tee*-aa
Australia *austrália* ⓕ ows-*traa*-lya
Australian Rules Football *Futebol* ⓜ
Australian Rules foo-te-*bol*
ows-*tra*-lee-ang roo-les
automatic teller machine (ATM) *caixa* ⓜ
automático kai-shaa ow-to-*maa*-tee-ko
autumn *outono* ⓜ o-*to*-no
avenue *avenida* ⓕ aa-ve-*nee*-daa
avocado *abacate* ⓜ aa-baa-*kaa*-te
awful *horrível* o-*hee*-vel

B

B&W (film) *preto e branco*
pre-to e *brang*-ko
baby *bebê* ⓜ&ⓕ be-*be*
baby food *comida* ⓕ *de bebê*
ko-*mee*-daa de be-*be*
baby powder *talco* ⓜ *tow*-ko
babysitter *babá* ⓕ baa-*baa*
back (position) *de costas de kos*-taas
back (body) *costas* ⓕ *kos*-taas
backpack *mochila* ⓕ mo-*shee*-la
bacon *bacon* ⓜ *bay*-kong
bad *ruim* hoo-*eeng*
bag *saco* ⓜ *saa*-ko
baggage *bagagem* ⓕ baa-*gaa*-zheng
baggage allowance *limité* ⓜ *de peso*
lee-*mee*-te de *pe*-zo
baggage claim *requerimento* ⓜ *de*
bagagem he-ke-ree-*meng*-to de
baa-*gaa*-zheng
bakery *padaria* ⓕ paa-daa-*ree*-aa
balance (account) *balanço* ⓜ baa-*lang*-so
balcony *varanda* ⓕ vaa-*rang*-daa
ball *bola* ⓕ *bo*-laa
ballet *balé* ⓕ ba-*le*
banana *banana* ⓕ baa-*na*-naa
band (music) *banda* ⓕ *(de música)*
bang-daa (de moo-zee-kaa)
bandage *curativo* ⓕ koo-raa-*tee*-vo
Band-Aid *band-aid* ⓜ bang-*day*-dee

bank *banco* ⓜ *bang*·ko
bank account *conta* ⓕ *bancária*
kong·taa bang·*kaa*·rya
banknote *nota* ⓕ *no*·taa
baptism *batismo* ⓜ baa·*tees*·mo
bar *bar* ⓜ baarr
bar work *trabalho* ⓜ *em bar*
traa·*ba*·lyo eng baarr
barber *barbeiro* ⓜ baar·*bay*·ro
baseball *baseball* ⓜ *bay*·ze·bol
basket *cesta* ⓕ *ses*·taa
basketball *basquete* ⓜ baas·*ke*·te
bathing suit *roupa* ⓕ *de banho*
ho·paa de *ba*·nyo
bathroom *banheiro* ⓜ ba·*nyay*·ro
battery *pilha* ⓕ *pee*·lyaa
be (temporary) *estar* es·*taarr*
be (ongoing) *ser* serr
beach *praia* ⓕ *prai*·aa
beach volleyball *vôlei* ⓜ *de praia*
vo·lay de porr·*yaa*
bean *feijão* ⓜ fay·*zhowng*
beansprout *broto* ⓜ *de feijão*
bro·to de fay·*zhowng*
beautiful *bonito/bonita* ⓜ/ⓕ
bo·*nee*·to/bo·*nee*·taa
beauty salon *salão* ⓜ *de beleza*
saa·*lowng* de be·*le*·zaa
because *por que* porr·*ke*
bed *cama* ⓕ *ka*·maa
bedding *roupa* ⓕ *de cama*
ho·paa de *ka*·maa
bedroom *quarto* ⓜ *kwaarr*·to
bee *abelha* ⓕ aa·*be*·lyaa
beef *bife* ⓜ *bee*·fe
beer *cerveja* ⓕ serr·*ve*·zhaa
beetroot *beterraba* ⓕ be·te·*haa*·baa
before *antes* *ang*·tes
beggar *pedinte* ⓜ&ⓕ pe·*deeng*·te
behind *atrás* aa·*traas*
below *abaixo* aa·*bai*·sho
best *melhor* me·*lyorr*
bet *aposta* ⓕ aa·*pos*·taa
better *melhor* me·*lyorr*
between *entre* *eng*·tre
bible *bíblia* ⓕ *bee*·blyaa
bicycle *bicicleta* ⓕ bee·see·*kle*·taa
big *grande* *grang*·de

bike *bicicleta* ⓕ bee·see·*kle*·taa
bike chain *corrente* ⓕ *de bicicleta*
ko·*heng*·te de bee·see·*kle*·tãa
bike lock *tranca* ⓕ *de bicicleta trang*·kaa
de bee·see·*kle*·taa
bike path *rota* ⓕ *de bicicleta*
ho·ta de bee·see·*kle*·taa
bike shop *loja* ⓕ *de bicicleta*
lo·zhaa de bee·see·*kle*·taa
bill (account) *conta* ⓕ *kong*·taa
binoculars *binóculos* ⓜ pl bee·no·*koo*·los
bird *pássaro* ⓜ paa·*saa*·ro
birth certificate *certidão* ⓕ *de nascimento*
serr·tee·*downg* de naa·see·*meng* to
birthday *aniversário* ⓜ aa·nee·verr·*saa*·ryo
biscuit *biscoito* ⓜ bees·*koy*·to
bite (dog) *mordida* ⓕ morr·*dee*·daa
bite (insect) *mordida* ⓕ morr·*dee*·daa
black *preto/preta* ⓜ/ⓕ *pre*·to/*pre*·taa
bladder *bexiga* ⓕ be·*shee*·gaa
blanket *cobertor* ⓜ ko·berr·*torr*
blind *cego/cega* ⓜ/ⓕ *se*·go/*se*·gaa
blister *bolha* ⓕ *bo*·lyaa
blocked *bloqueado/bloqueada* ⓜ/ⓕ
blo·ke·*aa*·do/blo·ke·*aa*·daa
blood *sangue* ⓜ *sang*·ge
blood group *grupo* ⓜ *sanguíneo*
groo·po sang·*gwee*·ne·o
blood pressure *pressão* ⓕ *arterial*
pre·*sowng* aar·te·ree·*ow*
blood test *exame* ⓜ *de sangue*
e·*za*·me de *sang*·ge
blue *azul* aa·*zool*
board (a plane, ship, etc) *subir a bordo*
soo·*beerr* aa *borr*·do
boarding house *casa* ⓕ *de cômodos* ·
pensão ⓕ *kaa*·zaa de *ko*·mo·dos ·
peng·*sowng*
boarding pass *boarding pass* ⓜ
borr·deeng paas
boat *barco* ⓜ *baar*·ko
body *corpo* ⓜ *korr*·po
bone *osso* ⓜ *o*·so
book *livro* ⓜ *lee*·vro
book (make a booking) *reservar*
he·zerr·*vaarr*
booked out *esgotado/esgotada* ⓜ/ⓕ
es·go·*taa*·do/es·go·*taa*·daa
book shop *livraria* ⓕ lee·vraa·*ree*·aa

boot (footwear) *bota* ① bo·taa
boots (footwear) *botas* ① pl bo·taas
border *borda* ① borr·daa
bored *entediado/entediada* ⑩/①
eng·te·dee·aa·do/eng·te·dee·aa·daa
boring *entediante* eng·te·dee·ang·te
borrow *emprestar* eng·pres·taarr
botanic garden *jardim* ⑩ *botânico*
zharr·deeng bo·ta·nee·ko
both *ambos/ambas* ⑩/①
ang·bos/ang·baas
bottle *garrafa* ① gaa·haa·faa
bottle opener *abridor* ⑩ *de garrafas*
aa·bree·dorr de gaa·haa·faas
bottle shop *loja* ① *de bebidas*
lo·zhaa de be·bee·daas
bottom (position) *fundo* foong·do
bottom (body) *traseiro* ⑩ traa·zay·ro
bowl *tigela* ① tee·zhe·laa
box *caixa* ① kai·shaa
boxer shorts *ciroula* ① se·ro·laa
boxing *boxe* ⑩ bo·kee·see
boy *menino* ⑩ me·nee·no
boyfriend *namorado* ⑩ na·mo·raa·do
bra *sutiã* ① soo·tee·ang
brake *freio* ⑩ fray·o
brandy *brandy* ⑩ brang·dee
brave *corajoso/corajosa* ⑩/①
ko·raa·zho·zo/ko·raa·zho·zaa
bread *pão* ⑩ powng
bread rolls *pães* ⑩ pl payngs
break *quebrar* ke·braarr
break down *pifar* • *enguiçar*
pee·faarr • eng·gee·saarr
breakfast *café* ⑩ *da manhã*
ka·fe da ma·nyang
breast (body) *peito* ⑩ sg pay·to
breasts (body) *seios* ⑩ pl say·os
breathe *respirar* hes·pee·raarr
bribe *suborno* ⑩ soo·borr·no
bridge *ponte* ① pong·te
briefcase *pasta* ① pas·taa
brilliant *brilhante* bree·lyang·te
bring *trazer* traa·zerr
broccoli *brocolis* ⑩ pl bro·ko·lees
brochure *brochura* ① bro·shoo·raa
broken *quebrado/quebrada* ⑩/①
ke·braa·do/ke·braa·daa
bronchitis *bronquite* ① brong·kee·te

brother *irmão* ⑩ eerr·mowng
brown *marron* maa·hong
bruise *hematoma* ⑩ e·maa·to·maa
brush (hair) *escova* ① es·ko·vaa
bucket *balde* ⑩ bow·de
Buddhist *Budista* boo·dees·taa
buffet *buffet* ⑩ boo·fe
bug *bicho* ⑩ bee·sho
build *construir* kongs·troo·eerr
builder *construtor* ⑩ kongs·troo·tor
building *prédio* ⑩ pre·dyo
bumbag *pochete* ① po·she·te
burn *queimadura* ① kay·maa·doo·raa
burnt *queimado/queimada* ⑩/①
kay·maa·do/kay·maa·daa
bus (city) *ônibus* ⑩ o·nee·boos
bus (intercity) *ônibus* ⑩ o·nee·boos
bus station *rodoviária* ①
ho·do·vee·aa·ryaa
bus stop *ponto* ⑩ *de ônibus*
pong·to de o·nee·boos
business *negócios* ⑩ pl ne·go·syos
business class *business class* ①
bee·zee·nes klaas
business person *homem/mulher* ⑩/①
de negócios o·meng/moo·lyerr de
ne·go·syos
business trip *viagem* ① *de negócios*
vee·aa·zheng de ne·goo·syos
busker *artista* ⑩&① *de rua*
aar·tees·taa de hoo·aa
busy *ocupado/ocupada* ⑩/①
oo·koo·paa·do/o·koo·paa·daa
but *mas* maas
butcher *açougueiro/açougueira* ⑩/①
aa·so·gay·ro/aa·so·gay·raa
butcher's shop *açougue* ⑩ aa·so·ge
butter *manteiga* ① man·tay·gaa
butterfly *borboleta* ① borr·bo·le·taa
buttons *botões* ⑩ pl bo·toyngs
buy *comprar* kong·praarr

C

cabbage *repolho* ⑩ he·po·lyo
cable car *bonde* ⑩ bong·de
cafe *café* ⑩ kaa·fe
cake *bolo* ⑩ bo·lo

cake shop *confeitaria* ①
  kong·fay·taa·*ree*·aa
calculator *calculadora* ①
  kow·koo·laa·*do*·raa
calendar *calendário* ⓜ kaa·leng·*daa*·ryo
camera *câmera* ① *ka*·me·raa
camera shop *loja* ① *de equipamentos*
  fotográficos lo·zhaa de
  e·kee·pa·*meng*·tos fo·to·*graa*·fee·kos
camp *acampar* aa·kang·*paarr*
camp site *local* ⓜ *para acampar* lo·kow
  paa·raa aa·kang·*paarr*
camping ground *acampamento* ⓜ
  aa·kang·paa·*meng*·to
camping store *loja* ① *de acampamento*
  lo·zhaa de aa·kam·paa·*meng*·to
can (be able) *poder* po·*derr*
can (have permission) *poder* po·*derr*
can (tin) *lata* ① *laa*·taa
can opener *abridor* ⓜ *de lata* aa·bree·*dorr*
  de *laa*·taa
Canada *Canadá* ⓜ kaa·naa·*daa*
cancel *cancelar* kang·se·*laarr*
cancer *câncer* ⓜ *kang*·serr
candle *vela* ① *ve*·laa
candy *bala* ① *baa*·laa
cantaloupe *melão* ⓜ me·*lowng*
capsicum *pimentão* ⓜ pee·meng·*towng*
car *carro* ⓜ *kaa*·ho
car hire *aluguel* ⓜ *de carro*
  aa·loo·*gel* de *kaa*·ho
car registration *registro* ⓜ *de carro*
  he·*zhees*·tro de *kaa*·ho
caravan *caravan* ① kaa·raa·*vang*
cardiac arrest *parada* ① *cardíaca*
  paa·*raa*·daa kaarr·*dee*·aa·kaa
cards (playing) *cartas* ① pl *kaarr*·tas
care (for someone) *gostar (de alguém)*
  gos·*taarr* (de ow·*geng*)
car park *estacionamento* ⓜ
  es·taa·syo·naa·*meng*·to
carpenter *carpinteiro* ⓜ karr·peeng·*tay*·ro
carrot *cenoura* ① se·no·raa
carry *carregar* kaa·he·*gaarr*
carton *caixa* ① *de papelão*
  kai·shaa de paa·pe·*lowng*
cash *em espécie* eng es·*pe*·sye
cash (a cheque) *descontar (um cheque)*
  des·kong·*taarr* (oom *she*·ke)

cash register *caixa* ① *registradora*
  kai·shaa he·gees·traa·*do*·raa
cashew *castanha* ① *de cajú* kas·*ta*·nyaa
  de kaa·*zhoo*
cashier *caixa* ⓜ&① *kai*·sha
casino *casino* ⓜ kaa·*see*·no
cassette *fita* ① *cassete* fee·taa kaa·*se*·te
castle *castelo* ⓜ kaas·*te*·lo
casual work *trabalho* ⓜ *ocasional*
  traa·*baa*·lyo o·kaa·zee·o·*now*
cat *gato/gata* ⓜ/① *gaa*·to/*gaa*·taa
cathedral *catedral* ① kaa·te·*drow*
Catholic *Católico/Católica* ⓜ/①
  kaa·to·*lee*·ko/kaa·to·*lee*·kaa
cauliflower *couve flor* ① *ko*·ve florr
cave *caverna* ① kaa·*verr*·naa
CD *CD* ⓜ se·*de*
celebration *comemoração* ①
  ko·me·mo·raa·*sowng*
cent *centavos* ⓜ pl seng·*taa*·vos
centimetre *centímetro* ⓜ seng·*tee*·me·tro
centre *centro* ⓜ *seng*·tro
ceramics *cerâmica* ① se·ra·*mee*·kaa
cereal *cereal* ⓜ se·re·*ow*
certificate *certificado* ⓜ
  serr·tee·fee·*kaa*·do
chain *corrente* ① ko·*heng*·te
chair *cadeira* ① kaa·*day*·raa
chairlift (skiing) *teleférico* ⓜ te·le·*fe*·ree·ko
championships *campeonatos* ⓜ pl
  kang·pe·o·*naa*·tos
chance *oportunidade* ①
  o·porr·too·nee·*daa*·de
change *trocar* tro·*kaarr*
change (coins) *troco* ⓜ *tro*·ko
changing room *provador* ⓜ pro·vaa·*dorr*
charming *charmoso/charmosa* ⓜ/①
  shaarr·*mo*·zo/shaarr·*mo*·zaa
chat up *conversar* kong·verr·*saarr*
cheap *barato/barata* ⓜ/①
  baa·*raa*·to/baa·*raa*·taa
cheat *traição* ① tra·ee·*sowng*
check *checar* she·*kaarr*
check-in (desk) *check in* ① she·*keeng*
checkpoint (border) *ponto* ⓜ *de controle*
  pong·to de kong·*tro*·le
cheque (banking) *cheque* ⓜ *she*·ke
cheque (bill) *conta* ① *kong*·taa
cheese *queijo* ⓜ *kay*·zho

cheese shop *queijaria* ① kay-zhaa-*ree*-aa

chef *chefe* ⓜ&① *de cozinha*
she-fe de ko-*zee*-nyaa

chemist *pharmacista* ⓜ&①
faarr-maa-*sees*-taa

cherry *cereja* ① se-re-*zhaa*

chess *xadrez* ⓜ shaa-*dres*

chess board *tabuleiro* ⓜ *de xadrez*
taa-boo-*lay*-ro de shaa-*dres*

chest (body) *peito* ⓜ *pay*-to

chestnut *castanha* ① *portuguesa*
kaas-*ta*-nyaa porr-*too*-ge-zaa

chewing gum *goma* ① *de mascar*
go-maa de maas-*kaarr*

chicken *galinha* ① gaa-*lee*-nyaa

chicken pox *catapora* ① kaa-taa-*po*-raa

chickpea *grão* ⓜ *de bico*
growng de *bee*-ko

child *criança* ⓜ&① kree-*ang*-saa

child seat *cadeira* ① *de criança*
kaa-*day*-raa de kree-*ang*-saa

childminding *cuidado* ⓜ *da criança*
kooy-*daa*-do de kree-*ang*-saa

children *crianças* ⓜ&① pl kree-*ang*-saas

chilli *pimenta* ① pee-*meng*-taa

chilli sauce *molho* ⓜ *de pimenta* mo-*lyo*
de pee-*meng*-taa

chiropractor *quiroprático/*
quiroprática ⓜ/① kee-ro-*praa*-tee-ko/
kee-ro-*praa*-tee-kaa

chocolate *chocolate* ⓜ sho-ko-*laa*-te

choose *escolher* es-ko-*lyerr*

Christian *Cristão/Cristã* ⓜ/① krees-*towng*/
krees-*tayng*

Christian name *nome* ⓜ *Cristão* •
primeiro nome ⓜ *no*-me krees-*towng* •
pree-*may*-ro *no*-me

Christmas Day *Dia* ⓜ *de Natal*
dee-aa de naa-*tow*

Christmas Eve *Noite* ① *de Natal* noy-te
de na-*tow*

church *igreja* ① ee-*gre*-zhaa

cider *cidra* ① *see*-draa

cigar *charuto* ⓜ shaa-*roo*-to

cigarette *cigarro* ⓜ see-*gaa*-ho

cigarette lighter *isqueiro* ⓜ ees-*kay*-ro

cinema *cinema* ⓜ see-*ne*-maa

circus *circo* ⓜ *seerr*-ko

citizenship *cidadania* ① see-daa-da-*nee*-aa

city *cidade* ① see-*daa*-de

city centre *centro* ⓜ *da cidade*
seng-tro daa see-*daa*-de

civil rights *direitos* ⓜ pl *civis*
dee-*ray*-tos see-*vees*

class (category) *classe* ① *klaa*-se

class system *sistema* ① *de classes*
sees-*te*-maa de *klaa*-ses

classical *clássico/clássica* ⓜ/①
klaa-see-ko/*klaa*-see-kaa

clean *limpo/limpa* ⓜ/①
leeng-po/*leeng*-paa

client *cliente* ⓜ&① klee-*eng*-te

cliff *penhasco* ⓜ pe-*nyaas*-ko

climb *subir* soo-*beerr*

cloakroom *guarda* ⓜ *volumes* gwaarr-daa
vo-*loo*-mes

clock *relógio* ⓜ he-*lo*-zhyo

close *fechar* fe-*shaarr*

closed *fechado/fechada* ⓜ/① fe-*shaa*-do/
fe-*shaa*-daa

clothesline *corda* ① *de roupa*
korr-daa de ho-paa

clothing *roupas* ① pl ho-paas

clothing store *loja* ① *de roupas*
lo-zhaa de ho-paas

cloud *nuvem* ① noo-*veng*

cloudy *nublado/nublada* ⓜ/①
noo-*blaa*-do/noo-*blaa*-daa

clutch (car) *embreagem* ①
eng-bre-*aa*-zheng

coach *técnico/técnica* ⓜ/①
te-kee-nee-ko/*te*-kee-nee-kaa

coast *costa* ① *kos*-taa

coat *casaco* ⓜ kaa-*zaa*-ko

cocaine *cocaína* ① ko-kaa-*ee*-naa

cockroach *barata* ① baa-*raa*-taa

cocoa *cacau* ⓜ ka-*kow*

coconut *côco* ⓜ *ko*-ko

coffee *café* ⓜ kaa-*fe*

coins *moedas* ① pl mo-*e*-daas

cold *frio* ⓜ *free*-o

cold *frio/fria* ⓜ/① *free*-o/*free*-aa

colleague *colega* ⓜ&① ko-*le*-gaa

collect call *ligação* ① *à cobrar*
lee-gaa-*sowng* aa ko-*braarr*

college *academia* ① •
universidade ① aa-kaa-de-*mee*-aa •
oo-nee-verr-see-*daa*-de

colour *cor* ① korr
comb *pente* Ⓜ peng·te
come *vir* veerr
comedy *comédia* ① ko·me·dyaa
comfortable *confortável* kong·forr·taa·vel
communications (profession)
 comunicação ① ko·moo·nee·kaa·sowng
communion *comunhão* ①
 ko·moo·nyowng
communist *comunista* Ⓜ&①
 ko·moo·nees·taa
companion *companheiro/companheira*
 Ⓜ/① kong·pa·nyay·ro/kong pa nyay raa
company *companhia* Ⓜ&①
 kong·paa·nhaa
compass *compasso* Ⓜ kong·paa·so
complain *reclamar* he·klaa·marr
computer *computador* Ⓜ
 kong·poo·taa·dorr
computer game *jogo* Ⓜ *de computador*
 zho·go de kong·poo·taa·dorr
concert *show* Ⓜ show
conditioner *condicionador* Ⓜ
 kong·dee·syo·naa·dorr
condom *camisinha* ① kaa·mee·zee·nyaa
confession *confissão* ① kong·fee·sowng
conjunctivitis *conjuntivite* ①
 kong·zhoong·tee·vee·te
confirm (a booking) *confirmar*
 kong·feerr·maarr
connection (phone) *conecção* ①
 ko·ne·kee·sowng
conservative *conservador/conservadora*
 Ⓜ/① kong·serr·vaa·dorr/
 kong·serr·vaa·do·raa
constipation *constipação* ①
 kongs·tee·paa·sowng
consulate *consulado* Ⓜ kong·soo·laa·do
contact lens solution *colírio* Ⓜ *para lentes
 de contato* ko·lee·ryo paa·raa leng·tes de
 kong·taa·to
contact lenses *lentes* Ⓜ pl *de contato*
 leng·tes de kong·taa·to
contraceptives *anticoncepcional* Ⓜ
 ang·tee·kong·sep·syo·now
contract *contrato* Ⓜ kong·traa·to
convenience store *mercearia* ①
 merr·se·aa·ree·aa
convent *convento* Ⓜ kong·veng·to

cook *cozinheiro/cozinheira* Ⓜ/①
 ko·zee·nyay·ro/ko zee·nyay·raa
cook *cozinhar* ko·zee·nyaarr
cookie *biscoito* Ⓜ bees·koy·to
corn *milho* Ⓜ mee·lyo
cornflakes *cereal* Ⓜ se·re·ow
corner *esquina* ① es·kee·naa
corrupt *corrupto/corrupta* Ⓜ/①
 koo·hoo·pee·to/koo·hoo·pee·taa
cost *custar* koos·taarr
cotton *algodão* Ⓜ ow·go·downg
cotton balls *bolas* Ⓜ pl *de algodão*
 bo·laas de ow·go·downg
cotton buds *cotonete* Ⓜ ko·to·ne·te
cough *tossir* to·seerr
cough medicine *xarope* Ⓜ shaa·ro·pe
count *contar* kong·taarr
counter (at bar) *balcão* Ⓜ bow·kowng
country *país* Ⓜ paa·ees
countryside *interior* Ⓜ eeng·te·ree·orr
coupon *cupom* Ⓜ koo·pong
courgette *abobrinha* ① aa·bo·bree·nyaa
court (legal) *corte* ① korr·te
court (tennis) *quadra* ① kwaa·draa
couscous *cuscuz* Ⓜ *marroquino*
 koos·koos maa·ho·kee·no
cover charge *couvert* Ⓜ *artístico*
 koo·verr aarr·tees·tee·ko
cow *vaca* ① vaa·kaa
cracker *biscoito* Ⓜ *d'água*
 bees·koy·to daa·gwaa
crafts *artesanato* Ⓜ aarr·te·zaa·naa·to
crash *batida* ① baa·tee·daa
crazy *louco/louca* Ⓜ/① lo·ko/lo·kaa
cream *creme* Ⓜ kre·me
creche *creche* ① kre·she
credit card *cartão* Ⓜ *de crédito*
 kaarr·towng de kre·dee·to
cricket (sport) *cricket* Ⓜ kree·ke·tee
crop *tosa* ① to·zaa
cross (religious) *cruz* ① kroos
crowded *lotado/lotada* Ⓜ/① lo·taa·do/
 lo·taa·daa
cucumber *pepino* Ⓜ pe·pee·no
cup *xícara* ① shee·kaa·raa
cupboard *armário* Ⓜ aarr·maa·ryo
currency exchange *câmbio* Ⓜ *de valores*
 kang·byo de vaa·lo·res
current (electricity) *corrente* ① ko·heng·te

current affairs *assuntos* ⓜ pl *atuais*
aa-*soong*-tos aa-*too*-ais

curry *caril* ⓜ kaa-*reel*

customs *alfândega* ⓕ aal-*fang*-de-gaa

cut *cortar* korr-*taarr*

cutlery *talheres* ⓜ pl taa-*lye*-res

CV *CV* ⓜ se-ve

cycle *andar de bicicleta* ang-*daarr* de
bee-see-*kle*-taa

cycling *ciclismo* ⓜ see-*klees*-mo

cyclist *ciclista* ⓜ&ⓕ see-*klees*-taa

cystitis *cistite* ⓕ sees-*tee*-te

D

dad *pai* ⓜ pai

dance *dançar* dang-*saarr*

dancing *dança* ⓕ *dang*-saa

dangerous *perigoso/perigosa* ⓜ/ⓕ
pe-ree-*go*-zo/pe-ree-*go*-zaa

dark *escuro/escura* ⓜ/ⓕ es-*koo*-ro/
es-*koo*-raa

date (appointment) *hora* ⓕ *marcada*
aw-raa maarr-*kaa*-daa

date (day) *data* ⓕ *daa*-taa

date (fruit) *tâmara* ⓕ *ta*-maa-raa

date (a person) *namorar* naa-mo-*raarr*

date of birth *data* ⓕ *de nascimento*
daa-taa de naa-see-*meng*-to

daughter *filha* ⓕ *fee*-lyaa

dawn *madrugada* ⓕ maa-droo-*gaa*-daa

day *dia* ⓜ *dee*-aa

day after tomorrow *depois* ⓜ *de amanhã*
de-*poys* de aa-maa-*nyang*

day before yesterday *antes* ⓜ *de ontem*
ang-tes de *ong*-teng

dead *morto/morta* ⓜ/ⓕ
morr-to/*morr*-taa

deaf *surdo/surda* ⓜ/ⓕ
soor-do/*soor*-daa

deal (cards) *dar* daarr

December *dezembro* de-*zeng*-bro

decide *decidir* de-see-*deer*

deep *profundo/profunda* ⓜ/ⓕ
pro-*foong*-do/pro-*foong*-daa

deforestation *desflorestamento* ⓜ
des-flo-res-taa-*meng*-to

degrees (temperature) *graus* ⓜ pl grows

delay *atraso* ⓜ aa-*traa*-zo

delicatessen *delicatessen* ⓕ
de-lee-kaa-*te*-seng

deliver *entregar* eng-tre-*gaarr*

democracy *democracia* ⓕ
de-mo-kraa-*see*-aa

demonstration *demonstração* ⓕ
de-mongs-traa-*sowng*

Denmark *Dinamarca* ⓕ
dee-naa-*maarr*-kaa

dental floss *fio* ⓜ *dental*
fee-o deng-*tow*

dentist *dentista* ⓜ&ⓕ deng-*tees*-taa

deodorant *desodorante* ⓜ
de-zo-do-*rang*-te

depart (leave) *partir* paarr-*teerr*

department store *loja* ⓕ *de
departamentos* lo-zhaa de
de-paarr-taa-*meng*-tos

departure *partida* ⓕ paarr-*tee*-daa

departure gate *portão* ⓜ *de partida*
porr-*towng* de paarr-*tee*-daa

deposit *depósito* de-*po*-zee-to

derailleur *câmbio* ⓜ *de marcha* kang-byo
de *maarr*-shaa

descendent *descendente* ⓜ&ⓕ
de-seng-*deng*-te

desert *deserto* ⓜ de-*zerr*-to

design *design*

dessert *sobremesa* ⓕ so-bre-*me*-zaa

destination *destino* ⓜ des-*tee*-no

details *detalhes* ⓜ pl de-*taa*-lyes

diabetes *diabetes* ⓕ dee-aa-*be*-tes

dial tone *linha* ⓕ *lee*-nyaa

diaper *fralda* ⓕ *frow*-daa

diaphragm *diafragma* ⓜ
dee-aa-*fraa*-gee-maa

diarrhoea *diarréia* ⓕ dee-aa-*hay*-aa

diary *diário* ⓜ dee-*aa*-ryo

dice *dados* ⓜ pl *daa*-dos

dictionary *dicionário* ⓜ dee-syo-*naa*-ryo

die *morrer* mo-*herr*

diet *dieta* ⓕ dee-*e*-taa

different *diferente* dee-fe-*reng*-te

difficult *difícil* dee-*fee*-seel

dining car *vagão* ⓜ *restaurante*
vaa-*gowng* hes-tow-*rang*-te

dinner *jantar* ⓜ zhang-*taarr*

direct *direto/direta* ⓜ/ⓕ
dee-*re*-to/dee-*re*-taa

direct-dial *ligação* ① *direta*
lee·gaa·*sowng* dee·*re*·taa
director *diretor/diretora* ⓜ/①
dee·re·*torr*/dee·re·*to*·raa
dirty *sujo/suja* ⓜ/① soo·zho/soo·zhaa
disabled *deficiente* de·fee·see·*eng*·te
disco *disco* ⓜ *dees*·ko
discount *desconto* des·*kong*·to
discrimination *discriminação* ①
dees·kree·mee·naa·*sowng*
disease *doença* ① do·*eng*·saa
disk (computer) *disk* ⓜ *deesk*
diving *mergulho* ⓜ merr·*goo*·lyö
diving equipment *equipamento* ⓜ
de mergulho e·kee·paa·*meng*·to de
merr·*goo*·lyo
dizzy *tonto/tonta* ⓜ/①
tong·to/*tong*·taa
do *fazer* faa·*zerr*
doctor *médico/médica* ⓜ/① *me*·dee·ko/
me·dee·kaa
documentary *documentário* ⓜ
do·koo·meng·*taa*·ryo
dog *cachorro* ⓜ/① kaa·*sho*·ho
dole *seguro social* ⓜ se·*goo* ro so·see·*ow*
doll *boneco/boneca* ⓜ/①
bo·*ne*·ko/bo·*ne*·kaa
dollar *dólar* ⓜ *do*·laarr
door *porta* ① *porr*·taa
dope (drugs) *bagulho* ⓜ baa·*goo*·lyo
double *duplo/dupla* ⓜ/①
doo·plo/*doo*·plaa
double bed *cama* ① *de casal*
ka·maa de kaa·*zow*
double room *quarto* ⓜ *de casa kwaarr*·to
de kaa·*zow*
down *baixo* bai·sho
downhill *para baixo* paa·raa hai·sho
dozen *dúzia* ① *doo*·zyaa
drama *drama* ⓜ *dra*·maa
dream *sonho* ⓜ so·nyo
dress *vestido* ⓜ ves·*tee*·do
dried *seco/seca* ⓜ/① *se*·ko/*se*·kaa
dried fruit *frutas* ① pl *secas*
froo·taas se·kaas
drink *bebida* ① be·*bee*·daa
drive *dirigir* dee·ree·*zheerr*
drivers licence *carteira* ① *de motorista*
kaar·*tay*·raa de mo·to·*rees*·taa

drug *droga* ① *dro*·gaa
drug addiction *vício* ⓜ *de drogas*
vee·syo de *dro*·gaas
drug dealer *traficante* ⓜ&①
traa·fee·*kang*·te
drug user *usuário/usuária* ⓜ/① *de*
drogas oo·zoo·*aa*·ryo/oo·zoo·*aa*·ryaa
de *dro*·gaas
drugs *drogas* ① pl *dro*·gaas
drum *bateria* ① baa·te·*ree*·aa
drunk *bêbado/bêbada* ⓜ/①
be·*baa*·do/be·*baa*·daa
dry *secar se kaarr*
dry *seco/seca* ⓜ/① *se*·ko/*se*·kaa
duck *pato/pata* ⓜ/① *paa*·to/*paa*·taa
dummy (for baby) *chupeta* ① shoo·*pe*·taa
DVD *DVD* ⓜ de·ve·*de*

E

each *cada* kaa·daa
ear *orelha* ① o·re·lyaa
early *cedo* se·do
earn *ganhar* ga·*nyaarr*
earplugs *tampões* ⓜ *de ouvido*
tang·*powng* de o·*vee*·do
earrings *brincos* ⓜ pl *breeng*·kos
Earth *Terra* ① *te*·haa
earthquake *terremoto* ⓜ te·he·*mo*·to
east *leste* ⓜ *les*·te
Easter *Páscoa* ① *paas*·kwaa
easy *fácil* faa·*seel*
eat *comer* ko·*merr*
economy class *classe* ① *econômica*
klaa·se e·ko·no·mee·kaa
ecstacy (drug) *êxtase* ⓜ *es*·taa·ze
eczema *eczema* ⓜ e·kee·ze·maa
editor *editor/editora* ⓜ/①
e·dee·*torr*/e·dee·*to*·raa
education *educação* ① e·doo·ka·*sowng*
egg *ovo* ⓜ *o*·vo
eggplant *beringela* ① be·reeng·zhe·laa
election *eleição* ① e·lay·*sowng*
electrical store *loja* ① *de aparelhos*
elétricos lo·zhaa de aa·paa·*re*·lyos
e·*le*·tree·kos
electricity *eletricidade* ①
e·le·tree·see·*daa*·de
elevator *elevador* ⓜ e·le·vaa·*dorr*

embarrassed *envergonhado/ envergonhada* ⓜ/ⓕ en·verr·go·*nyaa*·do/en·verr·go·*nyaa*·daa

embassy *embaixada* ⓕ eng·bai·*shaa*·daa

emergency *emergência* ⓕ e·merr·*zheng*·syaa

emotional *sensível* seng·*see*·vel

employee *empregado/ empregada* ⓜ/ⓕ eng·pre·*gaa*·do/ eng·pre·*gaa*·daa

employer *empregador/ empregadora* ⓜ/ⓕ eng·pre·gaa·*dorr*/ eng·pre·gaa·*do*·raa

empty *vazio/vazia* ⓜ/ⓕ vaa·*zee*·o/vaa·*zee*·aa

end *fim* ⓜ feeng

endangered species *espécies* ⓕ pl *ameaçadas de extinção* es·*pe*·syes aa·me·aa·*saa*·daas de es·teeng·*sowng*

engagement *noivado* ⓜ noy·*vaa*·do

engine *motor* ⓜ mo·*torr*

engineer *engenheiro/engenheira* ⓜ/ⓕ eng·zhe·*nyay*·ro/eng·zhe·*nyay*·raa

engineering *engenharia* ⓕ eng·zhe·nya·*ree*·aa

England *Inglaterra* ⓕ eeng·glaa·*te*·haa

English (language) *Inglês* ⓜ eeng·*gles*

enjoy (oneself) *aproveitar* aa·pro·vay·*taarr*

enough *suficiente* soo·fee·see·*eng*·te

enter *entrar* eng·*traarr*

entertainment guide *guia* ⓜ *de entretenimento* gee·aa de eng·tre·te·nee·*meng*·to

envelope *envelope* ⓜ eng·ve·*lo*·pe

environment *meio* ⓜ *ambiente* *may*·o ang·bee·*eng*·te

epilepsy *epilepsia* ⓕ e·pee·le·pe·*see*·aa

equal opportunity *oportunidades* ⓕ pl *iguais* o·porr·too·nee·*daa*·des ee·*gwaa*·ees

equality *igualdade* ⓕ ee·gwow·*daa*·de

equipment *equipamento* ⓜ e·kee·paa·*meng*·to

escalator *escada rolante* ⓕ es·*kaa*·daa ho·*lang*·te

euro *euro* ⓜ *e·oo*·ro

Europe *Europa* ⓕ e·oo·ro·paa

euthanasia *eutanásia* ⓕ e·oo·taa·*naa*·zyaa

evening *noite* ⓕ *noy*·te

everything *tudo* *too*·do

example *exemplo* ⓜ e·*zeng*·plo

excellent *excelente* e·se·*leng*·te

exchange *troca* ⓕ *tro*·kaa

exchange *trocar* tro·*kaarr*

exchange rate *taxa* ⓕ *de câmbio* *taa*·shaa de *kang*·byo

excluded *excluído/excluída* ⓜ/ⓕ es·kloo·*ee*·do/es·kloo·*ee*·daa

exhaust (car) *exaustor* ⓜ e·zows·*torr*

exhibition *exposição* ⓕ es·po·zee·*sowng*

exit *saída* ⓕ saa·*ee*·daa

expensive *caro/cara* ⓜ/ⓕ *kaa*·ro/*kaa*·raa

experience *experiência* ⓕ es·pe·ree·*eng*·syaa

exploitation *exploração* ⓕ es·plo·raa·*sowng*

express *expresso/expressa* ⓜ/ⓕ es·*pre*·so/ es·*pre*·saa

express mail *serviço* ⓜ *postal rápido* serr·*vee*·so pos·*tow* *haa*·pee·do

extension (visa) *extensão* ⓕ es·teng·*sowng*

eye *olho* ⓜ o·*lyo*

eye drops *colírio* ⓜ ko·*lee*·ryo

F

fabric *tecido* ⓜ te·*see*·do

face *rosto* ⓜ *hos*·to

face cloth *toalha* ⓕ *de rosto* to·*aa*·lyaa de *hos*·to

factory *fábrica* ⓕ *faa*·bree·kaa

factory worker *operário/operária* ⓜ/ⓕ o·pe·*raa*·ryo/o·pe·raa·ryaa

fall (autumn) *outono* ⓜ o·*to*·no

fall (down) *queda* ⓕ *ke*·daa

family *família* ⓕ faa·*mee*·lyaa

family name *sobrenome* ⓜ so·bre·*no*·me

famous *famoso/famosa* ⓜ/ⓕ faa·*mo*·zo/faa·*mo*·zaa

fan (machine) *ventilador* ⓜ veng·tee·laa·*dorr*

fan (sport, etc) *fã* ⓜ&ⓕ fang

fanbelt *correia* ⓕ ko·*hay*·aa

far *longe* *long*·zhe

farm *fazenda* ⓕ faa·*zeng*·daa

farmer *fazendeiro/fazendeira* ⓜ/ⓕ
faa‑zeng‑*day*‑ro/faa‑zeng‑*day*‑raa
fast *rápido/rápida* ⓜ/ⓕ
haa‑pee‑do/*haa*‑pee‑daa
fat *gordo/gorda* ⓜ/ⓕ gorr‑do/*gorr*‑daa
father *pai* ⓜ pai
father-in-law *sogro* ⓜ *so*‑gro
faucet *torneira* ⓕ torr‑*nay*‑raa
fault (someone's) *culpa* ⓕ *kool*‑paa
faulty *defeituoso/defeituosa* ⓜ/ⓕ
de‑fay‑too‑o‑zo/de‑fay‑too‑o‑zaa
February *fevereiro* fe‑ve‑*ray*‑ro
feed *alimentar* aa‑lee‑meng‑*taarr*
feel *sentir* seng‑*teerr*
feelings *sentimentos* ⓜ pl
seng‑tee‑*meng*‑tos
fence *cerca* ⓕ *serr*‑kaa
fencing (sport) *esgrima* ⓕ es‑*gree*‑maa
festival *festival* ⓜ fes‑tee‑*vow*
fever *febre* ⓕ *fe*‑bre
few *alguns/algumas* ⓜ/ⓕ
ow‑*goons*/ow‑*goo*‑maas
fiance *noivo* ⓜ *noy*‑vo
fiancee *noiva* ⓕ *noy*‑vaa
fiction *ficção* ⓕ feek‑*sowng*
fig *figo* ⓜ *fee*‑go
fight *luta* ⓕ *loo*‑ta
fill *encher* eng‑*sherr*
fillet *filé* ⓜ fee‑*le*
film (cinema) *filme* ⓜ *feel*‑me
film (photography) *filme* ⓜ *fotográfico*
feel‑me fo‑to‑*graa*‑fee‑ko
film speed *velocidade* ⓕ *do filme*
ve‑lo‑see‑*daa*‑de do *feel*‑me
filtered *filtrado/filtrada* ⓜ/ⓕ
feel *traa*‑do/feel‑*traa*‑daa
find *encontrar* eng‑kong‑*traarr*
fine (payment) *multa* ⓕ *mool*‑taa
fine (boa) *bom/boa* ⓜ/ⓕ bong/*bo*‑aa
finger *dedo* ⓜ *de*‑do
finish *término* ⓜ *terr*‑mee‑no
finish *terminar* terr‑mee‑*naarr*
fire *fogo* ⓜ *fo*‑go
firewood *lenha* ⓕ *le*‑nyaa
first *primeiro/primeira* ⓜ/ⓕ
pree‑*may*‑ro/pree‑*may*‑raa
first class *primeira classe* ⓕ
pree‑*may*‑raa *klaa*‑se

first-aid kit *kit* ⓜ *de primeiros socorros*
kee‑tee de pree‑*may*‑ros so‑*ko*‑hos
fish *peixe* ⓜ *pay*‑she
fish monger *peixeiro/peixeira* ⓜ/ⓕ
pay‑*shay*‑ro/pay‑*shay*‑raa
fish shop *peixaria* ⓕ pay‑sha‑*ree*‑aa
fishing *pesca* ⓕ *pes*‑kaa
flag *bandeira* ⓕ bang‑*day*‑raa
flannel *flanela* ⓕ fla‑*ne*‑laa
flashlight *flash* ⓜ *luminoso*
flash loo‑mee‑*no*‑zo
flat (apartment) *apartamento* ⓜ
aa‑paarr‑taa‑*meng*‑to
flat *plano/plana* ⓜ/ⓕ *pla*‑no/*pla*‑naa
flea *pulga* ⓕ *pool*‑gaa
flight *vôo* ⓜ *vo*‑o
flood *enchente* ⓕ eng‑*sheng*‑te
floor *chão* ⓜ showng
floor (storey) *andar* ⓜ ang‑*daarr*
florist (person) *florista* ⓜ&ⓕ flo‑*rees*‑taa
florist (shop) *floricultura* ⓕ
flo‑ree‑kool‑*too*‑raa
flour *farinha* ⓕ faa‑*ree*‑nyaa
flower *flor* ⓕ florr
fly *voar* vo‑*aarr*
foggy *nebuloso/nebulosa* ⓜ/ⓕ
ne‑boo‑lo‑zo/ne‑boo‑lo‑zaa
follow *seguir* se‑*geerr*
food *comida* ⓕ ko‑*mee*‑daa
foot *pé* ⓜ pe
football (soccer) *futebol* ⓜ foo‑te‑*bol*
footpath *calçada* ⓕ kow‑*saa*‑daa
foreign *estrangeiro/estrangeira* ⓜ/ⓕ
es‑trang‑*zhay*‑ro/es‑trang‑*zhay*‑raa
forest *floresta* ⓕ flo‑*res*‑taa
forever *para sempre* *paa*‑raa *seng*‑pre
forget *esquecer* es‑ke‑*serr*
forgive *perdoar* perr‑do‑*aarr*
fork *garfo* ⓜ *gaarr*‑fo
fortnight *quinzena* ⓕ keeng‑*ze*‑naa
fortune teller *vidente* ⓜ&ⓕ vee‑*deng*‑te
foul *falta* ⓕ *fow*‑taa
foyer *saguão* ⓜ saag‑*wowng*
fragile *frágil* *fraa*‑zheel
free (gratis) *gratuito/gratuita* ⓜ/ⓕ
graa‑too‑ee‑to/graa‑too‑ee‑taa
free (not bound) *livre* *lee*‑vre
freeze *congelar* kong‑zhe‑*laarr*
Friday *sexta-feira* ⓕ ses‑taa‑*fay*‑raa

fried frito/frita ⓜ/ⓕ *free*·to/*free*·taa
friend amigo/amiga ⓜ/ⓕ
  aa·*mee*·go/aa·*mee*·gaa
frost geada ⓕ zhe·*aa*·daa
fruit fruta ⓕ *froo*·taa
fruit picking colheita ⓕ de frutas
  ko·*lyay*·taa de *froo*·taas
fry fritar free·*taarr*
frying pan frigideira ⓕ free·zhee·*day*·raa
full cheio/cheia ⓜ/ⓕ *shay*·o/*shay*·aa
full-time tempo ⓜ integral
  teng·po eeng·te·*grow*
fun divertido/divertida ⓜ/ⓕ
  dee·verr·*tee*·do/dee·verr·*tee*·daa
funeral enterro ⓜ eng·*te*·ho
funny engraçado/engraçada ⓜ/ⓕ
  eng·graa·*saa*·do/eng·graa·*saa*·daa
furniture móveis ⓜ pl *mo*·vays
future futuro ⓜ foo·*too*·ro

G

game (sport) jogo ⓜ *zho*·go
garage oficina ⓕ o·fee·*see*·naa
garbage lixo ⓜ *lee*·sho
garden jardím ⓜ zhaarr·*deeng*
gardener jardineiro/jardineira ⓜ/ⓕ
  zhaarr·dee·*nay*·ro/zhaarr·dee·*nay*·raa
gardening jardinagem ⓕ
  zhaarr·dee·*naa*·zheng
garlic alho ⓜ *aa*·lyo
gas (for cooking) gás ⓜ gas
gas (petrol) gasolina ⓕ gaa·zo·*lee*·na
gas cartridge cartucho ⓜ de gás
  kaarr·*too*·sho de gaas
gastroenteritis gastrenterite ⓕ
  gaas·treng·te·*ree*·te
gate (airport, etc) portão ⓜ porr·*towng*
gauze gaze ⓕ *gaa*·ze
gay gay gay
Germany Alemanha ⓕ aa·le·*ma*·nyaa
get pegar pe·*gaarr*
gift presente ⓜ pre·*zeng*·te
gig apresentação ⓕ
  aa·pre·zeng·*taa*·sowng
gin gin ⓜ zheen
girl menina ⓕ me·*nee*·naa
girlfriend namorada ⓕ naa·mo·*raa*·daa
give dar daarr

glandular fever febre ⓕ glandular
  fe·bre glang·doo·*laar*
glass vidro ⓜ *vee*·dro
glasses (spectacles) óculos ⓜ pl o·*koo*·los
gloves luvas ⓕ pl *loo*·vaas
glue cola ⓕ *ko*·laa
go ir eerr
go out with sair saa·*eerr*
goal objetivo ⓜ o·bee·zhe·*tee*·vo
goal (sport) gol ⓜ gol
goalkeeper goleiro/goleira ⓜ/ⓕ
  go·*lay*·ro/go·*lay*·raa
goat bode ⓜ *bo*·de
god (general) deus ⓜ *de*·oos
goggles (skiing) óculos ⓜ pl de ski
  o·*koo*·los de es·*kee*
goggles (swimming) óculos ⓜ pl de
  natação o·*koo*·los de naa·taa·*sowng*
gold ouro ⓜ *o*·ro
golf ball bola ⓕ de golfe
  bo·laa de *gol*·fee
golf course campo ⓜ de golfe
  kang·po de *gol*·fee
good bom/boa ⓜ/ⓕ bong/*bo*·aa
Goodbye. Tchau/Adeus ⓜ
  tee·show/ aa·de·oos
government governo ⓜ go·*verr*·no
gram grama ⓕ *graa*·maa
grandchild neto/neta ⓜ/ⓕ
  ne·to/*ne*·taa
grandfather avô ⓜ aa·*vo*
grandmother avó ⓕ aa·*vaw*
grapefruit pomelo ⓜ po·*me*·lo
grapes uvas ⓕ pl *oo*·vaas
grass grama ⓕ *gra*·maa
grave túmulo ⓜ *too*·moo·lo
gray cinza *seeng*·zaa
great ótimo/ótima ⓜ/ⓕ
  o·*tee*·mo/o·*tee*·maa
green verde *verr*·de
greengrocer verdureiro/verdureira ⓜ/ⓕ
  verr·doo·*ray*·ro/verr·doo·*ray*·raa
grey cinza *seeng*·zaa
grocery mantimentos ⓜ pl
  mang·tee·*meng*·tos
groundnut amendoim ⓜ
  aa·meng·do·*eeng*
grow crescer kres·*serr*

g-string *biquíni* ⓜ *fio dental*
bee-kee-nee fyo deng-tow

guess *adivinhar* aa-dee-vee-nyaarr

guide (audio) *guia* ⓜ *auditivo*
gee-aa ow-dee-tee-vo

guide (person) *guia* ⓜ&ⓕ gee-aa

guide dog *cão-guia* ⓜ kowng-gee-aa

guidebook *guia* ⓜ gee-aa

guided tour *excursão* ⓕ *guiada*
es-koor-sowng gee-aa-daa

guilty *culpado/culpada* ⓜ/ⓕ kool-paa-do/
kool-paa-daa

guitar *violão* ⓜ vee-o-lowng

gum *gengiva* ⓕ zheng-zhee-vaa

gun *arma* ⓕ aarr-maa

gym *ginástica* ⓕ zhee-naas-tee-kaa

gymnastics *ginástica* ⓕ *olímpica*
gee-naas-tee-kaa o-leeng-pee-kaa

gynaecologist *ginecologista* ⓜ&ⓕ
zhee-ne-ko-lo-zhees-taa

H

hair *cabelo* ⓜ kaa-be-lo

hairbrush *escova* ⓕ es-ko-vaa

hairdresser *cabeleireiro/cabeleireira* ⓜ/ⓕ
kaa-be-lay-ray-ro/kaa-be-lay-ray-raa

halal *halal* aa-low

half *metade* ⓕ me-taa-de

hallucination *alucinação* ⓕ
aa-loo-see-naa-sowng

ham *presunto* ⓜ pre-zoong-to

hammer *martelo* ⓜ maarr-te-lo

hammock *rede* ⓕ he-de

hand *mão* ⓕ mowng

handbag *bolsa* ⓕ *de mão*
bol-saa de mowng

handball *handebol* ⓜ heng-de-bol

handicrafts *artesanato* ⓜ
aarr-te-zaa-naa-to

handlebars *corrimão* ⓜ ko-hee-mowng

handmade *feito à mão*
fay-to aa mowng

handsome *bonito/bonita* ⓜ/ⓕ
bo-nee-to/bo-nee-taa

happy *feliz* fe-lees

harassment *molestamento* ⓜ
mo-les-taa-meng-to

harbour *baía* ⓕ baa-ee-aa

hard *duro/dura* ⓜ/ⓕ doo-ro/doo-raa

hard-boiled *cozido/cozida* ⓜ/ⓕ
ko-zee-do/ko-zee-daa

hardware store *loja* ⓕ *de ferramentas*
lo-zhaa de fe-haa-meng-taas

hat *chapéu* ⓜ shaa-pe-oo

have *ter* terr

have a cold *estar resfriado* ⓜ/ⓕ
es-taarr hes-free-aa-do

have fun *divertir-se* dee-verr-teerr-se

hay fever *febre* ⓕ *do feno*
fe-bre do fe-no

hazelnut *avelã* ⓕ aa-ve-lang

he *ele* e-le

head *cabeça* ⓕ kaa-be-saa

headache *dor* ⓕ *de cabeça*
dorr de kaa-be-saa

headlight *faróis* ⓜ pl faa-roys

health *saúde* ⓕ sa-oo-de

hear *escutar* es-koo-taarr

hearing aid *aparelho* ⓜ *de surdez*
aa-paa-re-lyo de soorr-des

heart *coração* ⓜ ko-ra-sowng

heart attack *ataque* ⓜ *de coração*
aa-taa-ke de ko-ra-sowng

heart condition *problema* ⓜ *de coração*
pro-ble-maa de ko-ra-sowng

heating *aquecimento* ⓜ
aa-ke-see-meng-to

heater *estufa* ⓕ es-too-faa

heavy *pesado/pesada* ⓜ/ⓕ
pe-zaa-do/pe-zaa-daa

Hello. *Olá.* o-laa

Hello. (answering telephone) *Alô.* aa-lo

helmet *capacete* ⓜ kaa-paa-se-te

help *ajuda* ⓕ aa-zhoo-daa

help *ajudar* aa-zhoo-daarr

Help! *Socorro!* so-ko-ho

hepatitis *hepatite* ⓕ e-paa-tee-te

her *dela* de-laa

herbalist *botânico/botânica* ⓜ/ⓕ
bo-ta-nee-ko/bo-ta-nee-kaa

herb *erva* ⓕ err-vaa

here *aqui* aa-kee

heroin *heroína* ⓕ e-ro-ee-naa

herring *arenque* ⓜ aa-reng-ke

high *alto/alta* ⓜ/ⓕ ow-to/ow-taa

high school *segundo grau* ⓜ
se-goong-do grow

highchair *cadeira* ① *para refeição*
kaa-*day*-raa paa-raa he-fay-*sowng*
hike *caminhar* kaa-mee-*nyaarr*
hiking *caminhada* ① kaa-mee-*nyaa*-daa
hiking boots *botas* ① *para caminhadas*
bo-taas paa-raa kaa-mee-*nyaa*-daas
hiking route *rota* ① *de caminhada*
ho-taa de kaa-mee-*nyaa*-daa
hill *morro* ⓜ mo-ho
Hindu *Hindu* eeng-*doo*
hire *alugar* aa-loo-*gaarr*
his *dele* de-le
historical *histórico/histórica* ⓜ/①
ees-to-ree-ko/ees-to-ree-kaa
history *história* ① ees-to-rya
hitchhike *pegar carona*
pe-*gaarr* kaa-ro-naa
HIV *HIV* ⓜ aa-*gaa* ee ve
hockey *hockey* ⓜ ho-kay
holiday *férias* ① pl fe-ryaas
home *casa* ① *kaa*-zaa
homeless *desabrigado/*
desabrigada ⓜ/① de-zaa-bree-*gaa*-do/
de-zaa-bree-*gaa*-daa
homemaker *dona* ① *de casa*
do-naa de *kaa*-zaa
homeopathy *homeopatia* ①
o-me-o-paa-*tee*-aa
homosexual *homosexual* o-mo-sek-soo-*ow*
honey *mel* ⓜ mel
honeymoon *lua* ① *de mel*
loo-aa de mel
horoscope *horóscopo* ⓜ o-ros-ko-po
horse *cavalo* ⓜ kaa-*vaa*-lo
horse riding *cavalgada* ①
kaa-vaal-*gaa*-daa
hospital *hospital* ⓜ os-pee-*tow*
hospitality *hospitalidade* ①
os-pee-taa-lee-*daa*-de
hot *quente* keng-te
hot water *água* ① *quente*
aa-gwaa keng-te
hotel *hotel* ⓜ o-tel
house *casa* ① *kaa*-zaa
housework *trabalho* ⓜ *de casa*
traa-*baa*-lyo de *kaa*-zaa
how *como* ko-mo
how much *quanto* kwang-to
hug *abraçar* aa-braa-*saarr*

huge *enorme* e-norr-me
human resources *recursos* ⓜ pl *humanos*
he-koor-sos oo-ma-nos
human rights *direitos* ⓜ pl *humanos*
dee-ray-tos oo-ma-nos
humanities *humanidades* ① pl
oo-ma-nee-*daa*-des
hundred *cem* seng
hungry *faminto/faminta* ⓜ/①
faa-meeng-to/faa-*meeng*-taa
hunting *caça* ① *kaa*-saa
hurt *machucar* maa-shoo-*kaarr*
husband *marido* ⓜ maa-*ree*-do

I

I *eu* e-oo
ice *gelo* ⓜ zhe-lo
ice axe *quebrador* ⓜ *de gelo*
ke-braa-*dorr* de zhe-lo
ice cream *sorvete* ⓜ sorr-ve-te
ice-cream parlour *sorveteria* ①
sorr-ve-te-*ree*-aa
ice hockey *hockey* ⓜ *de gelo*
ho-kay de zhe-lo
identification *identificação* ①
ee-deng-tee-fee-kaa-*sowng*
identification card *carteira* ①
de identidade kaar-*tay*-raa de
ee-deng-tee-*daa*-de
idiot *idiota* ⓜ&① ee-dee-o-taa
if *se* se
ill *mal* mal
immigration *imigração* ①
ee-mee-graa-*sowng*
important *importante* eeng-porr-*tang*-te
in a hurry *com pressa* kong *pre*-saa
in front of *na frente de* naa *freng*-te de
included *incluso/inclusa* ⓜ/①
eeng-*kloo*-zo/eeng-*kloo*-zaa
income tax *imposto* ⓜ *de renda*
eeng-pos-to de *heng*-daa
India *Índia* ① *eeng*-dyaa
indicator *indicador* ⓜ eeng-dee-kaa-*dorr*
indigestion *indigestão* ①
eeng-dee-zhes-*towng*
indoors *adentro* aa-*deng*-tro
industry *indústria* ① eeng-*doos*-tryaa
infection *infecção* ① eeng-fek-*sowng*

inflammation *inflamação* ① eeng·fla·maa sowng
influenza *gripe* ① gree·pe
ingredient *ingrediente* ⑩ eeng·gre·dee·eng·te
inject *injetar* eeng·zhe·taarr
injection *injeção* ① eeng·zhe·sowng
injury *ferimento* ⑩ fe·ree·meng·to
inner tube *câmara* ① *de ar* ka·ma·raa de aarr
innocent *inocente* ee·no·seng·te
inside *dentro* deng·tro
instructor *instrutor/instrutora* ⑩/① eengs·troo·torr/eengs·troo·to·raa
insurance *seguro* ⑩ se·goo·ro
interesting *interessante* eeng·te·re·sang·te
intermission *intervalo* ⑩ eeng·terr·vaa·lo
international *internacional* eeng·terr·naa·syo·now
Internet *Internet* ① eeng·terr·ne·tee
Internet cafe *Internet café* ⑩ eeng·terr·ne·tee kaa·fe
interpreter *intérprete* ⑩&① eeng·terr·pre·te
interview *entrevista* ① eeng·tre·vees·taa
invite *convidar* kong·vee·daar
Ireland *Irlanda* ① eerr·lang·daa
iron (clothes) *ferro* ⑩ *de passa roupas* fe·ho de paa·saarr ho·paas
island *ilha* ① ee·lyaa
Israel *Israel* ees·haa·el
It *coisa* ① koy·zaa
IT (information technology) *IT* ⑩ ai·tee
itch *coceira* ① ko·say·raa
itemised *listado/listada* ⑩/① lees·taa·do/lees·taa·daa
itinerary *itinerário* ⑩ ee·tee·ne·raa·ryo
IUD *DIU* ⑩ dee·oo

J

jacket *jaqueta* ① zhaa·ke·taa
jail *prisão* ① pree·zowng
jam *geléia* ① zhe·le·yaa
January *janeiro* ⑩ zhaa·nay·ro
Japan *Japão* ⑩ zhaa·powng
jar *vidro* ⑩ vee·dro

jaw *mandíbula* ① mang·dee·boo·laa
jealous *ciumento/ciumenta* ⑩/① see·oo·meng·to/see·oo·meng·tàa
jeans *jeans* ⑩ zheens
jeep *jeep* ⑩ zhee·pe
jewellery *joalheria* ① zho·a·lye·ree·aa
Jewish *Judeu/Judia* ⑩/① zhoo·de·oo/zhoo·dee·aa
job *emprego* ⑩ eng·pre·go
jogging *corrida* ① ko·hee·daa
joke *piada* ① pee·aa·daa
journalist *jornalista* ⑩&① zhorr·naa·lees·taa
journey *viagem* ① vee·aa·zheng
judge *juiz/juíza* ⑩/① zhoo·ees/zhoo·ee·zaa
juice *suco* ⑩ soo·ko
July *julho* ⑩ zhoo·lyo
jump *pular* poo·laarr
jumper (sweater) *suéter* ① soo·e·terr
jumper leads *recarregador* ⑩ *de bateria* he·kaa·he·gaa·dorr de baa·te·ree·aa
June *junho* ⑩ zhoo·nyoo

K

ketchup *ketchup* ⑩ ke·tee·shoo·pee
key *chave* ① shaa·ve
keyboard *teclado* ⑩ te·klaa·do
kick (a ball) *chutar* shoo·taarr
kidney *rim* ⑩ pl heeng
kill *matar* maa·taarr
kilogram *kilograma* ⑩ kee·lo·gra·maa
kilometre *kilômetro* ⑩ kee·lo·me·tro
kind *bom/boa* ⑩/① bong/bo·aa
kindergarten *jardim* ⑩ *de infância* zhaarr·deeng de eeng·fang·syaa
king *rei* ⑩ hay
kiss *beijo* ⑩ bay·zho
kiss *beijar* bay·zhaarr
kitchen *cozinha* ① ko·zee·nyaa
kiwifruit *kiwi* ⑩ kee·wee
knee *joelho* ⑩ zho·e·lyo
knife *faca* ① faa·kaa
know *saber* saa·berr
kosher *kosher* ko·sherr

L

labourer *trabalhador/trabalhadora* ⓜ/ⓕ *de obra* traa-baa-lyaa-dorr/ traa-baa-lyaa-do-raa de o-braa
lace *renda* ⓕ heng-daa
lake *lago* ⓜ laa-go
lamb *ovelha* ⓕ o-ve-lyaa
land *terra* ⓕ te-haa
landlady *proprietária* ⓕ pro-pree-e-taa-ryaa
landlord *proprietário* ⓜ pro-pree-e-taa-ryo
language *língua* ⓕ leeng-gwaa
laptop *laptop* ⓜ le-pee-to-pee
large *grande* grang-de
last *último/última* ⓜ/ⓕ ool-tee-mo/ool-tee-maa
last (week) *passada (semana)* ⓕ paa-saa-daa (se-ma-naa)
late *atrasado/atrasada* ⓜ/ⓕ aa-traa-zaa-do/aa-traa-zaa-daa
laugh *rir* heerr
laundrette *lavanderia* ⓕ laa-vang-de-ree-aa
laundry (room) *área* ⓕ *de serviço* aa-re-aa de serr-vee-so
law *lei* ⓕ lay
lawyer *advogado/advogada* ⓜ/ⓕ aa-dee-vo-gaa-do/aa-dee-vo-gaa-daa
laxative *laxante* ⓜ la-shang-te
lazy *preguiçoso/preguiçosa* ⓜ/ⓕ pre-gee-so-zo/pre-gee-so-zaa
leader *líder* ⓜ&ⓕ lee-derr
leaf *folha* ⓕ fo-lyaa
learn *aprender* aa-preng-derr
leather *couro* ⓜ ko-ro
lecturer *professor/professora* ⓜ/ⓕ pro-fe-sorr/pro-fe-so-raa
ledge *parapeito* ⓜ paa-raa-pay-to
leek *alho* ⓜ *porró* aa-lyo po-ho
left (direction) *(à) esquerda* ⓕ (aa) es-kerr-daa
left luggage *achados e perdidos* ⓜ pl aa-shaa-dos e perr-dee-dos
left-wing *esquerdista* es-kerr-dees-taa
leg *perna* ⓕ perr-naa
legal *legal* le-gow
legislation *legislação* ⓕ le-zhees-la-sowng
legume *legumes* ⓜ pl le-goo-mes

lemon *limão* ⓜ lee-mowng
lemonade *limonada* ⓕ lee-mo-naa-daa
lens *lentes* ⓕ pl leng-tes
lentil *lentilha* ⓕ leng-tee-lyaa
lesbian *lésbica* ⓕ les-bee-kaa
less *menos* ⓜ me-nos
letter (mail) *carta* ⓕ kaarr-taa
lettuce *alface* ⓜ ow-faa-se
liar *mentiroso/mentirosa* ⓜ/ⓕ meng-tee-ro-zo/meng-tee-ro-zaa
library *biblioteca* ⓕ bee-blee-o-te-kaa
lice *piolho* ⓜ pee-o-lyo
licence *licença* ⓕ lee-seng-saa
license plate number *número* ⓜ *da placa* noo-me-ro daa plaa-kaa
lie (not stand) *deitar* day-taarr
life *vida* ⓕ vee-daa
life jacket *colete salva-vidas* ⓜ ko-le-te sow-vaa-vee-daas
lift (elevator) *elevador* ⓜ e-le-vaa-dorr
light *luz* ⓕ looz
light (not heavy) *leve* le-ve
light bulb *lâmpada* ⓕ lang-paa-daa
light meter *fotômetro* ⓜ fo-to-me-tro
lighter (cigarette) *isqueiro* ⓜ ees-kay-ro
like *gostar* gos-taarr
lime *limão* ⓜ lee-mowng
lip balm *bálsamo* ⓜ *para lábios* bow-sa-mo paa-raa laa-byos
lips *lábios* ⓜ pl laa-byos
lipstick *batom* ⓜ ba-tong
liquor store *loja* ⓕ *de bebidas* lo-zhaa de be-bee-daas
listen *escutar* es-koo-taarr
little (not much) *pouco/pouca* ⓜ/ⓕ po-ko/po-kaa
little (small) *pequeno/pequena* ⓜ/ⓕ pe-ke-no/pe-ke-naa
live (somewhere) *morar* mo-raarr
liver *fígado* ⓜ fee-gaa-do
lizard *lagarto* ⓜ laa-gaarr-to
local *local* lo-kow
lock *tranca* ⓕ trang-kaa
lock *trancar* trang-kaarr
locked *trancado/trancada* ⓜ/ⓕ trang-kaa-do/trang-kaa-daa
lollies *balas* ⓕ pl baa-laas
long *longo/longa* ⓜ/ⓕ long-go/long-gaa

look *ver* verr
look after *cuidar* kooy-*daarr*
look for *procurar* pro-koo-*raarr*
lookout *mirante* ⓜ mee-*rang*-te
loose *solto/solta* ⓜ/ⓕ *sol*-to/*sol*-taa
loose change *trocado* ⓜ tro-*kaa*-do
lose *perder* perr-*derr*
lost *perdido/perdida* ⓜ/ⓕ
   perr-*dee*-do/perr-*dee*-daa
lost property office *escritório* ⓜ *de*
   achados e perdidos es-kree-to-ryo de
   aa-*shaa*-dos e perr-*dee*-dos
(a) lot *muito/muita* ⓜ/ⓕ
   mweeng-to/*mweeng*-taa
loud *alto/alta* ⓜ/ⓕ *ow*-to/*ow*-taa
love *amor* ⓜ aa-*morr*
love *amar* aa-*maarr*
lover *amante* ⓜ&ⓕ aa-*mang*-te
low *baixo/baixa* ⓜ/ⓕ *bai*-sho/*bai*-shaa
lubricant *lubrificante* ⓜ
   loo-bree-fee-*kang*-te
luck *sorte* ⓕ *sorr*-te
lucky *sortudo/sortuda* ⓜ/ⓕ
   sorr-*too*-do/sorr-*too*-daa
luggage *bagagem* ⓕ baa-*gaa*-zheng
luggage locker *guarda* ⓜ *volumes*
   gwaar-daa vo-loo-mes
luggage tag *etiqueta* ⓕ *de bagagem*
   e-tee-*ke*-taa de baa-gaa-*zheng*
lump *nódulo* ⓜ *no*-doo-lo
lunch *almoço* ⓜ ow-*mo*-so
lung *pulmão* ⓜ pool-*mowng*
luxury *luxo* ⓜ *loo*-sho

M

machine *máquina* ⓕ *maa*-kee-naa
magazine *revista* ⓕ he-*vees*-taa
mail *correspondência* ⓕ
   ko-hes-pong-*deng*-syaa
mailbox *caixa* ⓕ *de correio*
   kai-shaa de ko-*hay*-o
main *principal* preeng-see-*pow*
main road *rua* ⓕ *principal*
   hoo-aa preeng-see-*pow*
make *fazer* faa-*zerr*
make-up *maquiagem* ⓕ
   maa-kee-*aa*-zheng

mammogram *mamograma* ⓜ
   maa-mo-*gra*-maa
man *homem* ⓜ o-*meng*
manager *gerente* zhe-*reng*-te
mandarin *tangerina* ⓕ tang-zhe-*ree*-naa
mango *manga* ⓕ *mang*-gaa
manual worker *trabalhador/trabalhadora*
   ⓜ/ⓕ *manual* traa-baa-lyaa-*dorr*/
   traa-baa-lyaa-*do*-raa maa-noo-*ow*
many *vários/várias* ⓜ/ⓕ
   vaa-ryos/*vaa*-ryaas
map *mapa* ⓕ *maa*-paa
March *março* *maar*-so
margarine *margarina* ⓕ
   maarr-gaa-*ree*-naa
marijuana *maconha* ⓕ maa-ko-*nyaa*
marital status *estado* ⓜ *civil*
   es-*taa*-do see-*veel*
market *mercado* ⓜ merr-*kaa*-do
marmalade *marmelada* ⓕ
   maarr-me-*laa*-daa
marriage *casamento* ⓜ kaa-zaa-*meng*-to
marry *casar* kaa-*zaarr*
martial arts *artes* ⓕ pl *marciais*
   aarr-tes maar-see-*ais*
mass (Catholic) *missa* ⓕ *mee*-saa
massage *massagem* ⓕ maa-*saa*-zheng
masseur *massagista* ⓜ&ⓕ
   maa-saa-*zhees*-taa
mat *capacho* ⓜ kaa-*paa*-sho
match (sport) *partida* ⓕ paarr-*tee*-daa
matches *fósforos* ⓜ pl fos-fu-ros
mattress *colchão* ⓜ kol-*showng*
May *maio* *maa*-yo
maybe *talvez* tow-*ves*
mayonnaise *maionese* ⓕ maa-yo-*ne*-ze
mayor *prefeito/prefeita* ⓜ/ⓕ
   pre-*fay*-to/pre-*fay*-taa
measles *sarampo* ⓜ saa-*rang*-po
meat *carne* ⓕ *kaar*-ne
mechanic *mecânico/mecânica* ⓜ/ⓕ
   me-ka-nee-ko/me-*ka*-nee-kaa
media *mídia* ⓕ *mee*-dyaa
medicine *medicina* ⓕ me-dee-*see*-naa
meditation *meditação* ⓕ
   me-dee-taa-*sowng*
meet *encontrar* eng-kong-*traarr*
melon *melão* ⓜ me-*lowng*
member *membro* ⓜ&ⓕ *meng*-bro

M

english–brazilian portuguese

205

menstruation *menstruação* ①
mengs·troo·aa·*sowng*

menu *cardápio* ⑩ kaarr·*daa*·pyo

message *mensagem* ① meng·*sa*·zheng

metal *metal* ⑩ me·*tow*

metre *metro* ⑩ *me*·tro

microwave *microondas* ⑩
mee·kro·*ong*·daas

midnight *meia-noite* ① *may*·aa·*noy*·te

migraine *enxaqueca* ① en·shaa·ke·*kaa*

military *militar* mee·lee·*taarr*

military service *serviço* ⑩ *militar*
serr·*vee*·so mee·lee·*taarr*

milk *leite* ⑩ *lay*·te

millimetre *milímetro* ① mee·*lee*·me·tro

million *milhão* ⑩ mee·*lowng*

mince *carne* ① *moída*
kaarr·ne mo·ee·daa

mineral water *água* ① *mineral*
aa·gwaa mee·ne·*row*

minute *minuto* ⑩ mee·*noo*·to

mirror *espelho* ⑩ es·*pe*·lyo

miscarriage *aborto* ⑩ *espontâneo*
aa·*borr*·to es·pong·*ta*·ne·o

miss (feel absence of) *sentir falta*
seng·*teerr* fow·*taa*

mistake *erro* ⑩ e·ho

mix *misturar* mees·too·*raar*

mobile phone *celular* ⑩ se·loo·*laarr*

modem *modem* ⑩ *mo*·deng

moisturiser *hidratante* ⑩ ee·draa·*tang*·te

monastery *monastério* ⑩ mo·naas·*te*·ryo

Monday *segunda-feira* ①
se·*goong*·daa·*fay*·raa

money *dinheiro* ⑩ dee·*nyay*·ro

monk *monge* ⑩ *mong*·zhe

month *mês* ⑩ mes

monument *monumento* ⑩
mo·noo·*meng*·to

moon *lua* ① *loo*·aa

more *mais* mais

morning *manhã* ① ma·*nyang*

morning sickness *enjôo* ⑩ en·*zho*·o

mosque *mosteiro* ⑩ mos·*tay*·ro

mosquito *mosquito* ⑩ mos·*kee*·to

mosquito coil *repelente* ⑩ *em aspiral*
he·pe·*leng*·te eng aas·pee·*row*

mosquito net *mosquiteiro* ⑩
mos·kee·*tay*·ro

mother *mamãe* ① ma·*mayng*

mother-in-law *sogra* ① so·graa

motorbike *motocicleta* ①
mo·to·see·*kle*·taa

motorboat *barco* ⑩ *à motor*
baar·ko aa mo·*torr*

motorway (tollway) *auto estrada* ①
ow·to es·*traa*·daa

mountain *montanha* ① mong·*ta*·nyaa

mountain bike *mountain bike* ⑩
maa·oong·*tayng* bai·kee

mountain path *trilha* ① *tree*·lyaa

mountain range *cordilheira* ①
korr·dee·*lyay*·raa

mountaineering *montanhismo* ⑩
mong·ta·*nyees*·mo

mouse *camundongo* ⑩
ka·moong·*dong*·go

mouth *boca* ① bo·kaa

movie *cinema* ⑩ see·ne·*maa*

mud *lama* ① *la*·maa

muesli *muesli* ⑩ *moos*·lee

mum *mãe* ① mayng

mumps *caxumba* ① kaa·*shoong*·baa

murder *assassinato* ⑩ aa·saa·see·*naa*·to

murder *assassinar* aa·saa·see·*naarr*

muscle *músculo* ⑩ *moos*·koo·lo

museum *museu* ⑩ mo·se·oo

mushroom *cogumelo* ⑩ ko·goo·*me*·lo

music *música* ① *moo*·zee·kaa

music shop *loja* ① *de música*
lo·zhaa de moo·zee·kaa

musician *músico/música* ⑩/①
moo·zee·ko/moo·zee·kaa

Muslim *Muçulmano/Muçulmana* ⑩/①
moo·sool·*ma*·no/moo·sool·*ma*·naa

mussel *mexilhão* ⑩ me·shee·*lyowng*

mustard *mustarda* ① moos·*taar*·daa

mute *mudo/muda* ⑩/①
moo·do/moo·daa

my *meu/minha* ⑩/① me·oo/mee·nyaa

N

nail clippers *cortador* ⑩ *de unhas*
korr·taa·*dorr* de oo·*nyaas*

name *nome* ⑩ *no*·me

napkin *guardanapo* ⑩ gwaar·daa·*naa*·po

nappy *fralda* ① *frow*·daa

nappy rash *irritação* ① *à fralda*
ee·hee·ta·*sowng* aa *frow*·daa

national park *parque* ⓜ *nacional*
paar·ke naa·syo·*now*

nationality *nacionalidade* ①
naa·syo·naa·lee·*daa*·de

nature *natureza* ① naa·too·re·*zaa*

naturopathy *naturopatia* ①
naa·too·ro·paa·*tee*·a

nausea *náusea* ① *now*·se·aa

near *perto/perta* ⓜ/① perr·to/perr·taa

nearby *por perto/perta* ⓜ/①
porr perr·to/perr·taa

nearest *mais perto/perta* ⓜ/①
mais perr·to/perr·taa

necessary *necessário/necessária* ⓜ/①
ne·se·*sa*·ryo/ne·se·*sa*·ryaa

necklace *colar* ⓜ ko·*laarr*

nectarine *pessego* ⓜ *pe*·se·go

need *precisar* pre·see·*zaarr*

needle (sewing) *agulha* ① aa·*goo*·lyaa

needle (syringe) *agulha* ① aa·*goo*·lyaa

negative *negativo/negativa* ⓜ/①
ne·gaa·*tee*·vo/ne·gaa·*tee*·vaa

neither *nenhum deles* ne·*yoom* de·les

net *rede* ① he·de

Netherlands *Países* ⓜ pl *Baixos*
paa·*ee*·zes bai·shos

never *nunca* noong·kaa

new *novo/nova* ⓜ/① *no*·vo/*no*·vaa

New Year's Day *Dia* ⓜ *de Ano Novo* dee·aa
de *a*·no *no*·vo

New Year's Eve *Véspera* ① *de Ano Novo*
ves·pe·raa de *a*·no *no*·vo

New Zealand *Nova Zelândia* ①
no·vaa ze·*lang*·dyaa

news *novidades · notícias* ① pl
no vee·*daa*·des · no·*tee*·syaas

news stand *jornaleiro* ⓜ zhorr·na·*lay*·ro

newsagency *jornaleiro* ⓜ zhorr·naa·*lay*·ro

newspaper *jornal* ⓜ zhorr·*now*

next *próximo/próxima* ⓜ/①
pro·see·mo/*pro*·see·maa

next to *ao lado de* ow *laa*·do de

nice *bacana* baa·*ka*·naa

nickname *apelido* ⓜ aa·pe·*lee*·do

night *noite* ① *noy*·te

no *não* nowng

noisy *barulhento/barulhenta* ⓜ/①
baa·roo·*lyeng*·to/baa·roo·*lyeng*·taa

none *nenhum* ne·*yoom*

non-smoking *não-fumante*
nowng·foo·*mang*·te

noodles *macarrão* ⓜ *chinês*
maa·kaa·*howng* shee·*nes*

noon *meio-dia* ⓜ *may*·o dee·aa

Norway *Noruega* ① no·roo·e·gaa

north *norte* ⓜ *norr*·te

nose *nariz* ⓜ naa·*rees*

not *não* nowng

notebook *caderno* ⓜ kaa·*derr*·no

nothing *nada* naa·daa

November *novembro* no·*veng*·bro

now *agora* aa·go·raa

nuclear energy *energia* ① *nuclear*
e·nerr·zhee·aa noo·kle·*aarr*

nuclear testing *teste* ⓜ *nuclear*
tes·te noo·kle·*aarr*

nuclear waste *resíduo* ⓜ *nuclear*
he·zee·doo·o noo·kle·*aarr*

number *número* ⓜ *noo*·me·ro

numberplate *número* ⓜ *da placa*
noo·me·ro daa *plaa*·kaa

nun *freira* ① *fray*·raa

nurse *enfermeira* ① eng·ferr·*may*·raa

nut *noz* ① noz

O

oats *aveia* ① aa·ve·aa

ocean *óceano* ⓜ o·se·a·no

October *outubro* o·too·bro

off (food) *estragado/estragada* ⓜ/①
es·traa·*gaa*·do/es·traa·*gaa*·daa

office *escritório* ⓜ es·kree·to·ryo

office worker *escriturário/escriturária*
ⓜ/① es·kree·too·*raa*·ryo/
es·kree·too·*raa*·ryaa

often *frequentemente*
fre·kweng·te·*meng*·te

oil *óleo* ⓜ o·lyo

old *velho/velha* ⓜ/① ve·lyo/ve·lyaa

olive *azeitona* ① aa·zay·to·naa

olive oil *azeite* ⓜ aa·*zay*·te

Olympic Games *Jogos Olímpidos* ⓜ pl
zho·gos o·*leeng*·pee·kos

on *sobre* so·bre

once *uma vez* oo·maa vez
one-way (ticket) *ida* ① ee·daa
onion *cebola* ① se·bo·laa
only *somente* so·meng·te
open *aberto/aberta* ⓜ/① aa·berr·to/aa·berr·taa
open *abrir* aa·breerr
opening hours *horário* ⓜ *de funcionamento* o·raa·ryo de foon·syo·naa·meng·to
opera *ópera* ① o·pe·raa
opera house *casa* ① *de ópera* kaa·zaa de o·pe·raa
operation *operação* ① o·pe·raa·sowng
operator *operador/operadora* ⓜ/① o·pe·raa·dorr/o·pe·raa·do·raa
opinion *opinião* ① o·pee·nee·owng
opposite *oposto/oposta* ⓜ/① o·pos·to/o·pos·taa
optometrist *optometrista* ⓜ&① o·pee·to·me·trees·taa
or *ou* o
orange (fruit) *laranja* ① laa·rang·zhaa
orange (colour) *laranja* laa·rang·zhaa
orange juice *suco* ⓜ *de laranja* soo·ko de laa·rang·zhaa
orchestra *orquestra* ① orr·kes·traa
order (command) *pedido* ⓜ pe·dee·do
order *pedir* pe·deerr
ordinary *ordinário/ordinária* ⓜ/① orr·dee·naa·ryo/orr·dee·naa·ryaa
orgasm *orgasmo* ⓜ orr·gaas·mo
original *original* o·ree·zhee·now
other *outro/outra* ⓜ/① o·tro/o·traa
our *nosso/nossa* ⓜ/① no·so/no·saa
outside *fora* fo·raa
ovarian cyst *cisto* ⓜ *no ovário* sees·to no o·vaa·ryo
ovary *ovário* ⓜ o·vaa·ryo
oven *forno* ⓜ forr·no
overcoat *sobretudo* ⓜ so·bre·too·do
overdose *overdose* ① o·verr·do·ze
owe *dever* de·verr
owner *dono/dona* ⓜ/① do·no/do·naa
oxygen *oxigênio* ⓜ ok·see·zhe·nyo
oyster *ostra* ① os·traa
ozone layer *camada* ① *de ozônio* kaa·maa·daa de o·zo·nyo

P

pacemaker *marca* ⓜ *passo* mar·kaa pa·so
pacifier *chupeta* ① shoo·pe·taa
package *embrulho* ⓜ eng·broo·lyo
packet *pacote* ⓜ pa·ko·te
padlock *cadeado* ⓜ kaa·de·aa·do
page *página* ① paa·zhee·naa
pain *dor* ⓜ dorr
painful *doloroso/dolorosa* ⓜ/① do·lo·ro·zo/do·lo·ro·zaa
painkiller *analgésico* ⓜ aa·now·ge·zee·ko
painter *pintor/pintora* ⓜ/① peeng·torr/peeng·to·raa
painting *pintura* ① peeng·too·raa
pair (couple) *par* ⓜ paarr
Pakistan *Paquistão* ⓜ paa·kees·towng
palace *palácio* ⓜ paa·laa·syo
pan *panela* ① paa·ne·laa
pants (trousers) *calças* ① pl kow·saas
panty liner *absorvente* ⓜ *higiênico* aab·sorr·veng·te ee·zhee·e·nee·ko
pantyhose *meia* ① *calça* may·aa kow·saa
pap smear *exame* ⓜ *papa nicolau* e·za·me paa·paa nee·ko·low
paper *papel* ⓜ paa·pel
paperwork *papelada* ① paa·pe·laa·daa
paraplegic *paraplégico/paraplégica* ⓜ/① paa·raa·ple·zhee·ko/paa·raa·ple·zhee·kaa
parcel *encomenda* ① eng·ko·meng·daa
parents *pais* ⓜ pl paa·ees
park *parque* ⓜ paarr·ke
park (vehicle) *estacionar* es·taa·syo·naarr
parliament *parlamento* ⓜ paarr·laa·meng·to
part (component) *parte* ① paarr·te
part-time *meio expediente* may·o es·pe·dee·eng·te
party (social gathering) *festa* ① fes·taa
party (politics) *partido* ⓜ paarr·tee·do
pass *passar* paa·saarr
passenger *passageiro/passageira* ⓜ/① paa·saa·zhay·ro/paa·saa·zhay·raa
passionfruit *maracujá* ⓜ maa·raa·koo·zhaa
passport *passaporte* ⓜ paa·saa·porr·te

passport number *número* ⓜ *do passaporte* noo·me·ro do paa·saa·porr·te
past *passado* ⓜ paa·saa·do
pasta *massas* ⓕ pl maa·saas
pastry *massa* ⓕ maa·saa
path *caminho* ⓜ kaa·mee·nyo
pay *pagar* paa·gaarr
payment *pagamento* ⓜ paa·gaa·meng·to
pea *ervilha* ⓕ err·vee·lyaa
peace *paz* ⓕ pas
peach *pêssego* ⓜ pe·se·go
peak (mountain) *pico* ⓜ pee·ko
peanut *amendoim* ⓜ aa·meng·do·eeng
pear *pêra* ⓕ pe·raa
pedal *pedal* ⓜ pe·dow
pedestrian *pedestre* ⓜ pe·des·tre
pen (ballpoint) *caneta* ⓕ ka·ne·taa
pencil *lápis* ⓜ laa·pees
penis *pênis* ⓜ pe·nees
penknife *canivete* ⓜ kaa·nee·ve·te
pensioner *pensionista* ⓜ&ⓕ peng·syo·nees·taa
people *pessoas* ⓕ pl pe·so·aas
pepper *pimenta* ⓕ pee·meng·taa
pepper (bell) *pimentão* ⓜ pee·meng·towng
per *por* porr
per cent *porcentagem* ⓕ porr·seng·taa·zheng
perfect *perfeito/perfeita* ⓜ/ⓕ perr·fay·to/perr·fay·taa
performance *performance* ⓕ perr·forr·mang·se
perfume *perfume* ⓜ perr·foo·me
period pain *cólica* ⓕ *menstrual* ko·lee·kaa mengs·troo·ow
permission *permissão* ⓕ perr·mee·sowng
permit *permissão* ⓕ per·mee·sowng
person *pessoa* ⓕ pe·so·aa
petition *petição* ⓕ pe·tee·sowng
petrol *petróleo* ⓜ pe·tro·lyo
pharmacy *farmácia* ⓕ faar·maa·syaa
phone book *lista* ⓕ *telefônica* lees·taa te·le·fo·nee·kaa
phone box *telefone* ⓜ *público* te·le·fo·ne poo·blee·ko
phonecard *cartão* ⓜ *telefônico* kaarr·towng te·le·fo·nee·ko
photograph *fotografia* ⓕ fo·to·graa·fee·aa

photographer *fotógrafo/fotógrafa* ⓜ/ⓕ fo·to·graa·fo/fo·to·graa·faa
photography *fotografia* ⓕ fo·to·graa·fee·aa
phrasebook *livro* ⓜ *de frases* lee·vro de fraa·zes
pickaxe *picareta* ⓕ pee·kaa·re·taa
pickles *pikles* ⓜ pl pee·kles
picnic *piquenique* ⓜ pee·ke·nee·ke
pie *torta* ⓕ torr·taa
piece *pedaço* ⓜ pe·da·so
pig *porco/porca* ⓜ/ⓕ porr·ko/porr·kaa
pill *pílula* ⓕ pee·loo·laa
Pill (the) *pílula* ⓕ pee·loo·laa
pillow *travesseiro* ⓜ traa·ve·say·ro
pillowcase *fronha* ⓕ fro·nyaa
pineapple *abacaxi* ⓜ aa·baa·kaa·shee
pink *rosa* ho·za
pistachio *pistáchio* ⓜ pees·taa·shyo
place *lugar* ⓜ loo·gaarr
place of birth *local* ⓜ *de nascimento* lo·kow de naas·see·meng·to
planet *planeta* ⓜ pla·ne·taa
plant *planta* ⓕ plang·taa
plastic *plástico/plástica* ⓜ/ⓕ plas·tee·ko/plas·tee·kaa
plate *prato* ⓜ praa·to
plateau *planalto* ⓜ pla·now·to
platform *plataforma* ⓕ plaa·taa·forr·maa
play (theatre) *peça* ⓕ pe·sãa
play *jogar* zho·gaarr
play (guitar) *tocar* to·kaarr
plug (bath) *tampa* ⓕ tang·paa
plug (electricity) *tomada* ⓕ to·maa·daa
plum *ameixa* ⓕ aa·may·shaa
poached *poché* po·she
pocket *bolso* ⓜ bol·so
pocket knife *canivete* ⓜ kaa·nee·ve·te
poetry *poesia* ⓕ po·e·zee·aa
point *ponto* ⓜ pong·to
point *apontar* aa·pong·taarr
poisonous *venenoso/venenosa* ⓜ/ⓕ ve·ne·no·zo/ve·ne·no·zaa
police *polícia* ⓕ po·lee·syaa
police station *delegacia* ⓕ *de polícia* de·le·gaa·see·aa de po·lee·sya
policy *regras* ⓕ pl he·graas
politician *político/política* ⓜ/ⓕ po·lee·tee·ko/po·lee·tee·kaa

politics *política* ① po-*lee*-tee-kaa
pollen *pólen* ⓜ po-leng
pollution *poluição* ① po-loo-ee-*sowng*
pool (game) *sinuca* ① see-*noo*-kaa
pool (swimming) *piscina* ① pee-*see*-naa
poor *pobre* po-bre
popular *popular* po-poo-*laarr*
pork *porco/porca* ⓜ/① porr-ko/porr-kaa
pork sausage *linguiça* ① *de porco*
leen-*gwee*-saa de porr-ko
port (sea) *porto* ⓜ porr-to
Portugal *Portugal* ⓜ porr-too-*gow*
positive *positivo/positiva* ⓜ/①
po-zee-*tee*-vo/po-zee-*tee*-vaa
possible *possível* po-*see*-vel
post office *correio* ⓜ ko-*hay*-o
postage *postagem* ① pos-*taa*-zheng
postcard *cartão* ⓜ *postal*
kaarr-*towng* pos-*tow*
postcode *código* ⓜ *postal*
ko-dee-go pos-*tow*
poster *cartaz* ⓜ kaarr-*taz*
pot (ceramics) *louça* ① pl *de barro*
lo-saa de baa-ho
pot (dope) *bagulho* ⓜ baa-*goo*-lyo
potato *batata* ① baa-*taa*-taa
pottery *cerâmica* ① se-*ra*-mee-kaa
pound (money) *libra* ① *lee*-braa
poverty *pobreza* ① po-bre-zaa
powder *pó* ⓜ po
power *poder* ⓜ po-*derr*
prawn *camarão* ⓜ kaa-maa-*rowng*
prayer *reza* ① he-zaa
prefer *preferir* pre-fe-*reerr*
pregnancy test kit *teste* ⓜ *de gravidez*
tes-te de graa-vee-*dez*
pregnant *grávida* ① *graa*-vee-daa
premenstrual tension *tensão* ①
pré-menstrual teng-*sowng*
pre-mengs-*troo*-ow
prepare *preparar* pre-paa-*raarr*
present (gift) *presente* ⓜ pre-*zeng*-te
present (time) *presente* ⓜ pre-*zeng*-te
president *presidente* ⓜ&①
pre-zee-*deng*-te
pressure *pressão* ① pre-*sowng*
pretty *bonito/bonita* ⓜ/①
bo-*nee*-to/bo-*nee*-taa
price *preço* ⓜ *pre*-so

priest *padre* ⓜ *paa*-dre
prime minister *primeiro ministro* ⓜ •
primeira ministra ① pree-*may*-ro
mee-*nees*-tro • pree-*may*-raa
mee-*nees*-traa
prison *prisão* ① pree-*zowng*
prisoner *prisioneiro/prisioneira* ⓜ/①
pree-zyo-*nay*-ro/pree-zyo-*nay*-raa
private *privado/privada* ⓜ/①
pree-*vaa*-do/pree-*vaa*-daa
produce *produzir* pro-doo-*zeerr*
profit *lucro* ⓜ *loo*-kro
program *programa* ⓜ pro-*gra*-maa
projector *projetor* ⓜ pro-zhe-*torr*
promise *prometer* pro-me-*terr*
protect *proteger* pro-te-*zherr*
protected *protegido/protegida* ①
pro-te-*zhee*-do/pro-te-*zhee*-daa
protest *protesto* ⓜ pro-*tes*-to
protest *protestar* pro-tes-*taarr*
provisions *provisões* ① pl pro-vee-*zoyngs*
prune *ameixa* ① *seca*
aa-*may*-shaa se-kaa
pub *bar* ⓜ baarr
public gardens *jardins* ⓜ pl *públicos*
zhaarr-*deengs* poo-blee-kos
public relations *relações* ① pl *públicas*
he-la-*soyngs* poo-blee-kaas
public telephone *telefone* ⓜ *público*
te-le-fo-ne poo-blee-ko
public toilet *banheiro* ⓜ *público*
ba-*nyay*-ro poo-blee-ko
publishing *editoração* ①
e-dee-to-raa-*sowng*
pull *puxar* poo-*shaarr*
pump *bomba* ① bong-baa
pumpkin *abóbora* ① aa-bo-bo-raa
puncture *furo* ⓜ foo-ro
pure *puro/pura* ⓜ/① poo-ro/poo-raa
purple *roxo/roxa* ⓜ/① ho-sho/ho-shaa
push *empurrar* eng-poo-*haarr*
put *colocar* ko-lo-*kaarr*

Q

quadriplegic *quadraplégico/*
quadraplégica ⓜ/①
kwaa-draa-*ple*-zhee-ko/
kwaa-draa-*ple*-zhee-kaa

qualifications *qualificações* ① pl
kwaa·lee·fee·kaa·soyngs

quality *qualidade* ① kwaa·lee·*daa*·de

quarantine *quarentena* ①
kwaa·reng·te·naa

quarter *quarto* ⓜ *kwaarr*·to

queen *rainha* ① haa·ee·nyaa

question *pergunta* ① · *questão* ①
perr·goong·taa · kes·*towng*

queue *fila* ① *fee*·laa

quick *rápido/rápida* ⓜ/①
haa·pee·do/*haa*·pee·daa

quiet *quieto/quieta* ⓜ/①
kee·e·to/kee·e·taa

quit *desistir* de·zees·*teerr*

R

rabbit *coelho* ⓜ ko·e·lyo

race (sport) *corrida* ① ko·*hee*·daa

racetrack *pista* ① *de corrida*
pees·taa de ko·*hee*·daa

racing bike *bicicleta* ① *de corrida*
bee·see·*kle*·taa de ko·*hee*·daa

racism *racismo* ⓜ haa·*sees*·mo

racquet *raquete* ① haa·*ke*·te

radiator *radiador* ⓜ haa·dee·aa·*dorr*

radish *rabanete* ⓜ haa·baa·*ne*·te

railway station *estação* ① *de trem*
es·taa·*sowng* de treng

rain *chuva* ① *shoo*·vaa

raincoat *casaco* ⓜ *de chuva*
kaa·*zaa*·ko de *shoo*·vaa

raisin *passas* ① pl *paa*·saas

rally *comício* ⓜ ko·*mee*·syo

rape *estrupo* ⓜ es·*troo*·po

rape *estrupar* es·troo·*paarr*

rare (food) *mal passado/passada* ⓜ/①
mow paa·*saa*·do/paa·*saa*·daa

rare (uncommon) *raro/rara* ⓜ/①
haa·ro/*haa*·raa

rash *irritação* ① *na pele*
ee·hee·taa·*sowng* naa *pe*·le

raspberry *framboesa* ① fraang·bo·e·zaa

rat *rato/ratazana* ⓜ/①
haa·to/haa·taa·*za*·naa

raw *cru/crua* ⓜ/① kroo/*kroo*·aa

razor *raspador* ⓜ haas·paa·*dorr*

razor blade *gilete* ① zhee·*le*·te

read *ler* lerr

ready *pronto/pronta* ⓜ/①
prong·to/*prong*·taa

real estate agent *agente* ⓜ&①
imobiliário aa·*zheng*·te
ee·mo·bee·lee·*aa*·ryo

realistic *realista* he·aa·*lees*·taa

reason *razão* ① haa·*zowng*

receipt *recibo* ⓜ he·*see*·bo

recently *recentemente* he·seng·te·*meng*·te

recommend *recomendar*
he·ko·meng·*daarr*

record *gravar* graa·*vaarr*

recording *gravação* ① graa·vaa·*sowng*

recyclable *reciclável* he·see·*klaa*·vel

recycle *reciclar* he·see·*klaar*

red *vermelho/vermelha* ⓜ/①
verr·*me*·lyo/verr·*me*·lyaa

referee *juiz/juiza* ⓜ/①
zhoo·ees/zhoo·ee·zaa

reference *referência* ① he·fe·*reng*·syaa

reflexology *reflexologia* ①
he·flek·so·lo·zhee·aa

refrigerator *geladeira* ① zhe·laa·*day*·raa

refugee *refugiado/refugiada* ⓜ/①
he·foo·zhee·*aa*·do/he·foo·zhee·*ga*·daa

refund *reembolso* ⓜ he·eng·*bol*·so

refuse *recusar* he·koo·*zaarr*

regional *regional* he·zhyo·*now*

registered mail *correio* ⓜ *registrado*
ko·*hay*·o he·zhees·*traa*·do

rehydration salts *sais* ⓜ pl *de hidratação*
sais de ee·draa·taa·*sowng*

reiki *reiki* ⓜ *hay*·kee

relationship *relacionamento* ⓜ
he·laa·syo·na·*meng*·to

relax *relaxar* he·la·*shaarr*

relic *rélica* ① he·*lee*·kaa

religion *religião* ① he·lee·zhee·*owng*

religious *religioso/religiosa* ⓜ/①
he·lee·zhee·*o*·zo/he·lee·zhee·*o*·zaa

remote *remoto/remota* ⓜ/①
he·*mo*·to/he·*mo*·taa

remote control *controle* ⓜ *remoto*
kong·*tro*·le he·*mo*·to

rent *alugar* aa·loo·*gaarr*

repair *consertar* kong·serr·*taarr*

republic *república* ① he·poo·blee·kaa

reservation (booking) *reserva* ①
he·zerr·vaa

rest *descansar* des·kang·saarr

restaurant *restaurante* ⓜ hes·tow·rang·te

resume (CV) *currículum* ⓜ
koo·hee·koo·loom

retired *aposentado/aposentada* ⓜ/①
aa·po·seng·taa·do/aa·po·seng·taa·daa

return *retornar* he·torr·naarr

return (ticket) *ida e volta*
ee·daa e vol·taa

review *revisão* ① he·vee·zowng

rhythm *ritmo* ⓜ hee·tee·mo

rib *costela* ① kos·te·laa

rice *arroz* ⓜ aa·hos

rich (wealthy) *rico/rica* ⓜ/①
hee·ko/hee·kaa

ride (car) *volta* ① vol·taa

ride (horse) *andar à cavalo*
ang·daarr aa kaa·vaa·lo

right (direction) *(à) direita*
(aa) dee·ray·taa

right (correct) *correto/correta* ⓜ/①
ko·he·to/ko·he·taa

right-wing *direitista* dee·ray·tees·taa

ring (on finger) *anel* ⓜ aa·nel

ring (phone) *tocar* to·kaarr

rip-off *roubo* ⓜ ho·bo

risk *risco* ⓜ hees·ko

river *rio* ⓜ hee·o

road *estrada* ① es·traa·daa

road map *mapa* ① *da estrada*
maa·paa daa es·traa·daa

rob *roubar* ho·baarr

rock *pedra* ① pe·draa

rock (music) *rock* ⓜ ho·kee

rock climbing *alpinismo* ⓜ
ow·pee·nees·mo

rock group *banda* ① *de rock*
bang·daa de ho·kee

rockmelon *melão* ⓜ me·lowng

roll (bread) *pão* ⓜ powng

rollerblading *patinaçao*
paa·tee·naa·sowng

romantic *romântico/romântica* ⓜ/①
ho·mang·tee·ko/ho·mang·tee·kaa

room *quarto* ⓜ kwaarr·to

room number *número* ⓜ *do quarto*
noo·me·ro do kwaarr·to

rope *corda* ① korr·daa

round *redondo/redonda* ⓜ/①
he·dong·do/he·dong·daa

route *rota* ① ho·taa

rowing *remo* ⓜ he·mo

rubbish *lixo* ⓜ lee·sho

rubella *rubéola* ① hoo·be·o·laa

rug *tapete* ① taa·pe·te

rugby *rugby* ⓜ hoo·gee·bee

ruins *ruínas* ① pl hoo·ee·naas

rule *regra* ① he·graa

rum *rum* ⓜ hoom

run *correr* ko·herr

running *corrida* ① ko·hee·daa

runny nose *coriza* ① ko·ree·zaa

S

sad *triste* trees·te

saddle *sela* ① se·laa

safe *seguro/segura* ⓜ/①
se·goo·ro/se·goo·raa

safe *cofre* ⓜ ko·fre

safe sex *sexo* ⓜ *com proteção*
sek·so kong pro·te·sowng

saint *santo/santa* ⓜ/①
sang·to/sang·taa

salad *salada* ① saa·laa·daa

salami *salaminho* ⓜ saa·laa·mee·nyo

salary *salário* ① saa·laa·ryo

sale *liquidação* ① lee·kee·daa·sowng

sales tax *imposto* ⓜ *sobre venda*
eeng·pos·to so·bre veng·daa

salmon *salmão* ① sow·mowng

salt *sal* ⓜ sow

same *mesmo/mesma* ⓜ/①
mes·mo/mes·maa

sand *areia* ① aa·re·yaa

sandal *sandália* ① sang·daa·lyaa

sanitary napkin *toalha* ① *higiênica*
to·aa·lyaa ee·zhee·e·nee·kaa

sardine *sardinha* ① saarr·dee·nyaa

Saturday *sábado* ⓜ saa·baa·do

sauce *molho* ⓜ mo·lyo

sauna *sauna* ① sow·naa

sausage *salsicha* ① sow·see·shaa

say *dizer* dee·zerr

scalp *couro* ⓜ *cabeludo*
ko·ro kaa·be·loo·do

scarf *lenço* ⓜ leng·so

school *escola* ⓕ es·ko·laa

science *ciências* ⓕ pl see·eng·syaas

scientist *cientista* ⓜ&ⓕ see·eng·tees·taa

scissors *tesoura* ⓕ te·zo·raa

score *contar os pontos* kong·*taarr* os *pong*·tos

scoreboard *painel* ⓜ *de marcação* pai·*nel* de maarr·kaa·*sowng*

Scotland *Escócia* ⓕ es·ko·syaa

scrambled *mexido/mexida* ⓜ/ⓕ me·*shee*·do/me·*shee*·daa

sculptor *escultor/escultor* ⓜ/ⓕ es·kool·*toorr*/es·kool·*too*·ra

sculpture *escultura* ⓕ es·kool·*too*·raa

sea *mar* ⓜ maarr

seasick *enjoado/enjoada* ⓜ/ⓕ en·zho·*aa*·do/en·zho·*aa*·daa

seaside *beira mar* ⓕ *bay*·raa maarr

season *estação* ⓕ es·taa·*sowng*

seat *assento* ⓜ aa·*seng*·to

seatbelt *cinto* ⓜ *de segurança* *seeng*·to de se·goo·*rang*·saa

second (time) *segundo* ⓜ se·*goong*·do

second *segundo/segunda* ⓜ/ⓕ se·*goong*·do/se·*goong*·daà

second-hand *de segunda mão* de se·*goong*·daa mowng

second-hand shop *loja* ⓕ *de segunda mão* *lo*·zhaa de se·*goon*·daa mowng

secretary *secretário/secretária* ⓜ/ⓕ se·kre·*taa*·ryo/se·kre·*taa*·ryaa

see *ver* verr

self-employed *autônomo/autônoma* ⓜ/ⓕ ow·*to*·no·mo/ow·*to*·no·maa

selfish *egoísta* e·go·*ees*·taa

self-service *auto-serviço* ⓜ ow·to·serr·*vee*·so

sell *vender* veng·*derr*

send *enviar* eng·vee·*garr*

sensible *sensível* seng·*see*·vel

sensual *sensual* seng·soo·ow

separate *separado/separada* ⓜ/ⓕ se·paa·*raa*·do/se·paa·*raa*·daa

September *setembro* se·*teng*·bro

serious *sério/séria* ⓜ/ⓕ *se*·ryo/*se*·ryaa

service charge *taxa* ⓕ *de serviço* *taa*·shaa de serr·*veee*·so

service station *posto* ⓜ *de gasolina* *pos*·to de gaa·zo·*lee*·naa

serviette *guardanapo* ⓜ gwaarr·daa·*naa*·po

several *diversos/diversas* ⓜ/ⓕ pl dee·*verr*·sos/dee·*verr*·saas

sew *costurar* kos·too·*raarr*

sex *sexo* ⓜ *sek*·so

sexism *machismo* ⓜ maa·*shees*·mo

sexy *sexy* sek·*see*

shadow *sombra* ⓕ *song*·braa

shampoo *xampú* ⓜ shang·*poo*

shape *forma* ⓕ *forr*·maa

share (with) *dividir* dee·vee·*deerr*

shave *fazer a barba* faa·*zerr* aa *baarr*·baa

shaving cream *creme* ⓜ *de barbear* *kre*·me de baarr·be·*aarr*

she *ela* e·laa

sheep *ovelha* ⓕ o·*ve*·lyaa

sheet (bed) *lençol* ⓜ leng·*sow*

shelf *prateleira* ⓕ praa·te·*lay*·raa

shiatsu *shiatsu* ⓜ shee·*aa*·tee·zoo

shingles (illness) *cobreiro* ⓜ ko·*bray*·ro

ship *navio* ⓜ naa·*vee*·o

shirt *camisa* ⓕ kaa·*mee*·zaa

shoe *sapato* ⓜ saa·*paa*·to

shoe shop *sapataria* ⓕ saa·paa·taa·*ree*·aa

shoot *atirar* aa·tee·*raarr*

shop *loja* ⓕ *lo*·zhaa

shopping centre *shopping centre* ⓜ *sho*·peeng *seng*·terr

short *curto/curta* ⓜ/ⓕ *koor*·to/*knor*·taa

shortage *escassez* ⓕ es·kaa·*ses*

shorts *bermuda* ⓕ berr·*moo*·daa

shoulder *ombro* ⓜ pl *ong*·bro

shout *gritar* gree·*taarr*

show *mostrar* mos·*traarr*

shower *chuveiro* ⓜ shoo·*vay*·ro

shrine *relicário* ⓜ he·lee·*kaa*·ryo

shut *fechado/fechada* ⓜ/ⓕ fe·*shaa*·do/fe·*shaa*·daa

shy *tímido/tímida* ⓜ/ⓕ *tee*·mee·do/*tee*·mee·daa

sick *doente* do·*eng*·te

side *lado* ⓜ *laa*·do

sign *aviso* ⓜ aa·*vee*·zo

signature *assinatura* ⓕ aa·see·naa·*too*·raa

silk *seda* ⓕ *se*·daa

silver *prata* ⓕ *praa*·taa

similar *parecido/parecida* ⓜ/ⓕ
paa·re·*see*·do/paa·re·*see*·daa

simple *simples seeng*·ples

since *desde des*·de

sing *cantar* kang·*taarr*

Singapore *Cingapura* seen·gaa·*poo*·raa

singer *cantor/cantora* ⓜ/ⓕ
kang·*torr*/kang·*to*·raa

single *solteiro/solteira* ⓜ/ⓕ
sol·*tay*·ro/sol·*tay*·raa

singlet *camiseta* ⓕ kaa·mee·*ze*·taa

sister *irmã* ⓕ eer·*ma*

sit *sentar* seng·*taarr*

size *tamanho* ⓜ ta·*ma*·nyo

skate *andar de skate*
ang·*daarr* de ees·*kay*·te

skateboarding *skate* ⓜ ees·*kay*·te

ski *esquiar* es·kee·*aarr*

skiing *esqui* ⓜ es·*kee*

skim milk *leite* ⓜ *desnatado*
lay·te des·naa·*taa*·do

skin *pele* ⓕ *pe*·le

skirt *saia* ⓕ *saa*·yaa

skull *crânio* ⓜ *kra*·nyo

sky *céu* ⓜ *se*·oo

sleep *dormir* dorr·*meerr*

sleeping bag *saco* ⓜ *de dormir*
saa·ko de dorr·*meerr*

sleeping berth *leito* ⓜ *lay*·to

sleeping car *vagão* ⓜ *de dormir*
va·*gowng* de dorr·*meerr*

sleeping pills *pílula* ⓕ *para dormir*
pee·loo·laa paa·raa dorr·*meerr*

sleepy *sonolento/sonolenta* ⓜ/ⓕ
so·no·*leng*·to/so·no·*leng*·taa

slide (film) *slide* ⓜ ees·*lai*·de

slow *devagar* de·vaa·*gaarr*

slowly *vagarosamente*
vaa·gaa·ro·zaa·*meng*·te

small *pequeno/pequena* ⓜ/ⓕ
pe·*ke*·no/pe·*ke*·na

smell *cheiro* ⓜ *shay*·ro

smile *sorrir* so·*heerr*

smoke *fumar* foo·*maarr*

snack *lanche* ⓜ *lang*·she

snail *lesma* ⓕ *les*·maa

snake *cobra* ⓕ *ko*·braa

snorkelling *snorkel* ⓜ ees·*norr*·kel

snow *neve* ⓕ *ne*·ve

snow pea *vagem* ⓕ *chinesa vaa*·zheng
shee·ne·zaa

snowboarding *snowboarding* ⓜ
snow·*borr*·deeng

soap *sabonete* ⓜ saa·bo·*ne*·te

soap opera *novela* ⓕ no·ve·laa

soccer *futebol* ⓜ foo·te·*bol*

social welfare *seguro* ⓜ *social*
se·*goo*·ro so·see·ow

socialist *socialista* so·see·aa·*lees*·taa

sock *meia* ⓕ *may*·aa

soft drink *refrigerante* ⓜ
he·free·zhe·*rang*·te

soft-boiled *mole mo*·le

soldier *soldado* ⓜ&ⓕ sol·*daa*·do

some *alguns/algumas* ⓜ/ⓕ
ow·*goons*/ow·*goo*·maas

someone *alguém* ow·*geng*

something *alguma coisa*
ow·*goo*·maa koy·zaa

sometimes *às vezes* aas *ve*·zes

son *filho* ⓜ *fee*·lyo

song *canção* ⓕ kang·*sowng*

soon *em breve* eng *bre*·ve

sore *dolorido/dolorida* ⓜ/ⓕ
do·lo·*ree*·do/do·lo·*ree*·daa

soup *sopa* ⓕ *so*·paa

sour cream *creme* ⓜ *azedo*
kre·me aa·ze·do

south *sul* ⓜ sool

souvenir *souvenir* ⓜ soo·ve·*neerr*

souvenir shop *loja* ⓕ *de souvenir*
lo·zhaa de soo·ve·*neerr*

soy milk *leite* ⓜ *de soja lay*·te de so·zhaa

soy sauce *molho* ⓜ *de soja*
mo·lyo de so·zhaa

space *espaço* ⓜ es·*pa*·so

Spain *Espanha* ⓕ es·*pa*·nyaa

sparkling wine *vinho* ⓜ *espumante*
vee·nyo es·poo·*mang*·te

speak *falar* faa·*laarr*

special *especial* es·pe·see·*ow*

specialist *especialista* ⓜ&ⓕ
es·pe·see·aa·*lees*·taa

speed *velocidade* ⓕ ve·lo·see·*daa*·de

speed limit *limite* ⓜ *de velocidade*
lee·*mee*·te de ve·lo·see·*daa*·de

speedometer *mostrador* ⓜ *de velocidade*
mos·traa·*dorr* de ve·lo·see·*daa*·de

spider *aranha* ① aa·ra·nyaa
spinach *espinafre* ⑩ es·pee·naa·fre
spoiled *mimado/mimada* ⑩/①
mee·maa·do/mee·maa·daa
spoke (wheel) *trave* ① *de roda*
traa·ve de ho·daa
spoon *colher* ① ko·lyerr
sport *esporte* ⑩ es·porr·te
sports store *loja* ① *de esportes*
lo·zhaa de es·porr·tes
sportsperson *esportista* ⑩&①
es·porr·tees·taa
sprain *torcimento* ⑩ • *deslocamento* ⑩
torr·see·meng·to • des·lo·kaa·meng·to
spring (coil) *molas* ① pl mo·laas
spring (season) *primavera* ①
pree·maa·ve·raa
square (town) *praça* ① praa·saa
stadium *estádio* ⑩ es·taa·dyo
stairway *escadaria* ① es·kaa·daa·ree·aa
stale *velho/velha* ⑩/① ve·lyo/ve·lyaa
stamp *selo* ⑩ se·lo
standby ticket *bilhete* ⑩ *de stand by*
bee·lye·te de ees·tang·dee bai
(four-)star (quatro) estrelas ① pl (kwaa·tro)
es·tre·laas
star *estrela* ① es·tre·laa
start *começo* ⑩ ko·me·so
start *começar* ko·me·saarr
station *estação* ① es·taa·sowng
stationery shop *papelaria* ①
paa·pe·laa·ree·aa
statue *estátua* ① es·taa·twaa
stay (at a hotel) *ficar* fee·kaarr
stay (in one place) *ficar* fee·kaarr
steak (beef) *bife* ⑩ bee·fe
steal *roubar* ho·baarr
steep *íngreme* eeng·gre·me
step *passo* ⑩ paa·so
stereo *estéreo* ⑩ es·te·ryo
still water *água* ① *sem gás*
aa·gwaa seng gaas
stock (food) *caldo* ⑩ kow·do
stockings *meias* ① pl *finas*
may·aas fee·naas
stomach *estômago* ⑩ es·to·maa·go
stomachache *dor* ⑩ *de estômago*
dorr de es·to·maa·go
stone *pedra* ① pe·draa

stoned (drugged) *fumado/fumada* ⑩/①
foo·maa·do/foo·maa·daa
stop (bus) *ponto* ⑩ *de ônibus*
pong·to de o·nee·boos
stop (cease) *parar* paa·raarr
stop (prevent) *evitar* e·vee·taarr
Stop! *Pare!* paa·re
storm *tempestade* ① teng·pes·taa·de
story *estória* ① es·to·ryaa
stove *fogão* ⑩ fo·gowng
straight *direto/direta* ⑩/①
dee·re·to/dee·re·taa
strange *estranho/estranha* ⑩/①
es·tra·nyo/es·tra·nyaa
stranger *estranho/estranha* ⑩/①
es·tra·nyo/es·tra·nyaa
strawberry *morango* ⑩ mo·rang·go
stream *vapor* ⑩ vaa·porr
street *rua* ① hoo·aa
strike *ataque* ⑩ aa·taa·ke
string *barbante* ⑩ baarr·bang·te
stroke (health) *derrame* ⑩ de·ha·me
strong *forte* forr·te
stubborn *teimoso/teimosa* ⑩/①
tay·mo·zo/tay·mo·zaa
student *estudante* ⑩&① es·too·dang·te
studio *estúdio* ⑩ es·too·dyo
stupid *burro/burra* ⑩/①
boo·ho/boo·haa
style *estilo* ⑩ es·tee·lo
subtitles *sub-títulos* ⑩ pl
soo·bee·tee·too·los
suburb *bairro* ⑩ bai·ho
sugar *açúcar* ⑩ aa·soo·kaarr
suitcase *mala* ① maa·laa
sultana *passas* ① pl pa·saas
summer *verão* ⑩ ve·rowng
sun *sol* ⑩ sol
Sunday *domingo* ⑩ do·meeng·go
sunblock *proteção* ① *contra sol*
pro·te·sowng kong·traa sol
sunburnt *queimado/queimada* ⑩/①
de sol kay·maa·do/kay·maa·daa de sol
sunglasses *óculos* ⑩ pl *de sol*
o koo·los de sol
sunny *ensolarado/ensolarada* ⑩/①
eng·so·laa·raa·do/eng·so·laa·raa·daa
sunrise *nascer* ① *do sol* naa·serr do sol
sunset *pôr* ⑩ *do sol* porr do sol

sunstroke *insolação* ① eeng·so·laa·*sowng*

supermarket *supermercado* ⓜ
soo·perr·merr·*kaa*·do

superstition *superstição* ①
soo·pers·tee·*sowng*

supporter (sport) *torcedor/
torcedora* ⓜ/① torr·se·*dorr*/
torr·se·do·raa

supporter (politics) *apoio* ⓜ *ao
partido* aa·*po*·yo ow paarr·*tee*·do

surf *surfar* soorr·*faarr*

surface mail *correspondência* ① *via
terrestre* ko·hes·pong·*deng*·syaa vee·aa
te·*hes*·tre

surfboard *prancha* ① *de surfe* prang·shaa
de soorr·fee

surfing *surfe* ⓜ *soor*·fee

surname *sobrenome* ⓜ so·bre·*no*·me

surprise *surpresa* ① soorr·*pre*·zaa

sweater *suéter* ① soo·e·terr

Sweden *Suécia* ① soo·e·syaa

sweet *doce do*·se

sweets *doces* ⓜ pl *do*·ses

swelling *inchaço* ① eeng·*shaa*·so

swim *nadar* naa·*daarr*

swimming pool *piscina* ① pee·*see*·naa

swimsuit *roupa* ① *de banho*
ho·paa de *ba*·nyo

Switzerland *Suíça* ① soo·ee·saa

synagogue *sinagoga* ① see·naa·*go*·gaa

synthetic *sintético/sintética* ⓜ/①
seeng·te·tee·ko/seeng·te·tee·kaa

syringe *seringa* ① se·*reeng*·gaa

T

table *mesa* ① *me*·zaa

table tennis *tênis* ① *de mesa*
te·nees de *me*·zaa

tablecloth *toalha* ① *de mesa* to·aa·lyaa
de *me*·zaa

tail *rabo* ⓜ *haa*·bo

tailor *alfaiate* ⓜ ow·faa·*yaa*·te

take *levar* le·*vaarr*

take (photo) *tirar* tee·*raarr*

talk *falar* faa·*laarr*

tall *alto/alta* ⓜ/① ow·to/ow·taa

tampon *tampão* ⓜ tang·*powng*

tanning lotion *loção* ① *de bronzear*
lo·*sowng* de brong·ze·*aarr*

tap *torneira* ① torr·*nay*·raa

tap water *água* ① *da torneira*
aa·gwaa daa torr·*nay*·raa

tasty *gostoso/gostosa* ⓜ/①
gos·to·zo/gos·to·zaa

tax *imposto* ⓜ eeng·*pos*·to

taxi *táxi* ① *taak*·see

taxi stand *fila* ① *de táxi*
fee·laa de *taak*·see

tea *chá* ① shaa

teacher *professor/professora* ⓜ/①
pro·fe·sorr/pro·fe·so·raa

team *time* ⓜ *tee*·me

teaspoon *colher* ① *de chá*
ko·*lyerr* de shaa

technique *técnica* ① te·kee·nee·kaa

teeth *dentes* ⓜ pl *deng*·tes

telegram *telegrama* ① te·le·*gra*·maa

telephone *telefone* ⓜ te·le·*fo*·ne

telephone *telefonar* te·le·fo·*naarr*

telephone centre *central* ① *telefônica*
seng·*trow* te·le·fo·nee·kaa

telescope *telescópio* ① te·les·ko·pyo

television *televisão* ① te·le·vee·*sowng*

tell *dizer* dee·*zerr*

temperature *temperatura* ①
teng·pe·raa·*too*·raa

temple *têmpora* ① *teng*·po·raa

tennis *tênis* ⓜ *te*·nees

tennis court *quadra* ① *de tênis*
kwaa·draa de *te*·nees

tent *barraca* ① baa·*haa*·kaa

tent peg *estaca* ① es·*taa*·kaa

terrible *terrível* te·*hee*·vel

test *teste* ⓜ *tes*·te

thank *agradecer* aa·graa·de·*serr*

theatre *teatro* ⓜ te·*aa*·tro

their *deles* de·les

they *eles* e·les

thick *grosso/grossa* ⓜ/① gro·so/gro·saa

thief *ladrão/ladra* ⓜ/①
laa·*drowng*/*laa*·dra

thin *fino/fina* ⓜ/① *fee*·no/*fee*·naa

think *pensar* peng·*saarr*

third *terceiro/terceira* ⓜ/①
terr·*say*·ro/terr·*say*·raa

thirsty *sedento/sedenta* ⓜ/ⓕ
se-*deng*-to/se-*deng*-taa

this *este/esta* ⓜ/ⓕ *es*-te/*es*-taa

throat *garganta* ⓕ gaarr-*gang*-taa

thrush (health) *cândida* ⓕ • *corrimento* ⓜ
kang-dee-daa • ko-hee-*meng*-to

Thursday *quinta-feira* ⓕ kween-ta-*fay*-raa

ticket *bilhete* ⓜ bee-*lye*-te

ticket machine *máquina* ⓕ *de vender passagem* maa-kee-naa de *veng*-derr paa-*saa*-zheng

ticket office *bilheteria* ⓕ bee-lye-te-*ree*-aa

tide *maré* ⓕ maa-*re*

tight *apertado/apertada* ⓜ/ⓕ
aa-perr-*taa*-do/aa-perr-*taa*-daa

time *tempo* ⓜ *teng*-po

time difference *diferença* ⓕ *de horário*
dee-fe-*reng*-saa de o-*raa*-ryo

timetable *horário* ⓕ o-*raa*-rio

tin (can) *lata* ⓕ *laa*-taa

tin opener *abridor* ⓜ *de lata*
aa-bree-dorr de *laa*-taa

tiny *mínimo/mínima* ⓜ/ⓕ
mee-nee-mo/mee-nee-maa

tip (gratuity) *gorjeta* ⓕ gorr *zhe*-taa

tired *cansado/cansada* ⓜ/ⓕ
kang-*saa*-do/kang-*saa*-daa

tissue *lencinho* ⓜ *de papel*
leng-*see*-nyo de paa-*pel*

toast *torrada* ⓕ to-*haa*-daa

toaster *torradeira* ⓕ to-haa-*day*-raa

tobacco *tabaco* ⓜ taa-*baa*-ko

tobacconist *tabaconista* ⓕ
taa-baa-ko-*nees*-taa

tobogganing *tobogã* ⓜ to-bo-*gang*

today *hoje* o-zhe

toe *dedos* ⓜ pl *do pé de*-dos do pe

tofu *tofu* ⓜ to-*foo*

together *junto/junta* ⓜ/ⓕ
zhoong-to/*zhoong*-taa

toilet *banheiro* ⓜ ba-*nyay*-ro

toilet paper *papel* ⓜ *higiênico*
paa-*pel* ee-gee-e-nee-ko

tomato *tomate* ⓜ to-*maa*-te

tomato sauce *molho* ⓜ *de tomate*
mo-lyo de to-*maa*-te

tomorrow *amanhã* aa-ma-*nyang*

tomorrow afternoon *amanhã à tarde*
aa-ma-*nyang* aa *taarr*-de

tomorrow evening *amanhã à noite*
aa-ma-*nyang* aa noy-te

tomorrow morning *amanhã de manhã*
aa-ma-*nyang* de ma-*nyang*

tonight *hoje à noite* o-zhe aa noy-te

too (also) *também* tang-*beng*

too (much) *demais* de-*mais*

tooth *dente* ⓜ *deng*-te

toothache *dor* ⓕ *de dente*
dorr de *deng*-te

toothbrush *escova* ⓕ *de dentes*
es-*ko*-vaa de *deng*-tes

toothpaste *pasta* ⓕ *de dentes*
pas-taa de *deng*-tes

toothpick *palito* ⓜ *de dentes*
paa-*lee*-to de *deng*-tes

torch (flashlight) *lanterna* ⓕ lang-*terr*-naa

touch *tocar* to-*kaarr*

tour *excursão* ⓕ es-koorr-*sowng*

tourist *turista* ⓜ&ⓕ too-rees-taa

tourist office *escritório* ⓜ *de turismo*
es-kree-to-ryo de too-rees-mo

towards *em direção à*
eng dee-re-sowng aa

towel *toalha* ⓕ to *aa* lyaa

tower *torre* ⓕ to he

toxic waste *resíduo* ⓜ *tóxico*
he-zee-dwo tok-see-ko

toy shop *loja* ⓕ *de brinquedos*
lo-zhaa de breeng-ke-dos

track (path) *caminho* ⓜ kaa-*mee*-nyo

track (sport) *pista* ⓕ *pees*-taa

trade *comércio* ⓜ ko-*merr*-syo

traffic *tráfico* ⓜ traa-fee-ko

traffic light *sinal* ⓜ *de trânsito*
see-now de trang-zee-to

trail *vestígio* ⓜ ves-*tee*-zhyo

train *trem* ⓜ treng

train station *estação* ⓕ *de trem*
es-taa-sowng de treng

tram *bonde* ⓜ bong-de

transit lounge *sala* ⓕ *de trânsito*
saa-laa de trang-zee-to

translate *traduzir* traa-doo-*zeerr*

transport *transporte* ⓜ trans-*porr*-te

travel *viajar* vee-aa-*zhaarr*

travel agency *agência* ⓕ *de viagens*
aa-*zheng*-syaa de vee-*aa*-zhengs

travel sickness *enjôo* ⓜ *de viagem*
eng·jo·o de vee·aa·zheng
travellers cheques *travellers cheques* ⓜ pl traa·ve·ler she·kes
tree *árvore* ⓕ aarr·vo·re
trip (journey) *viagem* ⓕ vee·aa·zheng
trousers *calças* ⓕ pl kow·saas
truck *caminhão* ⓜ kaa·mee·nyowng
trust *crer* krerr
try (attempt) *tentar* teng·taarr
T-shirt *camiseta* ⓕ kaa·mee·ze·taa
tube (tyre) *câmara* ⓕ ka·maa·raa
Tuesday *terça-feira* ⓕ terr·saa·fay·raa
tumour *tumor* ⓜ too·morr
tuna *atum* ⓜ aa·toong
tune *tom* ⓜ tong
turkey *perú* ⓜ pe·roo
turn *virar* vee·raarr
TV *tevé* ⓕ te·ve
tweezers *pinça* ⓕ peeng·saa
twice *duas vezes* doo·aas ve·zes
twin beds *camas* ⓕ pl *gêmeas*
ka·maas zhe·me·aas
twins *gêmeos/gêmeas* ⓜ/ⓕ
zhe·me·os/zhe·me·aas
type *tipo* ⓜ tee·po
typical *típico/típica* ⓜ/ⓕ
tee·pee·ko/tee·pee·kaa
tyre *pneu* ⓜ pee·ne·oo

U

ultrasound *ultrasom* ⓜ ool·traa·song
umbrella *guarda-chuva* ⓜ
gwaarr·daa·shoo·vaa
uncomfortable *desconfortável*
des·kong·forr·taa·vel
understand *compreender*
kong·pre·eng·derr
underwear *roupa* ⓕ *de baixo*
ho·paa de bai·sho
unemployed *desempregado/*
desempregada ⓜ/ⓕ
de·zeng·pre·gaa·do/
de·zeng·pre·gaa·daa
unfair *injusto/injusta* ⓜ/ⓕ
eeng·zhoos·to/eeng·zhoos·taa
uniform *uniforme* ⓜ oo·nee·forr·me
universe *universo* ⓜ oo·nee·verr·so

university *universidade* ⓕ
oo·nee·verr·see·daa·de
unleaded *sem chumbo* seng shoong·bo
unsafe *inseguro/insegura* ⓜ/ⓕ
eeng·se·goo·ro/eeng·se·goo·raa
until *até* aa·te
unusual *atípico/atípica* ⓜ/ⓕ
aa·tee·pee·ko/aa·tee·pee·kaa
up *em cima* eng see·maa
uphill *para cima* paa·raa see·maa
urgent *urgente* oorr·zheng·te
urinary infection *infecção* ⓕ *urinária*
een·fek·sowng oo·ree·naa·ryaa
the USA *os EUA* ⓜ pl os e·waa
useful *útil* oo·til

V

vacant *vago/vaga* ⓜ/ⓕ
vaa·go/vaa·gaa
vacation *férias* ⓕ pl fe·ryaas
vaccination *vacina* ⓕ vaa·see·naa
vagina *vagina* ⓕ vaa·zhee·naa
validate *validar* vaa·lee·daarr
valley *vale* ⓜ vaa·le
valuable *valioso/valiosa* ⓜ/ⓕ
vaa·lee·o·zo/vaa·lee·o·zaa
value (price) *valor* vaa·lorr
van *van* ⓜ van
veal *bezerro/bezerra* ⓜ/ⓕ
be·ze·ho/be·ze·haa
vegetable *legumes* ⓜ pl le·goo·mes
vegetarian *vegetariano/*
vegetariana ⓜ/ⓕ ve·zhe·taa·ree·a·no/
ve·zhe·taa·ree·a·naa
vein *veia* ⓕ ve·aa
venereal disease *doença* ⓕ *venérea*
do·eng·saa ve·ne·ryaa
venue *local* ⓜ lo·kow
very *muito/muita* ⓜ/ⓕ
mweeng·to/mweeng·taa
video tape *fita* ⓕ *de vídeo*
fee·taa de vee·de·o
view *vista* ⓕ vees·taa
village *vilarejo* ⓜ vee·laa·re·zho
vine *vinho* ⓜ vee·nyo
vinegar *vinagre* ⓜ vee·naa·gre
vineyard *vinha* ⓕ vee·nyaa
virus *vírus* ⓜ vee·roos

visa *visto* ⓜ vees·to
visit *visitar* vee·zee·taarr
vitamin *vitamina* ⓕ vee·taa·mee·naa
vodka *vodka* ⓕ vo·dee·kaa
voice *voz* ⓕ voz
volleyball (sport) *vôlei* ⓜ vo·lay
volume *volume* ⓜ vo·loo·me
vote *votar* vo·taarr

W

wage *salário* ⓜ saa·laa·ryo
wait *esperar* es·pe·raarr
waiter *garçon/garçonete* ⓜ/ⓕ gaarr·song/
  gaarr·so·ne·te
waiting room *sala* ⓕ *de espera*
  saa·laa de es·pe·raa
walk *andar* ang·daarr
wall (outer) *parede* ⓕ paa·re·de
want *querer* ke·rerr
war *guerra* ⓕ ge·haa
wardrobe *armário* ⓜ aarr·maa·ryo
warm *morno/morna* ⓜ/ⓕ
  morr·no/morr·naa
warn *avisar* aa·vee·zaarr
wash *lavar* laa·vaarr
wash cloth (flannel) *pano* ⓜ *de limpeza*
  pa·no de leeng·pe·zaa
washing machine *máquina* ⓕ *de lavar*
  roupa maa·kee·naa de laa·vaarr ho·paa
watch *relógio* ⓜ he·lo·zhyo
watch *cuidar • vigiar*
  kooy·daarr • vee·zhee·aarr
water *água* ⓕ aa·gwaa
water bottle *garrafa* ⓕ *d'água*
  gaa·haa·faa daa·gwaa
waterfall *cachoeira* ⓕ kaa·sho·ay·raa
watermelon *melancia* ⓕ me·lang·see·aa
waterproof *a prova d'água*
  aa pro·vaa daa·gwaa
waterskiing *eski* ⓜ *aquático*
  es·kee aa·kwaa·tee·ko
wave *onda* ⓕ ong·daa
way *caminho* ⓜ kaa·mee·nyo
we *nós* nos
weak *fraco/fraca* ⓜ/ⓕ fraa·ko/fraa·kaa
wealthy *rico/rica* ⓜ/ⓕ hee·ko/hee·kaa
wear *vestir* ves·teerr
weather *tempo* ⓜ teng·po

wedding *casamento* ⓜ kaa·zaa·meng·to
wedding cake *bolo* ⓜ *de casamento*
  bo·lo de kaa·zaa·meng·to
wedding present *presente* ⓜ
  de casamento pre·zeng·te de
  kaa·zaa·meng·to
Wednesday *quarta-feira* ⓕ
  kwaarr·taa·fay·raa
week *semana* ⓕ se·ma·naa
weekend *final* ⓜ *de semana*
  fee·now de se·ma·naa
weigh *pesar* pe·zaarr
weight *peso* ⓜ pe·zo
weights *pesos* ⓜ pl pe·zos
welcome *receber* he·se·berr
welfare *bem* ⓜ *social* beng so·see·ow
well *bem* ⓜ beng
west *oeste* ⓜ o·es·te
wet *molhado/molhada* ⓜ/ⓕ
  mo·lyaa·do/mo·lyaa·daa
what *que* ke
wheel *roda* ⓕ ho·daa
wheelchair *cadeira* ⓕ *de rodas* kaa·day·raa
  de ho·daas
when *quando* kwang·do
where *onde* ong·de
whisky *whisky* ⓜ oo·ees·kee
white *branco/branca* ⓜ/ⓕ
  brang·ko/brang·kaa
who *quem* keng
wholemeal bread *pão* ⓜ *integral*
  powng eeng·te·grow
why *por que* porr ke
wide *largo/larga* ⓜ/ⓕ
  laarr·go/laarr·gaa
wife *esposa* ⓕ es·po·zaa
win *ganhar* ga·nyaarr
wind *vento* ⓜ veng·to
window *janela* ⓕ zhaa·ne·laa
windscreen *parabrisa* ⓜ paa·raa·bree·zaa
windsurfing *windsurfe* ⓜ wind·soorr·fee
wine *vinho* ⓜ vee·nyo
wings *asas* ⓕ pl aa·zaas
winner *ganhador/ganhadora* ⓜ/ⓕ
  ga·nyaa·dorr/ga·nyaa·do·raa
winter *inverno* ⓜ eeng·verr·no
wire *arame* ⓜ aa·ra·me
wish *desejar* de·ze·zhaarr
with *com* kong

within (an hour) *dentro de (uma hora)* deng·tro de (oo·maa aw·raa)

without *sem* seng

woman *mulher* ① moo·lyerr

wonderful *maravilhoso/maravilhosa* ⓜ/① maa·raa·vee·lyo·zo/maa·raa·vee·lyo·zaa

wood *madeira* ① maa·day·raa

wool *lã* ① lang

word *palavra* ① paa·laa·vraa

work *trabalho* ⓜ traa·baa·lyo

work *trabalhar* traa·baa·lyaarr

work experience *experiência* ① de trabalho es·pe·ree·eng·syaa de traa·baa·lyo

work permit *permissão* ① para trabalhar perr·mee·sowng paa·raa traa·baa·lyaarr

workout *resolução* ① he·zo·loo·sowng

workshop *oficina* ① o·fee·see·naa

world *mundo* ⓜ moong·do

World Cup *Copa do Mundo* ① ko·paa do moong·do

worms *minhocas* ① pl mee·nyo·kaas

worried *preocupado/preocupada* ⓜ/① pre·o·koo·paa·do/pre·o·koo·paa·daa

worship *reverenciar* he·ve·reng·see·aarr

wrist *punho* ⓜ poo·nyo

write *escrever* es·kre·verr

writer *escritor/escritora* ⓜ/① es·kree·torr/es·kree·to·raa

wrong *errado/errada* ⓜ/① e·haa·do/e·haa·daa

Y

year *ano* ⓜ a·no

yellow *amarelo/amarela* ⓜ/① aa·maa·re·lo/aa·maa·re·laa

yes *sim* seeng

yesterday *ontem* ong·teng

(not) yet *ainda (não)* aa·eeng·daa (nowng)

yoga *ioga* ① ee·o·gaa

yogurt *iogurte* ⓜ ee·o·goorr·te

you *você/vocês* sg/pl vo·se/vo·ses

young *jovem* zho·veng

your *seu/sua* ⓜ/① se·oo/soo·aa

youth hostel *albergue* ⓜ da juventude ow·berr·ge daa zhoo·veng·too·de

Z

zodiac *zodíaco* ⓜ zo·dee·aa·ko

zoo *zoológico* ⓜ zo·o·lo·zhee·ko

zucchini *abobrinha* ① aa·bo·bree·nyaa

brazilian portuguese–english

Nouns in the dictionary have their gender indicated by ⑩ or ①. If it's a plural noun, you'll also see pl. Where a word that could be either a noun or a verb has no gender indicated, it's the verb. For all words relating to local food, see the **culinary reader**, page 159.

A

a bordo aa *horr*-do *aboard*

à direita ① aa dee-*ray*-taa *right (direction)*

à esquerda ① aa es-*kerr*-daa *left (direction)*

a prova d'água aa *pro*-vaa *daa*-gwaa *waterproof*

abacate ⑩ aa-baa-*kaa*-te *avocado*

abacaxi ⑩ aa-baa-kaa-*shee* *pineapple*

abaixo aa-*bai*-sho *below*

abelha ① aa-*be*-lyaa *bee*

aberto/aberta ⑩/① aa-*berr*-to/aa-*berr*-taa *open*

abóbora ① aa-*bo*-bo-raa *pumpkin*

abobrinha ① aa-bo-*bree*-nyaa *courgette • zucchini*

aborto ⑩ aa-*borr*-to *abortion*

— **espontâneo** es-*pong*-ta-ne-o *miscarriage*

abraçar aa braa-*saarr* *hug*

abridor ⑩ **de garrafas** aa-bree-*dorr* de *gaa-haa*-faas *bottle opener*

abridor ⑩ **de lata** aa-*bree*-dorr de *laa*-taa *can opener • tin opener*

abril aa-*breel* *April*

abrir aa-*breerr* *open*

absorvente ⑩ **higiênico** aab-sorr-*veng*-te ee-zhee-e-nee-ko *panty liner*

academia aa-kaa-de-*mee*-aa *college*

acampamento ⑩ aa kang-paa-*meng*-to *camping ground*

acampar aa-kang-*paarr* *camp*

achados e perdidos ⑩ pl aa-*shaa*-dos e perr-*dee*-dos *left luggage*

acidente ⑩ aa-see-*deng*-te *accident*

açougue ⑩ aa-so-ge *butcher's shop*

açougueiro/açougueira ⑩/① aa-so-*gay*-ro/aa-so-*gay*-raa *butcher*

açúcar ⑩ aa-*soo*-kaarr *sugar*

acupuntura ① aa-koo-poom-*too*-raa *acupuncture*

adaptador ⑩ aa-daa-pee-taa-*dorr* *adaptor*

adentro aa-*deng*-tro *indoors*

adivinhar aa-dee-vee-*nyaarr* *guess*

administração ① aa-dee-mee-nees-traa-*sowng* *administration*

admitir aa-dee-mee-*teerr* *admit (acknowledge)*

adulto/adulta ⑩/① aa-*dool*-to/aa-*dool*-taa *adult*

advogado/advogada ⑩/① aa-dee-vo-*gaa*-do/aa-dee-vo-*gaa*-daa *lawyer*

aeróbica ① aa-e-ro-bee-kaa *aerobics*

aeroplano ⑩ aa-e-ro-*pla*-no *aeroplane*

aeroporto ⑩ aa-e-ro-*porr*-to *airport*

África ① aa-free-kaa *Africa*

agência ① **de viagens** aa-*zheng*-syaa de vee-*aa*-zhengs *travel agency*

agente ⑩&① **imobiliário** aa-*zheng* te ee-mo-bee-lee-*aa*-ryo *real estate agent*

agora aa-*go*-raa *now*

agosto aa-*gos*-to *August*

agradecer aa-graa-de-*serr* *thank*

agricultura ① aa-gree-kool-*too*-raa *agriculture*

água ① *aa*-gwaa *water*

— **da torneira** daa torr *nay*-raa *tap water*

— **mineral** mee-ne-*row* *mineral water*

— **quente** *keng*-te *hot water*

— **sem gás** seng gaas *still water*

agulha ① aa-*goo*-lyaa *needle (sewing/syringe)*

Aids ① *ai*-dees *AIDS*

ainda (não) aa-*eeng*-daa (nowng) *(not) yet*

ajuda ① aa-*zhoo*-daa *help*

ajudar aa-zhoo-*daarr* *help*

albergue ⓜ da juventude ow-*berr*-ge da zhoo-veng-*too*-de *youth hostel*

álcool ⓜ ow-kol *alcohol*

Alemanha ① aa-le-*ma*-nyaa *Germany*

alergia ① aa-lerr-*zhee*-aa *allergy*

alface ⓜ ow-*faa*-se *lettuce*

alfaiate ⓜ ow-faa-*yaa*-te *tailor*

alfândega ① aal-*fang*-de-gaa *customs*

algodão ⓜ ow-go-*downg* *cotton*

alguém ow-*geng* *someone*

alguma coisa ow-*goo*-maa *koy*-zaa *something*

alguns/algumas ⓜ/① ow-*goons*/ow-*goo*-maas *few • some*

alho ⓜ aa-lyo *garlic*

alimentar aa-lee-meng-*taarr* *feed*

almoço ⓜ ow-*mo*-so *lunch*

alpinismo ⓜ ow-pee-*nees*-mo *rock climbing*

altar ⓜ ow-*taarr* *altar*

altitude ① ow-tee-*too*-de *altitude*

alto/alta ⓜ/① ow-to/ow-taa *high • loud • tall*

alucinação ① aa-loo-see-naa-*sowng* *hallucination*

alugar aa-loo-*gaarr* *hire • rent*

aluguel ⓜ de carro aa-loo-*gel* de *kaa*-ho *car hire*

amanhã aa-ma-*nyang* *tomorrow*

— **à noite** aa *noy*-te *tomorrow evening*

— **à tarde** aa *taarr*-de *tomorrow afternoon*

— **de manhã** de ma-*nyang* *tomorrow morning*

amante ⓜ&① aa-*mang*-te *lover*

amar aa-*maarr* *love*

amarelo/amarela ⓜ/① aa-maa-*re*-lo/aa-maa-*re*-laa *yellow*

ambos/ambas ⓜ/① ang-bos/ang-baas *both*

ameixa ① aa-*may*-shaa *plum*

— **seca** *se*-kaa *prune*

amêndoa ① aa-*meng*-dwaa *almond*

amendoim ⓜ aa-meng-do-*eeng* *groundnut • peanut*

amigo/amiga ⓜ/① aa-*mee*-go/aa-*mee*-gaa *friend*

amor ⓜ aa-*morr* *love*

analgésico ⓜ aa-now-*ge*-zee-ko *painkiller*

anarquista ⓜ&① aa-naarr-*kees*-taa *anarchist*

ancião/anciã ⓜ/① ang-see-*owng*/ang-see-*ang* *ancient*

andar ⓜ ang-*daarr* *floor (storey)*

andar ang-*daarr* *walk*

— **a cavalo** aa kaa-*vaa*-lo *ride (horse)*

— **de bicicleta** de bee-see-*kle*-taa *cycle*

— **de skate** de ees-*kay*-te *skate*

anel ⓜ aa-*nel* *ring (on finger)*

anemia ① aa-ne-*mee*-aa *anaemia*

animal ⓜ&① aa-nee-*mow* *animal*

aniversário ⓜ aa-nee-verr-*saa*-ryo *birthday*

ano ⓜ *a*-no *year*

antes ang-tes *before*

antes de ontem ang-tes de *ong*-teng *day before yesterday*

antibióticos ⓜ pl ang-tee-bee-o-tee-kos *antibiotics*

anticoncepcional ⓜ ang-tee-kong-sep-syo-*now* *contraceptives*

antigo/antiga ⓜ/① ang-*tee*-go/ang-*tee*-gaa *antique*

antinuclear ang-tee-noo-kle-*aarr* *antinuclear*

anti-séptico ⓜ ang-tee-*sep*-tee-ko *antiseptic*

anúncio ⓜ aa-*noom*-see-o *advertisement*

ao lado de ow *laa*-do de *next to*

aparelho ⓜ de surdez aa-paa-*re*-lyo de soorr-*des* *hearing aid*

apartamento ⓜ aa-paarr-taa-*meng*-to *apartment • flat*

apelido ⓜ aa-pe-*lee*-do *nickname*

apêndice ⓜ aa-*peng*-dee-se *appendix (body)*

apertado/apertada ⓜ/① aa-perr-*taa*-do/aa-perr-*taa*-daa *tight*

apoio ⓜ ao partido aa-*po*-yo ow paarr-*tee*-do *supporter (politics)*

apontar aa·pong·*taarr* point

aposentado/aposentada ⓜ/ⓕ aa·po·seng·*taa*·do/aa·po·seng·*taa*·daa retired

aposta ⓕ aa·*pos*·taa bet

aprender aa·preng·*derr* learn

apresentação ⓕ aa·pre·seng·taa·*sowng* gig

aproveitar aa·pro·vay·*taarr* enjoy (oneself)

aquecimento ⓜ aa·ke·see·*meng*·to heating

aqui aa·*kee* here

ar ⓜ *aarr* air

ar condicionado ⓜ aarr kong·dee·syo·*naa*·do air-conditioning

arame ⓜ aa·*ra*·me wire

aranha ⓕ aa·*ra* nyaa spider

área ⓕ **de serviço** aa·re·aa de serr·*vee*·so laundry (room)

areia ⓕ aa·*re* yaa sand

arenque ⓜ aa·*reng*·ke herring

arma ⓕ *aarr*·maa gun

armário ⓜ aarr·*maa*·ryo cupboard • wardrobe

aromaterapia ⓕ aa·ro·maa·te·raa·*pee*·aa aromatherapy

arqueológico/arqueológica ⓜ/ⓕ aarr·ke·o·*lo*·zhee·ko/ aarr·ke·o·*lo*·zhee·kaa archaeological

arquiteto/arquiteta ⓜ/ⓕ aarr·*kee*·te·to/aarr·*kee*·te·taa architect

arquitetura ⓕ aar·kee·te·*too*·raa architecture

arroz ⓜ aa·*hos* rice

arte ⓕ *aarr*·te art

artes ⓕ pl **marciais** *aarr*·tes maar·see·*ais* martial arts

artesanato ⓜ aarr·te·zaa·*naa*·to crafts • handicrafts

artista ⓜ&ⓕ aar·*tees*·taa artist — **de rua** de hoo·aa busker

árvore ⓕ *aarr*·vo·re tree

às vezes aas *ve*·zes sometimes

asas ⓕ pl *aa*·zaas wings

Ásia ⓕ *aa*·zyaa Asia

asma ⓕ *aas*·maa asthma

aspargo ⓜ aas·*paarr*·go asparagus

aspirina ⓕ aas·pee·*ree*·naa aspirin

assassinar aa·saa·see·*naarr* murder

assassinato ⓜ aa·saa·see·*naa*·to murder

assento ⓜ aa·*seng*·to seat

assinatura ⓕ aa·see·naa·*too*·raa signature

assuntos ⓜ pl **atuais** aa·*soong*·tos aa·too·*ais* current affairs

ataque ⓜ aa·*taa*·ke strike — **de coração** de ko·ra·*sowng* heart attack

até aa·*te* until

atípico/atípica ⓜ/ⓕ aa·*tee*·pee·ko/aa·*tee*·pee·kaa unusual

atlrar aa·tee·*raarr* shoot

ativista ⓜ&ⓕ aa·tee·*vees*·taa activist

atletismo ⓜ aat·le·*tees*·mo athletics

atmosfera ⓕ aa·tee·mos·*fe*·raa atmosphere

atrás aa·*traas* behind

atrasado/atrasada ⓜ/ⓕ aa·traa·*zaa*·do/aa·traa·*zaa*·daa late

atraso ⓜ aa·*traa*·zo delay

através aa·traa·*ves* across

atum ⓜ aa·*toong* tuna

austrália ⓕ ows·*traa*·lya Australia

auto estrada ⓕ ow·to es·*traa*·daa motorway (tollway)

autônomo/autônoma ⓜ/ⓕ ow·*to*·no·mo/ow·*to*·no·maa self-employed

auto-serviço ⓜ ow·to·serr·*vee*·so self-service

aveia ⓕ aa·*ve*·aa oats

avelã ⓕ aa·ve·*lang* hazelnut

avenida ⓕ aa·ve·*nee*·daa avenue

avião ⓜ aa·vee·*owng* airplane

avisar aa·vee·*zaarr* warn

aviso ⓜ aa·*vee*·zo sign

avó ⓕ aa·*vaw* grandmother

avô ⓜ aa·*vo* grandfather

azeite ⓜ aa·*zay*·te olive oil

azeltuna ⓕ aa·zay·*too*·naa olive

azul aa·*zool* blue

B

babá ⓕ baa·*baa* babysitter

bacana baa·*ka*·naa nice

bacon ⓜ *bay*·kong bacon

B

brazilian portuguese–english

223

bagagem ① baa-*gaa*-zheng
  baggage • luggage
bagulho ⓜ baa-*goo*-lyo dope (drugs)
baía ① baa-*ee*-aa harbour
bairro ⓜ *bai*-ho suburb
baixo *bai*-sho down
baixo/baixa ⓜ/① *bai*-sho/*bai*-shaa low
bala ① *baa*-laa candy
balanço ⓜ baa-*lang*-so balance (account)
balas ① pl *baa*-laas lollies
balcão ⓜ bow-*kowng* balcony •
  counter (at bar)
balde ⓜ *bow*-de bucket
balé ⓜ ba-*le* ballet
bálsamo ⓜ **para lábios** *bow*-sa-mo
  paa-raa *laa*-byos lip balm
banana ① baa-*na*-naa banana
banco ⓜ *bang*-ko bank
banda ① **(de música)** *bang*-daa (de
  moo-zee-kaa) band (music)
band-aid ⓜ *bang*-*day*-dee Band-Aid
bandeira ① *bang*-*day*-raa flag
banheira ① ba-*nyay*-raa bath
banheiro ⓜ ba-*nyay*-ro bathroom • toilet
  — **público** ba-*nyay*-ro poo-*blee*-ko
  public toilet
bar ⓜ baarr bar • pub
barata ① baa-*raa*-taa cockroach
barato/barata ⓜ/①
  baa-*raa*-to/baa-*raa*-taa cheap
barbante ⓜ baarr-*bang*-te string
barbeiro ⓜ baar-*bay*-ro barber
barco ⓜ *baar*-ko boat
barco à motor *baar*-ko aa mo-*torr*
  motorboat
barraca ① baa-*haa*-kaa tent
barulhento/barulhenta ⓜ/①
  baa-roo-*lyeng*-to/baa-roo-*lyeng*-taa noisy
baseball ⓜ *bay*-ze-bol baseball
basquete ⓜ baas-*ke*-te basketball
batata ① baa-*taa*-taa potato
bateria ① baa-te-*ree*-aa drum
batida ① baa-*tee*-daa crash
batismo ⓜ baa-*tees*-mo baptism
batom ⓜ ba-*tong* lipstick
bêbado/bêbada ⓜ/①
  be-*baa*-do/be-*baa*-daa drunk
bebê ⓜ&① be-*be* baby

bebida ① be-*bee*-daa drink
beijar bay-*zhaarr* kiss
beijo ⓜ *bay*-zho kiss
beira mar ① *bay*-raa maarr seaside
bem beng well
bem ⓜ **social** beng so-see-*ow* welfare
beringela ① be-reeng-*zhe*-la
  aubergine • eggplant
bermuda ① berr-*moo*-daa shorts
beterraba ① be-te-*haa*-baa beetroot
bexiga ① be-*shee*-gaa bladder
bezerro/bezerra ⓜ/①
  be-*ze*-ho/be-*ze*-haa veal
bíblia ① *bee*-blyaa bible
biblioteca ① bee-blee-o-*te*-kaa library
bicho ⓜ *bee*-sho bug
bicicleta ① bee-see-*kle*-taa bicycle • bike
  — **de corrida** de ko-*hee*-daa racing bike
bife ⓜ *bee*-fe beef • steak
bilhete ⓜ bee-*lye*-te ticket
  — **de stand by** de ees-*tang*-dee bai
  standby ticket
bilheteria ① bee-lye-te-*ree*-aa ticket office
binóculos ⓜ pl bee-*no*-koo-los binoculars
biquíni ⓜ **fio dental** bee-*kee*-nee fyo
  deng-*tow* g-string
biscoito ⓜ bees-*koy*-to biscuit • cookie
  — **d'água** *daa*-gwaa cracker
bloqueado/bloqueada ⓜ/①
  blo-ke-*aa*-do/blo-ke-*aa*-daa blocked
boarding pass ⓜ *borr*-deeng paas
  boarding pass
boca ① *bo*-kaa mouth
bode ⓜ *bo*-de goat
bola ① *bo*-laa ball
  — **de golfe** de *gol*-fee golf ball
bolas ① pl **de algodão**
  bo-laas de ow-go-*downg* cotton balls
bolha ① *bo*-lyaa blister
bolo ⓜ *bo*-lo cake
  — **de casamento** de kaa-zaa-*meng*-to
  wedding cake
bolsa ① **de mão** *bol*-saa de mowng
  handbag
bolso ⓜ *bol*-so pocket
bom/boa ⓜ/① bong/*bo*-aa
  fine • good • kind
bomba ① *bong*-baa pump

Santa Clara County Library District
1-800-286-1991
www.sccld.org

Terminal: GI-SELFCK3
Date: 07/18/2022 4:04:04 PM

Member: J. S***********
Membership Number: *********57

Current Fine: $0.00
On Loan:1 (0 Overdue)
On Hold:0 (0 Available to pickup)

Today's Borrowed Items: (1)

33305213827128
Brazilian Portuguese.

Due Date: 08/08/2022

24/7 Telecirc: 1-800-471-0991
Thank you for visiting our library

bonde ⑩ *bong*-de *cable car • tram*

boneco/boneca ⑩/① bo-*ne*-ko/bo-*ne*-kaa *doll*

bonito/bonita ⑩/① bo-*nee*-to/bo-*nee*-taa *handsome • beautiful*

borboleta ① borr-bo-*le*-taa *butterfly*

borda ① *borr*-daa *border*

borracha ① bo-*haa*-shaa *gum*

bota ① bo-*taa boot (footwear)*

botânico/botânica ⑩/① bo-*ta*-nee-ko/bo-*ta*-nee-kaa *herbalist*

botas ① pl bo-*taas boots (footwear)*

botões ⑩ pl bo-*toyngs buttons*

boxe ⑩ *bo*-kee-see *boxing*

braço ⑩ *braa*-so *arm*

branco/branca ⑩/① *brang*-ko/*brang*-kaa *white*

brandy ⑩ *brang*-dee *brandy*

brilhante bree-*lyang*-te *brilliant*

brincos ⑩ pl *breeng*-kos *earrings*

brochura ① bro-*shoo*-raa *brochure*

brócolis ⑩ pl *bro*-ko-lees *broccoli*

bronquite ① brong-*kee*-te *bronchitis*

broto ⑩ **de feijão** *bro*-to de fay-*zhowng beansprout*

Budista boo-*dees*-taa *Buddhist*

buffet ⑩ boo-*fe buffet*

burro/burra ⑩/① *boo*-ho/*boo*-haa *stupid*

business class ① bee-zee-*nes* klaas *business class*

C

cabeça ① kaa-*be*-saa *head*

cabeleireiro/cabeleireira ⑩/① kaa-be-lay-*ray*-ro/kaa-be-lay-*ray*-raa *hairdresser*

cabelo ⑩ kaa-*be*-lo *hair*

caça ① *kaa*-saa *hunting*

cacau ⑩ ka-*kow cocoa*

cachoeira ① kaa-sho-*ay*-raa *waterfall*

cachorro ⑩/① kaa-*sho*-ho *dog*

cada *kaa*-daa *each*

cadeado ⑩ kaa-de-*aa*-do *padlock*

cadeira ① kaa-*day*-raa *chair*

— **de criança** de kree-*ang*-saa *child seat*

— **de rodas** de ho-daas *wheelchair*

— **para refeição** paa-raa he-*fay*-sowng *highchair*

caderno ⑩ kaa-*derr*-no *notebook*

café ⑩ kaa-*fe cafe • coffee*

— **da manhã** da ma-*nyang breakfast*

caixa ① *kai*-shaa *box • cashier*

— **automático** ow-to-*maa*-tee-ko *automatic teller machine (ATM)*

— **registradora** he-gees-traa-*do*-raa *cash register*

— **de correio** de ko-*hay*-o *mailbox*

— **de papelão** de paa-pe-*lowng carton*

calçada ① kow-*saa*-daa *footpath*

calças ① pl *kow*-saas *pants • trousers*

calculadora ① kow-koo-laa-*do*-raa *calculator*

caldo ⑩ *kow*-do *stock (food)*

calendário ⑩ kaa-leng-*daa*-ryo *calendar*

cama ① *ka*-maa *bed*

— **de casal** de kaa-*zow double bed*

camada ① **de ozônio** kaa-*maa*-daa de o-zo-nyo *ozone layer*

câmara ① *ka*-maa-raa *tube (tyre)*

— **de ar** de aarr *inner tube*

camarão ⑩ kaa-maa-*rowng prawn*

camas ① pl **gêmeas** *ka*-maas zhe-me-aas *twin beds*

câmbio ⑩ **de marcha** *kang*-byo de *maarr*-shaa *derailleur*

câmbio ⑩ **de valores** *kang*-byo de vaa-*lo*-res *currency exchange*

câmera ① *ka*-me-raa *camera*

caminhada ① kaa-mee-*nyaa*-daa *hiking*

caminhão ⑩ kaa-mee-*nyowng truck*

caminhar kaa-mee-*nyaarr hike*

caminho ⑩ kaa-*mee*-nyo *path • track • way*

camisa ① kaa-*mee*-zaa *shirt*

camiseta ① kaa-mee-*ze*-taa *singlet • T-shirt*

camisinha ① kaa-mee-*zee* nyaa *condom*

campeonatos ⑩ pl kang-pe-o-*naa*-tos *championships*

campo ① **de golfe** *kang*-po de *gol*-fee *golf course*

camundongo ⓜ ka-moong-*dong*-go
 mouse
Canadá ⓜ kaa-naa-*daa* Canada
canção ⓕ kang-*sowng* song
cancelar kang-se-*laarr* cancel
câncer ⓜ *kang*-serr cancer
cândida ⓕ *kang*-dee-daa thrush (health)
caneta ⓕ ka-*ne*-taa pen (ballpoint)
canivete ⓜ kaa-nee-*ve*-te
 penknife • pocket knife
cansado/cansada ⓜ/ⓕ
 kang-*saa*-do/kang-*saa*-daa tired
cantar kang-*taarr* sing
cantor/cantora ⓜ/ⓕ
 kang-*torr*/kang-*to*-raa singer
cão-guia ⓜ kowng-*gee*-aa guide dog
capacete ⓜ kaa-paa-*se*-te helmet
capacho ⓜ kaa-*paa*-sho mat
caravan ⓕ kaa-raa-*vang* caravan
cardápio ⓜ kaarr-*daa*-pyo menu
caril ⓜ kaa-*reel* curry
carne ⓕ *kaar*-ne meat
 — moída mo-ee-daa mince
caro/cara ⓜ/ⓕ *kaa*-ro/*kaa*-raa expensive
carpinteiro ⓜ karr-peeng-*tay*-ro carpenter
carregar kaa-he-*gaarr* carry
carro ⓜ *kaa*-ho car
carta ⓕ *kaarr*-taa letter (mail)
cartão ⓜ kaarr-*towng* credit card
 — de crédito de kre-dee-to credit card
 — postal kaarr-*towng* pos-*tow* postcard
 — telefônico kaarr-*towng*
 te-le-fo-nee-ko phonecard
cartas ⓕ pl *kaarr*-tas cards (playing)
cartaz ⓜ kaarr-*taz* poster
carteira ⓕ **de identidade** kaar-*tay*-raa de
 ee-deng-tee-*daa*-de identification card
carteira ⓕ **de motorista** kaar-*tay*-raa de
 mo-to-*rees*-taa drivers licence
cartucho ⓜ **de gás** kaarr-*too*-sho de gaas
 gas cartridge
casa ⓕ *kaa*-zaa home • house
 — de cômodos de ko-mo-dos
 boarding house
 — de ópera de o-pe-raa opera house
casaco ⓜ kaa-*zaa*-ko coat
 — de chuva de shoo-vaa raincoat

casamento ⓜ kaa-zaa-*meng*-to
 marriage • wedding
casar kaa-*zaarr* marry
casino ⓜ kaa-*see*-no casino
castanha ⓕ **de cajú** kas-*ta*-nyaa de
 kaa-*zhoo* cashew
castanha ⓕ **portuguesa** kaas-*ta*-nyaa
 porr-too-ge-*zaa* chestnut
castelo ⓜ kaas-*te*-lo castle
catapora ⓕ kaa-taa-*po*-raa chicken pox
catedral ⓕ kaa-te-*drow* cathedral
Católico/Católica ⓜ/ⓕ
 kaa-to-lee-ko/kaa-to-lee-kaa Catholic
cavalgada ⓕ kaa-vaal-*gaa*-daa
 horse riding
cavalo ⓜ kaa-*vaa*-lo horse
caverna ⓕ kaa-*verr*-naa cave
caxumba ⓕ kaa-*shoong*-baa mumps
CD ⓜ se-*de* CD
cebola ⓕ se-*bo*-laa onion
cedo se-do early
cego/cega ⓜ/ⓕ se-go/se-gaa blind
celular ⓜ se-loo-*laarr* mobile phone
cem seng hundred
cenoura ⓕ se-no-raa carrot
centavos ⓜ pl seng-*taa*-vos cent
centímetro ⓜ seng-tee-me-tro centimetre
central ⓕ **telefônica** seng-*trow*
 te-le-fo-nee-kaa telephone centre
centro ⓜ *seng*-tro centre
 — da cidade daa see-*daa*-de city centre
cerâmica ⓕ se-*ra*-mee-kaa
 ceramics • pottery
cerca ⓕ *serr*-kaa fence
cereal ⓜ se-re-*ow* cereal
cereja ⓕ se-*re*-zhaa cherry
certidão ⓕ **de nascimento**
 serr-tee-*downg* de naa-see-*meng*-to birth
 certificate
certificado ⓜ serr-tee-fee-*kaa*-do
 certificate
cerveja ⓕ serr-*ve*-zhaa beer
cesta ⓕ *ses*-taa basket
céu ⓜ se-oo sky
chá ⓜ shaa tea
chão ⓜ showng floor
chapéu ⓜ shaa-*pe*-oo hat

charmoso/charmosa ⓜ/ⓕ
    shaarr·mo·zo/shaarr·mo·zaa charming
charuto ⓜ shaa·roo·to cigar
chave ⓕ shaa·ve key
checar she·kaarr check
check in ⓜ she·keeng check-in (desk)
chefe ⓜ&ⓕ de cozinha she·fe de
    ko·zee·nyaa chef
chegada(s) ⓕ sg/pl she·gaa·daa(s) arrival
chegar she·gaarr arrive
cheio/cheia ⓜ/ⓕ shay·o/shay·aa full
cheiro ⓜ shay·ro smell
cheque ⓜ she·ke cheque (banking)
chocolate ⓜ sho·ko·laa·te chocolate
chupeta ⓕ shoo·pe·taa dummy • pacifier
chutar shoo·taarr kick (a ball)
chuva ⓕ shoo·vaa rain
chuveiro ⓜ shoo·vay·ro shower
ciclismo ⓜ see·klees·mo cycling
ciclista ⓜ&ⓕ see·klees·taa cyclist
cidadania ⓕ see·daa·da·nee·aa citizenship
cidade ⓕ see·daa·de city
cidra ⓕ see·draa cider
ciências ⓕ pl see·eng·syaas science
cientista ⓜ&ⓕ see·eng·tees·taa scientist
cigarro ⓜ see·gaa·ho cigarette
cinema ⓜ see·ne·maa cinema • movie
Cingapura seen·gaa·poo·raa Singapore
cinto ⓜ de segurança seeng·to de
    se·goo·rang·saa seatbelt
cinza seeng·zaa gray
cinzeiro ⓜ seen·zay·ro ashtray
circo ⓜ seerr·ko circus
ciroula ⓕ se·ro·laa boxer shorts
cistite ⓕ sees·tee·te cystitis
cisto ⓜ no ovário sees·to no o·vaa·ryo
    ovarian cyst
ciumento/ciumenta ⓜ/ⓕ
    see·oo·meng·to/see·oo·meng·taa jealous
classe ⓕ klaa·se class (category)
    — econômica e·ko·no·mee·kaa
    economy class
clássico/clássica ⓜ/ⓕ
    klaa·see·ko/klaa·see·kaa classical
cliente ⓜ&ⓕ klee·eng·te client
cobertor ⓜ ko·berr·torr blanket
cobra ⓕ ko·braa snake
cobreiro ⓜ ko·bray·ro shingles (illness)

cocaína ⓕ ko·kaa·ee·naa cocaine
coceira ⓕ ko·say·raa itch
côco ⓜ ko·ko coconut
código ⓜ postal ko·dee·go pos·tow
    postcode
coelho ⓜ ko·e·lyo rabbit
cofre ⓜ ko·fre safe
cogumelo ⓜ ko·goo·me·lo mushroom
coisa ⓕ koy·zaa it
cola ⓕ ko·laa glue
colar ⓜ ko·laarr necklace
colchão ⓜ kol·showng mattress
colega ⓜ&ⓕ ko·le·gaa colleague
colete salva-vidas ⓜ ko·le·te
    sow·vaa·vee·daas life jacket
colheita ⓕ de frutas ko·lyay·taa de
    froo·taas fruit picking
colher ⓕ ko·lyerr spoon
    — de chá de shaa teaspoon
cólica ⓕ menstrual ko·lee·kaa
    mengs·troo·ow period pain
colírio ⓜ ko·lee·ryo eye drops
colocar ko·lo·kaarr put
com kong with
com pressa kong pre·saa in a hurry
começar ko·me·saarr start
começo ⓜ ko·me·so start
comédia ⓕ ko·me·dyaa comedy
comemoração ⓕ ko·me·mo·raa·sowng
    celebration
comer ko·merr eat
comércio ⓜ ko·merr·syo trade
comício ⓜ ko·mee·syo rally
comida ⓕ ko·mee·daa food
    — de bebê de be·be baby food
como ko·mo how
companheiro/companheira ⓜ/ⓕ
    kong·pa·nyay·ro/kong·pa·nyay·raa
    companion
companhia ⓕ kong·paa·nhaa company
compasso ⓜ kong·paa·so compass
comprar kong·praarr buy
compreender kong·pre·eng·derr
    understand
computador ⓜ kong·poo·taa·dorr
    computer
comunhão ⓕ ko·moo·nyowng
    communion

comunicação ① ko-moo-nee-kaa-*sowng* communication • communications (profession)

comunista ⓜ&① ko-moo-nees-*taa* communist

concordar kong-korr-*daarr* agree

condicionador ⓜ kong-dee-syo-naa-*dorr* conditioner

conecção ① ko-ne-kee-*sowng* connection (phone)

confeitaria ① kong-fay-taa-*ree*-aa cake shop

confirmar kong-feerr-*maarr* confirm (a booking)

confissão ① kong-fee-*sowng* confession

confortável kong-forr-*taa*-vel comfortable

congelar kong-zhe-*laarr* freeze

conjuntivite ① kong-zhoong-tee-*vee*-te conjunctivitis

conselho ⓜ kong-se-lyo advice

consertar kong-serr-*taarr* repair

conservador/conservadora ⓜ/① kong-serr-vaa-*dorr*/kong-serr-vaa-*do*-raa conservative

constipação ① kongs-tee-paa-*sowng* constipation

construir kongs-troo-*eerr* build

construtor ⓜ kongs-troo-*tor* builder

consulado ⓜ kong-soo-*laa*-do consulate

consulta ① kong-*sool*-taa appointment

conta ① kong-*taa* bill • cheque
— **bancária** bang-*kaa*-rya bank account

contar kong-*taarr* count

contar os pontos kong-*taarr* os *pong*-tos score

contrato ⓜ kong-*traa*-to contract

controle ⓜ **remoto** kong-*tro*-le he-*mo*-to remote control

convento ⓜ kong-*veng*-to convent

conversar kong-verr-*saarr* chat

convidar kong-vee-*daar* invite

Copa do Mundo ① *ko*-paa do *moong*-do World Cup

cor ⓜ korr colour

coração ⓜ ko-ra-*sowng* heart

corajoso/corajosa ⓜ/① ko-raa-*zho*-zo/ko-raa-*zho*-zaa brave

corda ① *korr*-daa rope
— **de roupa** de ho-*paa* clothesline

cordilheira ① korr-dee-*lyay*-raa mountain range

coriza ① ko-*ree*-zaa runny nose

corpo ⓜ *korr*-po body

corredor ⓜ ko-he-*dorr* aisle

correia ① ko-*hay*-aa fanbelt

correio ⓜ ko-*hay*-o post office
— **registrado** he-zhees-*traa*-do registered mail

corrente ① ko-*heng*-te chain • current (electricity)
— **de bicicleta** de bee-see-*kle*-taa bike chain

correr ko-*herr* run

correspondência ① ko-hes-pong-*deng*-syaa mail
— **via aéreo/aérea** ⓜ/① *vee*-aa aa-e-re-o/aa-e-re-aa airmail
— **via terrestre** *vee*-aa te-*hes*-tre surface mail

correto/correta ⓜ/① ko-*he*-to/ko-*he*-taa right (correct)

corrida ① ko-*hee*-daa jogging • race • running

corrimão ⓜ ko-hee-*mowng* handlebars

corrimento ⓜ ko-hee-*meng*-to thrush (health)

corrupto/corrupta ⓜ/① koo-hoo-pee-to/koo-hoo-pee-taa corrupt

cortador ⓜ **de unhas** korr-taa-*dorr* de oo-nyaas nail clippers

cortar korr-*taarr* cut

corte ① *korr*-te court (legal)

costa ① *kos*-taa coast

costas ① *kos*-taas back (body)

costela ① kos-*te*-laa rib

costurar kos-too-*raarr* sew

cotonete ⓜ ko-to-ne-te cotton buds

couro ⓜ *ko*-ro leather
— **cabeludo** kaa-be-loo-do scalp

couve ① **flor** *ko*-ve florr cauliflower

couvert ⓜ **artístico** koo-*verr* aarr-*tees*-tee-ko cover charge

cozido/cozida ⓜ/① ko-*zee*-do/ko-*zee*-daa hard-boiled

cozinha ① ko-*zee*-nyaa *kitchen*
cozinhar ko-zee-*nyaar cook*
cozinheiro/cozinheira ⑩/①
ko-zee-*nyay*-ro/ko-zee-*nyay*-raa *cook*
crânio ⑩ *kra*-nyo *skull*
creche ① *kre*-she *creche*
creme ⑩ *kre*-me *cream*
— azedo aa-*ze*-do *sour cream*
— de barbear de baarr-be-*aarr*
shaving cream
crer krerr *trust*
crescer kres-*serr grow*
criança kree-*ang*-saa *child*
crianças pl kree-*ang*-saas *children*
cricket ⑩ *kree*-ke-tee *cricket (sport)*
Cristão/Cristã ⑩/①
krees-*towng*/krees-*tayng Christian*
cru/crua ⑩/① kroo/*kroo*-aa *raw*
cruz ① kroos *cross (religious)*
cuidado ⑩ da criança kooy-*daa*-do de
kree-*ang*-saa *childminding*
cuidar kooy-*daarr look after • watch*
culpa ① *kool*-paa *(someone's) fault*
culpado/culpada ⑩/① kool-*paa*-do/
kool-*paa*-daa *guilty*
cupom ⑩ koo-*pong* *coupon*
curativo ⑩ koo-raa-*tee*-vo *bandage*
currículum ⑩ koo-*hee*-koo-loom
resume (CV)
curto/curta ⑩/① *koor*-to/*koor*-taa *short*
cuscuz ⑩ marroquino koos-*koos*
maa-ho-*kee*-no *couscous*
custar koos-*taarr cost*
CV ① se-*ve CV*

D

dados ⑩ pl *daa*-dos *dice*
damasco ⑩ daa-*maas*-ko *apricot*
dança ① *dang*-saa *dancing*
dançar dang-*saarr dance*
dar daarr *give • deal (cards)*
data ① *daa*-taa *date (day)*
— de nascimento de naa-see-*meng*-to
date of birth
de costas de *kos*-taas *back (position)*
de segunda mão de se-*goong*-daa
mowng *second-hand*

---

decidir de-see-*deer decide*
dedo ⑩ *de*-do *finger*
— do pé do pe *toe*
defeituoso/defeituosa ⑩/①
de-fay-too-*o*-zo/de-fay-too-*o*-zaa *faulty*
deficiente de-fee-see-*eng*-te *disabled*
deitar day-*taarr lie (not stand)*
dela de-*laa her*
dele de-*le his*
delegacia ① de polícia de-le-gaa-*see*-aa
de po-*lee*-sya *police station*
deles de-*les their*
delicatessen ① de-lee-kaa-*te*-seng
delicatessen
demais de-*mais too (much)*
democracia ① de-mo-kraa-*see*-aa
democracy
demonstração ① de-mongs-traa-*sowng*
demonstration
dente(s) ⑩ *deng*-te(s) *tooth (teeth)*
dentista ⑩&① deng-*tees*-taa *dentist*
dentro *deng*-tro *inside*
— de (uma hora) de (*oo*-maa *aw*-raa)
within (an hour)
depois de-*poys after*
— de amanhã de aa-maa-*nyang*
day after tomorrow
depósito ⑩ de-po-*zee*-to *deposit*
derrame ⑩ de-*ha*-me *stroke (health)*
desabrigado/desabrigada ⑩/①
de-zaa-bree-*gaa*-do/de-zaa-bree-*gaa*-daa
homeless
descansar des-kang-*saarr rest*
descendente ⑩&① de-seng-*deng*-te
descendent
desconfortável des-kong-forr-*taa*-vel
uncomfortable
descontar (um cheque) des-kong-*taarr*
(oom she-ke) *cash (a cheque)*
desconto ⑩ des-*kong*-to *discount*
desde *des*-de *since*
desejar de-ze-*zhaarr wish*
deserto ⑩ de-*zerr*-to *desert*
desflorestamento ⑩
des-flo-res-taa-*meng*-to *deforestation*
design ⑩ *design design*
desistir de-zees-*teerr quit*

deslocamento ⓜ des·lo·kaa·*meng*·to
sprain

desodorante ⓜ de·zo·do·*rang*·te
deodorant

despertador ⓜ des·perr·taa·*dorr*
alarm clock

destino ⓜ des·*tee*·no *destination*

detalhes ⓜ pl de·*taa*·lyes *details*

deus ⓜ *de*·oos *god*

devagar de·vaa·*gaarr* *slow*

dever de·*verr* *owe*

dezembro de·*zeng*·bro *December*

dia ⓘ *dee*·aa *day*

Dia ⓜ **de Ano Novo** *dee*·aa de *a*·no *no*·vo
New Year's Day

Dia ⓜ **de Natal** *dee*·aa de naa·*tow*
Christmas Day

diabetes ⓘ dee·aa·*be*·tes *diabetes*

diafragma ⓜ dee·aa·*fraa*·gee·maa
diaphragm

diário ⓜ dee·*aa*·ryo *diary*

diarréia ⓘ dee·aa·*hay*·aa *diarrhoea*

dicionário ⓜ dee·syo·*naa*·ryo *dictionary*

dieta ⓘ dee·*e*·taa *diet*

diferença ⓘ **de horário** dee·fe·*reng*·saa
de o·*raa*·ryo *time difference*

diferente dee·fe·*reng*·te *different*

difícil dee·*fee*·seel *difficult*

Dinamarca ⓘ dee·naa·*maarr*·kaa
Denmark

dinheiro ⓜ dee·*nyay*·ro *money*

(à) direita ⓘ (aa) dee·*ray*·taa *right*
(direction)

direitista dee·ray·*tees*·taa *right-wing*

direto/direta ⓜ/ⓘ dee·*re*·to/dee·*re*·taa
direct • straight

diretor/diretora ⓜ/ⓘ dee·*re*·torr/
dee·*re*·to·raa *director*

direitos ⓜ pl **civis** dee·*ray*·tos see·*vees*
civil rights

direitos ⓜ pl **humanos** dee·*ray*·tos
oo·*ma*·nos *human rights*

dirigir dee·ree·*zheerr* *drive*

disco ⓜ *dees*·ko *disco*

discriminação ⓘ
dees·kree·mee·naa·*sowng*
discrimination

discutir dees·koo·*teerr* *argue*

disk ⓜ deesk *disk (computer)*

DIU ⓜ *dee*·oo *IUD*

diversos/diversas ⓜ/ⓘ pl
dee·*verr*·sos/dee·*verr*·saas *several*

divertido/divertida ⓜ/ⓘ
dee·verr·*tee*·do/dee·verr·*tee*·daa *fun*

divertir-se dee·verr·*teerr*·se *have fun*

dividir dee·vee·*deerr* *share (with)*

dizer dee·*zerr* *say • tell*

doce *do*·se *sweet*

documentário ⓜ do·koo·meng·*taa*·ryo
documentary

doença ⓘ do·*eng*·saa *disease*
— **venérea** ve·ne·*ryaa* *venereal disease*

doente do·*eng*·te *sick*

dólar ⓜ *do*·laarr *dollar*

dolorido/dolorida ⓜ/ⓘ
do·lo·*ree*·do/do·lo·*ree*·daa *sore*

doloroso/dolorosa ⓜ/ⓘ
do·lo·*ro*·zo/do·lo·*ro*·zaa *painful*

domingo ⓜ do·*meeng*·go *Sunday*

dona ⓘ **de casa** *do*·naa de *kaa*·zaa
homemaker

dono/dona ⓜ/ⓘ *do*·no/*do*·naa *owner*

dor ⓘ dorr *pain*
— **de cabeça** de kaa·*be*·saa *headache*
— **de dente** de *deng*·te *toothache*
— **de estômago** de es·*to*·maa·go
stomachache

dormir dorr·*meerr* *sleep*

drama ⓜ *dra*·maa *drama*

droga ⓘ *dro*·gaa *drug*

duas vezes *doo*·aas *ve*·zes *twice*

duplo/dupla ⓜ/ⓘ *doo*·plo/*doo*·plaa
double

duro/dura ⓜ/ⓘ *doo*·ro/*doo*·raa *hard*

dúzia ⓘ *doo*·zyaa *dozen*

DVD ⓜ de·ve·*de* *DVD*

E

e e *and*

eczema ⓜ e·ke·*ze*·maa *eczema*

editor/editora ⓜ/ⓘ
e·dee·*torr*/e·dee·to·raa *editor*

editoração ⓘ e·dee·to·raa·*sowng*
publishing

educação ⓘ e·doo·ka·*sowng* *education*

egoísta e·go·*ees*·taa *selfish*

ela e·laa *she*

ele e·le *he*

eleição ① e·lay·*sowng election*

eles e·les *they*

eletricidade ① e·le·tree·see·*daa*·de *electricity*

elevador ⑩ e·le·vaa·*dorr elevator* • *lift (elevator)*

em eng *in*

  — **em breve** *bre*·ve *soon*

  — **cima** *see*·maa *up*

  — **direção à** dee·re·*sowng* aa *towards*

  — **espécie** es·*pe*·sye *cash*

  — **frente** *freng*·te *ahead*

embaixada ① eng·bai·*shaa*·daa *embassy*

embaixador/embaixadora ⑩/①
eng·bai·shaa·*dorr*/eng·bai·shaa·*do*·raa *ambassador*

embreagem ① eng·bre·*aa*·zheng *clutch (car)*

embrulho ⑩ eng·*broo*·lyo *package*

emergência ① e·merr·*zheng*·syaa *emergency*

empregado/empregada ⑩/①
eng·pre·*gaa*·do/eng·pre·*gaa*·daa *employee*

empregador/empregadora ⑩/①
eng·pre·gaa·*dorr*/eng·pre·gaa·*do*·raa *employer*

emprego ⑩ eng·*pre*·go *job*

emprestar eng·pres·*taarr borrow*

empurrar eng·poo·*haarr push*

enchente ① eng·*sheng*·te *flood*

encher eng·*sherr fill*

encomenda ① eng·ko·*meng*·daa *parcel*

encontrar eng·kong·*traarr* find • *meet*

endereço ⑩ eng·de·*re*·so *address*

energia ① **nuclear** e·nerr·*zhee*·aa noo·kle·*aarr nuclear energy*

enfermeira ① eng·ferr·*may*·raa *nurse*

engenharia ① eng·zhe·nya·*ree*·aa *engineering*

engenheiro/engenheira ⑩/①
eng·zhe·*nyay*·ro/eng·zhe·*nyay*·raa *engineer*

engraçado/engraçada ⑩/①
eng·graa·*saa*·do/eng·graa·*saa*·daa *funny*

enguiçar eng·gee·*saarr break down*

enjoado/enjoada ⑩/①
en·zho·*aa*·do/en·zho·*aa*·daa *seasick*

enjôo ⑩ en·*zho*·o *morning sickness*

  — **de viagem** de vee·*aa*·zheng *travel sickness*

enorme e·*norr*·me *huge*

ensolarado/ensolarada ⑩/①
eng·so·laa·*raa*·do/eng·so·laa·*raa*·daa *sunny*

entediado/entediada ⑩/①
eng·te·dee·*aa*·do/eng·te·dee·*aa*·daa *bored*

entediante eng·te·dee·*ang*·te *boring*

enterro ⑩ eng·*te*·ho *funeral*

entrar eng·*traarr enter*

entre *eng*·tre *between*

entregar eng·tre·*gaarr deliver*

entrevista ① eeng·tre·*vees*·taa *interview*

envelope ⑩ eng·ve·*lo*·pe *envelope*

envergonhado/envergonhada ⑩/①
en·verr·go·*nyaa*·do/en·verr·go·*nyaa*·daa *embarrassed*

enviar eng·vee·*aarr send*

enxaqueca ① en·shaa·*ke*·kaa *migraine*

epilepsia ① e·pee·le·pee·*see*·aa *epilepsy*

equipamento ⑩ e·kee·paa·*meng*·to *equipment*

  — **de mergulho** de merr·*goo*·lyo *diving equipment*

errado/errada ⑩/① e·*haa*·do/e·*haa*·daa *wrong*

erro ⑩ e·ho *mistake*

ervilha ① err·*vee*·lyaa *pea*

escada ① **rolante** es·*kaa*·daa ho·*lang*·te *escalator*

escadaria ① es·kaa·daa·*ree*·aa *stairway*

escassez ① es·kaa·*ses shortage*

Escócia ① es·ko·*syaa Scotland*

escola ① es·ko·*laa school*

escolher es·ko·*lyerr choose*

escova ① es·ko·vaa *brush (hair)*

  — **de dentes** de *deng*·tes *toothbrush*

escrever es·kre·*verr write*

escritor/escritora ⓜ/ⓕ
es·kree·torr/es·kree·to·raa *writer*
escritório ⓜ es·kree·to·ryo *office*
— **de achados e perdidos** de
aa·shaa·dos e perr·dee·dos
lost-property office
— **de turismo** de too·rees·mo
tourist office
escriturário/escriturária ⓜ/ⓕ
es·kree·too·raa·ryo/es·kree·too·raa·ryaa
office worker
escultor/escultora ⓜ/ⓕ
es·kool·torr/es·kool·too·ra *sculptor*
escultura ⓕ es·kool·too·raa *sculpture*
escuro/escura ⓜ/ⓕ es·koo·ro/es·koo·raa
dark
escutar es·koo·taarr *hear • listen*
esempregado/desempregada ⓜ/ⓕ
de·zeng·pre·gaa·do/
de·zeng·pre·gaa·daa *unemployed*
esgotado/esgotada ⓜ/ⓕ es·go·taa·do/
es·go·taa·daa *booked out*
esgrima ⓕ es·gree·maa *fencing (sport)*
eski ⓜ **aquático** es·kee aa·kwaa·tee·ko
waterskiing
espaço ⓜ es·pa·so *space*
Espanha ⓕ es·pa·nyaa *Spain*
especial es·pe·see·ow *special*
especialista ⓜ&ⓕ es·pe·see·aa·lees·taa
specialist
espécies ⓕ pl **ameaçadas de extinção**
es·pe·syes aa·me·aa·saa·daas de
es·teeng·sowng *endangered species*
espelho ⓜ es·pe·lyo *mirror*
esperar es·pe·raarr *hope • wait*
espinafre ⓜ es·pee·naa·fre *spinach*
esporte ⓜ es·porr·te *sport*
esportista ⓜ&ⓕ es·porr·tees·taa
sportsperson
esposa ⓕ es·po·zaa *wife*
esquecer es·ke·serr *forget*
(à) esquerda ⓕ (aa) es·kerr·daa *left
(direction)*
esquerdista es·kerr·dees·taa *left-wing*
esqui ⓜ es·kee *skiing*
esquiar es·kee·aarr *ski*
esquina ⓕ es·kee·naa *corner*
esta ⓕ es·taa *this*

estaca ⓕ es·taa·kaa *tent peg*
estação ⓕ es·taa·sowng *season • station*
— **de trem** de treng *railway station*
estacionamento ⓜ
es·taa·syo·naa·meng·to *car park*
estacionar es·taa·syo·naarr *park (vehicle)*
estádio ⓜ es·taa·dyo *stadium*
estado ⓜ **civil** es·taa·do see·veel
marital status
estar es·taarr *be (temporary)*
— **resfriado** hes·free·aa·do *have a cold*
estátua ⓕ es·taa·twaa *statue*
este ⓜ es·te *this*
estéreo ⓜ es·te·ryo *stereo*
estilo ⓜ es·tee·lo *style*
estômago ⓜ es·to·maa·go *stomach*
estória ⓕ es·to·ryaa *story*
estrada ⓕ es·traa·daa *road*
estragado/estragada ⓜ/ⓕ
es·traa·gaa·do/es·traa·gaa·daa *off (food)*
estrangeiro/estrangeira ⓜ/ⓕ
es·trang·zhay·ro/es·trang·zhay·raa
foreign
estranho/estranha ⓜ/ⓕ es·tra·nyo/
es·tra·nyaa *strange • stranger*
estrela ⓕ es·tre·laa *star*
estrupar es·troo·paarr *rape*
estrupo ⓜ es·troo·po *rape*
estudante ⓜ&ⓕ es·too·dang·te *student*
estúdio ⓜ es·too·dyo *studio*
estufa ⓕ es·too·faa *heater*
etiqueta ⓕ **de bagagem** e·tee·ke·taa de
baa·gaa·zheng *luggage tag*
eu e·oo *I*
EUA ⓜ pl e·waa *USA*
euro ⓜ e·oo·ro *euro*
Europa ⓕ e·oo·ro·paa *Europe*
eutanásia ⓕ e·oo·taa·naa·zyaa
euthanasia
evitar e·vee·taarr *stop (prevent)*
exame ⓜ **de sangue** e·za·me de sang·ge
blood test
exame ⓜ **papa nicolau** e·za·me paa·paa
nee·ko·low *pap smear*
exaustor ⓜ e·zows·torr *exhaust (car)*
excelente e·se·leng·te *excellent*
excluído/excluída ⓜ/ⓕ es·kloo·ee·do/
es·kloo·ee·daa *excluded*

excursão ① es·koorr·*sowng* tour
— guiada ① *gee aa* daa *guided tour*
exemplo ① e·*zeng*·plo *example*
experiência ① es·pe·ree·*eng*·syaa
experience
exploração ① es·plo·raa·*sowng*
exploitation
exposição ① es·po·zee·*sowng* exhibition
expresso/expressa ⓜ/①
es·*pre*·so/es·*pre*·saa *express*
êxtase ⓜ es·*taa*·ze *ecstasy (drug)*
extensão ① es·teng·*sowng*
extension
exterior es·te·ree·*orr* abroad

F

fã ⓜ&① *fang* fan *(sport, etc)*
fábrica ① *faa*·bree·kaa *factory*
faca ① *faa*·kaa *knife*
fácil *faa*·seel *easy*
falar *faa·laarr* speak • *talk*
falta ① *fow*·taa *foul*
família ① faa·*mee*·lyaa *family*
faminto/faminta ⓜ/① faa·*meeng*·to/
faa·*meeng*·taa *hungry*
famoso/famosa ⓜ/① faa·*mo*·zo/
faa·*mo*·zaa *famous*
farinha ① faa·*ree*·nyaa *flour*
farmácia ① faar·*maa*·syaa *pharmacy*
faróis ⓜ pl faa·*roys* *headlight*
fazenda ① faa·*zeng*·daa *farm*
fazendeiro/fazendeira ⓜ/①
faa·zeng·*day*·ro/faa·zeng·*day*·raa *farmer*
fazer faa·*zerr* do • *make*
febre ① *fe*·bre *fever*
— do feno do *fe*·no *hay fever*
— glandular glang·doo·*laar*
glandular fever
fechado/fechada ⓜ/① fe·*shaa*·do/
fe·*shaa*·daa *closed* • *shut*
fechar fe·*shaarr* close
feijão ① fay·*zhowng* bean
feito/feita ⓜ/① à mão *fay*·to/*fay*·taa aa
mowng *handmade*
feliz fe·*lees* happy
férias ① pl *fe*·ryaas holiday • *vacation*
ferimento ⓜ fe·ree·*meng*·to *injury*

ferro ⓜ de passa roupas *fe*·ho de
*paa·saarr ho·*paas iron *(clothes)*
festa ① *fes*·taa party *(social gathering)*
festival ⓜ fes·tee·*vow* *festival*
fevereiro fe·ve·*ray*·ro *February*
ficar fee·*kaarr* stay
ficção ① feek·*sowng* *fiction*
fígado ⓜ *fee*·gaa·do *liver*
figo ⓜ *fee*·go fig
fila ① *fee*·laa *queue*
— de táxi de *taak*·see *taxi stand*
filé ⓜ fee·*le* *fillet*
filha ① *fee*·lyaa *daughter*
filho ⓜ *fee*·lyo son
filme ⓜ *feel*·me film *(cinema)*
— fotográfico fo·to·*graa*·fee·ko
film *(photography)*
filtrado/filtrada ⓜ/① feel·*traa*·do/
feel·*traa*·daa *filtered*
fim ⓜ *feeng* *end*
final ⓜ de semana fee·*now* de se·*ma*·naa
weekend
fino/fina ⓜ/① *fee*·no/*fee*·naa thin
fio ⓜ dental *fee*·o deng·*tow* *dental floss*
fita ① cassete *fee*·taa kaa·*se*·te *cassette*
fita ① de vídeo *fee*·taa de *vee*·de·o
video tape
flanela ① fla·*ne*·laa *flannel*
flash ⓜ luminoso flash loo·mee·*no*·zo
flashlight
flor ① *florr* *flower*
floresta ① flo·*res*·taa *forest*
floricultura ① flo·ree·kool·*too*·raa
florist (shop)
florista ⓜ&① flo·*rees*·taa *florist (person)*
fogão ⓜ fo·*gowng* *stove*
fogo ⓜ *fo*·go *fire*
folha ① *fo*·lyaa *leaf*
fora *fo*·raa *outside*
forma ① *forr*·maa *shape*
formiga ① torr·*mee*·gaa *ant*
forno ⓜ *forr*·no *oven*
forte *forr*·te *strong*
fósforos ⓜ pl fos·*fo*·ros *matches*
fotografia ① fo·to·graa·*fee*·aa *photograph* •
photography
fotógrafo/fotógrafa ⓜ/① fo·to·*graa*·fo/
fo·to·*graa*·faa *photographer*

fotômetro ⓜ fo·to·me·tro *light meter*
fraco/fraca ⓜ/ⓕ *fraa·ko/fraa·kaa* weak
frágil *fraa·zheel* fragile
fralda ⓕ *frow·daa* diaper • nappy
framboesa ⓕ frang·bo·e·zaa *raspberry*
freio ⓜ *fray·o* brake
freira ⓕ *fray·raa* nun
frequentemente fre·kweng·te·meng·te *often*
frigideira ⓕ free·zhee·day·raa *frying pan*
frio ⓜ *free·o* cold
frio/fria ⓜ/ⓕ *free·o/free·aa* cold
fritar free·*taarr* fry
frito/frita ⓜ/ⓕ *free·to/free·taa* fried
fronha ⓕ *fro·nyaa* pillowcase
fruta ⓕ *froo·taa* fruit
frutas ⓕ pl **secas** *froo·taas se·kaas* dried fruit
fumado/fumada ⓜ/ⓕ foo·*maa·*do/ foo·*maa·*daa *stoned (drugged)*
fumar foo·*maarr* smoke
furo ⓜ *foo·ro* puncture
futebol ⓜ **americano** foo·te·*bol* aa·me·ree·*ka·no* American football
futebol ⓜ foo·te·*bol* football • soccer
futuro ⓜ foo·*too·ro* future

G

galeria ⓕ **de arte** gaa·le·*ree·*aa de *aarr·*te art gallery
galinha ⓕ gaa·*lee·nyaa* chicken
ganhador/ganhadora ⓜ/ⓕ ga·nyaa·*dorr/*ga·nyaa·*do·raa* winner
ganhar ga·*nyaarr* earn • win
garçon/garçonete ⓜ/ⓕ gaarr·*song/*gaarr·so·*ne·te* waiter
garfo ⓜ *gaarr·fo* fork
garganta ⓕ gaarr·*gang·taa* throat
garrafa ⓕ gaa·*haa·faa* bottle
— d'água *daa·gwaa* water bottle
gás ⓜ gas *gas (for cooking)*
gasolina ⓕ gaa·zo·*lee·na* gas (petrol)
gastrenterite ⓕ gaas·treng·te·*ree·te* gastroenteritis
gato/gata ⓜ/ⓕ *gaa·to/gaa·taa* cat
gay gay *gay*
gaze ⓕ *gaa·ze* gauze

geada ⓕ zhe·*aa·daa* frost
geladeira ⓕ zhe·laa·*day·raa* refrigerator
geléia ⓕ zhe·*le·yaa* jam
gelo ⓜ *zhe·lo* ice
gêmeos/gêmeas ⓜ/ⓕ *zhe·me·os/zhe·me·aas* twins
gengiva ⓕ zheng·*zhee·vaa* gum (part of mouth)
gerente ⓜ&ⓕ zhe·*reng·te* manager
gilete ⓕ zhee·*le·te* razor blade
gin ⓜ zheen *gin*
ginástica ⓕ zhee·*naas·*tee·kaa *gym*
— olímpica o·*leeng·*pee·kaa *gymnastics*
ginecologista ⓜ&ⓕ zhee·ne·ko·lo·*zhees·*taa gynaecologist
gol ⓜ gol *goal (sport)*
goleiro/goleira ⓜ/ⓕ go·*lay·*ro/go·*lay·*raa goalkeeper
goma ⓕ **de mascar** go·maa de maas·*kaarr* chewing gum
gordo/gorda ⓜ/ⓕ *gorr·*do/*gorr·daa* fat
gorgeta ⓕ gorr·*zhe·taa* tip (gratuity)
gostar gos·*taarr* like
gostar (de alguém) gos·*taarr* (de ow·*geng*) care (for someone)
gostoso/gostosa ⓜ/ⓕ gos·*to·zo/*gos·*to·zaa* tasty
governo ⓜ go·*verr·no* government
grama ⓕ *graa·maa* gram • grass
grande *grang·de* large • big
grão ⓜ **de bico** growng de *bee·ko* chickpea
gratuito/gratuita graa·*too·ee·to/* graa·*too·ee·taa* free (gratis)
graus ⓜ pl grows degrees (temperature)
gravação ⓕ graa·vaa·*sowng* recording
gravar graa·*vaarr* record
grávida ⓕ *graa·*vee·daa pregnant
gripe ⓕ *gree·pe* influenza
gritar gree·*taarr* shout
grosso/grossa ⓜ/ⓕ *gro·so/gro·saa* thick
grupo ⓜ **sanguíneo** *groo·po* sang·*gwee·*ne·o blood group
guarda ⓕ **de volumes** *gwaarr·*daa vo·*loo·*mes cloakroom • luggage locker
guarda-chuva ⓜ *gwaarr·*daa·*shoo·*vaa umbrella

guardanapo ⓜ gwaar·daa·*naa*·po
nupkin • serviette

guerra ⓕ ge·haa *war*

guia ⓜ/ⓕ gee·aa *guide (person)*

guia ⓜ gee·aa *guidebook*
— **auditivo** ⓜ ow·dee·*tee*·vo
guide (audio)
— **de entretenimento** de
eng·tre·te·nee·*meng*·to
entertainment guide

guitarra ⓕ gee·*taa*·haa *guitar*

H

há (três dias) aa (tres *dee*·aas)
(three days) ago

halal aa·*low* *halal*

handebol ⓜ heng·de·bol *handball*

hematoma ⓜ e·maa·*to*·maa *bruise*

hepatite ⓕ e·paa·*tee*·te *hepatitis*

heroína ⓕ e·ro·ee·naa *heroin*

hidratante ⓜ ee·draa·*tang*·te *moisturiser*

Hindu eeng·*doo* *Hindu*

história ⓕ ees·*to*·rya *history*

histórico/histórica ⓜ/ⓕ ees·*to*·ree·kõ/
ees·*to*·ree·kaa *historical*

HIV ⓜ aa·*gaa* ee ve *HIV*

hockey ⓜ *ho*·kay *hockey*

hoje *o*·zhee *today*

hoje à noite *o*·zhee aa *noy*·te *tonight*

homem ⓜ *o*·meng *man*
— **de negócios** de ne·*go*·syos
businessman

homeopatia ⓕ o·me·o·paa·*tee*·aa
homeopathy

homosexual o·mo·sek·soo·*ow*
homosexual

hora ⓕ **marcada** *aw*·raa maarr·*kaa*·daa
date (appointment)

horário ⓜ o·*raa*·rio *timetable*

horário ⓜ **de funcionamento** o·*raa*·ryo
de foon·syo·naa·*meng*·to *opening hours*

horóscopo ⓜ o·*ros*·ko·po *horoscope*

horrível o·*hee*·vel *awful*

hospedagem ⓕ os·pe·*daa*·zheng
accommodation

hospital ⓜ os·pee·*tow* *hospital*

hospitalidade ⓕ os·pee·taa·lee·*daa*·de
hospitality

hotel ⓜ o·*tel* *hotel*

humanidades ⓕ pl oo·ma·nee·*daa*·des
humanities

I

ida ⓕ ee·daa *one-way (ticket)*

ida e volta ee·daa e *vol*·taa *return (ticket)*

idade ⓕ ee·*daa*·de *age*

identificação ⓕ ee·deng·tee·fee·kaa·*sowng*
identification

idiota ⓜ&ⓕ ee·dee·o·taa *idiot*

igreja ⓕ ee·*gre*·zhaa *church*

igualdade ⓕ ee·gwow·*daa*·de *equality*

ilha ⓕ ee·lyaa *island*

imigração ⓕ ee·mee·graa·*sowng*
immigration

importante eeng·*porr*·*tang*·te *important*

imposto ⓜ eeng·*pos*·to *tax*
— **de renda** de heng·daa *income tax*
— **sobre venda** so·bre *veng*·daa
sales tax

inchaço ⓜ eeng·*shaa*·so *swelling*

incluso/inclusa ⓜ/ⓕ eeng·*kloo*·zo/
eeng·*kloo*·zaa *included*

Índia ⓕ eeng·*dyaa* *India*

indicador ⓜ eeng·dee·kaa·*dorr* *indicator*

indigestão ⓕ eeng·dee·zhes·*towng*
indigestion

indústria ⓕ eeng·*doos*·tryaa *industry*

infecção ⓕ eeng·fek·*sowng* *Infection*
— **urinária** oo·ree·naa·ryaa
urinary Infection

inflamação ⓕ eenq·fla·maa·*sowng*
inflammation

Inglaterra ⓕ eeng·glaa·*te*·haa *England*

Inglês ⓜ eeng·*gles* English *(language)*

ingrediente ⓜ eeng·gre·*dee*·eng·te
ingredient

ingreme eeng·*gre*·me *steep*

injeção ⓕ eeng·zhe·*sowng* *injection*

injetar eeng·zhe·*taarr* *inject*

injusto/injusta ⓜ/ⓕ eeng·*zhoos*·to/
eeng·*zhoos*·taa *unfair*

inocente ee·no·*seng*·te *innocent*

inseguro/insegura ⓜ/ⓕ eeng·se·goo·ro/
eeng·se·goo·raa *unsafe*
insolação ⓕ eeng·so·laa·*sowng sunstroke*
instrutor/instrutora ⓜ/ⓕ
eengs·troo·*torr*/eengs·troo·to·raa
instructor
interessante eeng·te·re·*sang*·te *interesting*
interior ⓜ eeng·te·ree·*orr countryside*
internacional eeng·terr·naa·syo·*now*
international
Internet ⓕ eeng·terr·*ne*·te *Internet*
intérprete ⓜ&ⓕ eeng·*terr*·pre·te
interpreter
intervalo ⓜ eeng·terr·*vaa*·lo *intermission*
inverno ⓜ eeng·*verr*·no *winter*
ioga ⓕ ee·*o*·gaa *yoga*
iogurte ⓕ ee·o·*goorr*·te *yogurt*
ir eerr *go*
Irlanda ⓕ eerr·*lang*·daa *Ireland*
irmã ⓕ eer·*ma sister*
irmão ⓜ eerr·*mowng brother*
irritação ⓕ ee·hee·ta·*sowng irritation*
  — **à fralda** aa *frow*·daa *nappy rash*
  — **na pele** naa *pe*·le *rash*
isqueiro ⓜ ees·*kay*·ro *cigarette lighter*
Israel ⓜ ees·haa·*el Israel*
IT ⓜ ai·*tee* IT *(information technology)*
itinerário ⓜ ee·tee·ne·*raa*·ryo *itinerary*

J

já zhaa *already*
janeiro ⓜ zhaa·*nay*·ro *January*
janela ⓕ zhaa·*ne*·laa *window*
jantar ⓜ zhang·*taarr dinner*
Japão ⓜ zhaa·*powng Japan*
jaqueta ⓕ zhaa·*ke*·taa *jacket*
jardim ⓜ zhaarr·*deeng garden*
  — **botânico** bo·*ta*·nee·ko
  botanic garden
  — **de infância** de eeng·*fang*·syaa
  kindergarten
jardineiro/jardineira ⓜ/ⓕ
  zhaarr·dee·*nay*·ro/zhaarr·dee·*nay*·raa
  gardener
jardins ⓜ pl **públicos** zhaarr·*deengs*
  poo·blee·kos *public gardens*
jeans ⓜ zheens *jeans*

jeep ⓜ *zhee*·pe *jeep*
joalheria ⓕ zho·a·lye·*ree*·aa *jewellery*
joelho ⓜ zho·*e*·lyo *knee*
jogar zho·*gaarr play*
jogo ⓜ *zho*·go *game (sport)*
  — **de computador** de
  kong·poo·taa·*dorr computer game*
Jogos Olímpicos ⓜ pl *zho*·gos
  o·*leeng*·pee·kos *Olympic Games*
jornal ⓜ zhorr·*now newspaper*
jornaleiro ⓜ zhorr·na·*lay*·ro
  news stand · newsagency
jornalista ⓜ&ⓕ zhorr·naa·*lees*·taa
  journalist
jovem *zho*·veng *young*
Judeu/Judia ⓜ/ⓕ zhoo·*de*·oo/
  zhoo·*dee*·aa *Jewish*
juiz/juíza ⓜ/ⓕ zhoo·*ees*/zhoo·*ee*·zaa
  judge · referee
julho ⓜ *zhoo*·lyo *July*
junho ⓜ *zhoo*·nyoo *June*
junto/junta ⓜ/ⓕ zhoong·to/zhoong·taa
  together

K

ketchup ⓜ ke·tee·*shoo*·pee *ketchup*
kilograma ⓜ kee·lo·*gra*·maa *kilogram*
kilômetro ⓜ kee·*lo*·me·tro *kilometre*
kit ⓜ **de primeiros socorros** *kee*·tee de
  pree·*may*·ros so·ko·hos *first-aid kit*
kiwi ⓜ kee·*wee kiwifruit*
kosher ko·*sherr kosher*

L

lã ⓕ lang *wool*
lábios ⓜ pl *laa*·byos *lips*
lado ⓜ *laa*·do *side*
ladrão/ladra ⓜ/ⓕ *laa*·drowng/*laa*·dra
  thief
lagarto ⓜ laa·*gaarr*·to *lizard*
lago ⓜ *laa*·go *lake*
lama ⓕ *la*·maa *mud*
lâmpada ⓕ *lang*·paa·daa *light bulb*
lanche ⓜ *lang*·she *snack*
lanterna ⓕ lang·*terr*·naa *torch (flashlight)*
lápis ⓜ *laa*·pees *pencil*

laptop ⓜ le·pee·to·*pee laptop*

laranja ⓕ laa·*rang*·zhaa *orange*

laranja laa·*rang*·zhaa *orange*

largo/larga ⓜ/ⓕ *laarr*·go/*laarr*·gaa *wide*

lata ⓕ *laa*·taa *can • tin*

lavanderia ⓕ laa·vang·de·*ree*·aa *laundrette*

lavar la·*vaarr wash*

laxante ⓜ la·*shang*·te *laxative*

legal le·*gow legal*

legislação ⓕ le·zhees·la·*sowng legislation*

legumes ⓜ pl le·*goo*·mes *legumes • vegetables*

lei ⓕ lay *law*

leite ⓜ *lay*·te *milk*

   — de soja de so·zhaa *soy milk*

   — desnatado des·naa·*taa*·do *skim milk*

leito ⓜ *lay*·to *sleeping berth*

lencinho ⓜ **de papel** leng·*see*·nyo de paa·*pel tissue*

lenço ⓜ *leng*·so *scarf*

lençol ⓜ leng *sow sheet (bed)*

lenha ⓕ *le*·nyaa *firewood*

lentes ⓕ pl *leng*·tes *lenses*

   — de contato de kong·*taa*·to *contact lenses*

lentilha ⓕ leng·*tee*·lyaa *lentil*

ler *lerr read*

lésbica ⓕ *les*·bee·kaa *lesbian*

lesma ⓕ *les*·maa *snail*

leste ⓜ *les*·te *east*

levar le·*vaarr take*

leve *le*·ve *light (not heavy)*

libra ⓕ *lee*·braa *pound (money)*

licença ⓕ lee·*seng*·saa *licence*

líder ⓜ&ⓕ *lee*·derr *leader*

ligação ⓕ **à cobrar** lee·gaa·*sowng* aa ko·*braarr collect call*

ligação ⓕ **direta** lee·gaa·*sowng* dee·*re*·taa *direct-dial call*

limão ⓜ lee·*mowng lemon • lime*

limite ⓜ **de peso** lee·*mee*·te de *pe*·zo *baggage allowance*

limite ⓜ **de velocidade** lee·*mee*·te de ve·lo·see·*daa*·de *speed limit*

limonada ⓕ lee·mo·*naa*·daa *lemonade*

limpo/limpa ⓜ/ⓕ *leeng*·po/*leeng*·paa *clean*

língua ⓕ *leeng*·gwaa *language • tongue*

linguiça ⓕ **de porco** leen·*gwee*·saa de *porr*·ko *pork sausage*

linha ⓕ *lee*·nyaa *dial tone*

linha aérea ⓕ pl *lee*·nyaa aa·*e*·re·aa *airline*

liquidação ⓕ lee·kee·daa·*sowng sale*

lista ⓕ **telefônica** *lees*·taa te·le·*fo*·nee·kaa *phone book*

listado/listada ⓜ/ⓕ *lees*·taa do/ *lees*·taa·daa *itemised*

livraria ⓕ lee·vraa·*ree*·aa *book shop*

livre *lee*·vre *free (not bound)*

livro ⓜ *lee*·vro *book*

   — de frases de *fraa*·zes *phrasebook*

lixo ⓜ *lee*·sho *garbage • rubbish*

local lo·*kow local*

local ⓜ lo·*kow venue*

   — de nascimento de naas·see·*meng*·to *place of birth*

   — para acampar paa·raa aa·kang·*paarr camp site*

loção ⓕ **de bronzear** lo·*sowng* de brong·ze·*aarr tanning lotion*

loja ⓕ *lo*·zhaa *shop*

   — de aparelhos elétricos de aa·paa·*re*·lyos e·*le*·tree·kos *electrical store*

   — de bebidas de be·*bee*·daas *bottle shop • liquor store*

   — de bicicleta de bee·see·*kle*·taa *bike shop*

   — de brinquedos de breeng·*ke*·dos *toy shop*

   — de departamentos de de·paarr·taa·*meng*·tos *department store*

   — de equipamentos fotográficos de e·kee·pa·*meng*·tos fo·to·*graa*·fee·kos *camera shop*

   — de esportes de es·*porr*·tes *sports store*

   — de ferramentas de fe·haa·*meng*·taas *hardware store*

   — de música de *moo*·zee·kaa *music shop*

— de roupas de *ho*·paas *clothing store*
— de segunda mão de se·*goon*·daa mowng *second-hand shop*
— de souvenir de soo·ve·*neerr souvenir shop*
— de acampamento de aa·kam·paa·*meng*·to *camping store*
longe *long*·zhe *far*
longo/longa ⓜ/ⓕ *long*·go/*long*·gaa *long*
lotado/lotada ⓜ/ⓕ lo·*taa*·do/lo·*taa*·daa *crowded*
louça ⓕ **de barro** *lo*·saa de *baa*·ho *pot (ceramics)*
louco/louca ⓜ/ⓕ *lo*·ko/*lo*·kaa *crazy*
lua ⓕ *loo*·aa *moon*
— de mel de mel *honeymoon*
lubrificante ⓜ loo·bree·fee·*kang*·te *lubricant*
lucro ⓜ *loo*·kro *profit*
lugar ⓜ loo·*gaarr place*
luta ⓕ *loo*·ta *fight*
luvas ⓕ pl *loo*·vaas *gloves*
luxo ⓜ *loo*·sho *luxury*
luz ⓕ looz *light*

M

maçã ⓕ maa·*sang apple*
macarrão ⓜ **chinês** maa·kaa·*howng* shee·*nes noodles*
machismo ⓜ maa·*shees*·mo *sexism*
machucar maa·shoo·*kaarr hurt*
maconha ⓕ maa·*ko*·nyaa *marijuana*
madeira ⓕ maa·*day*·raa *wood*
madrugada ⓕ maa·droo·*gaa*·daa *dawn*
mãe ⓕ mayng *mum*
maio *maa*·yo *May*
maionese ⓕ maa·yo·*ne*·ze *mayonnaise*
mais mais *more*
— perto/perta ⓜ/ⓕ *perr*·to/*perr*·taa *nearest*
mal mal *ill*
mal passado/passada ⓜ/ⓕ mow paa·*saa*·do/paa·*saa*·daa *rare (food)*
mala ⓕ *maa*·laa *suitcase*
mamãe ⓕ ma·*mayng mother*
mamograma ⓜ maa·mo·*gra*·maa *mammogram*

mandíbula ⓕ mang·*dee*·boo·laa *jaw*
manga ⓕ *mang*·gaa *mango*
manhã ⓕ ma·*nyang morning*
manteiga ⓕ man·*tay*·gaa *butter*
mantimentos ⓜ pl mang·tee·*meng*·tos *groceries*
mão ⓕ mowng *hand*
mapa ⓕ *maa*·paa *map*
— da estrada daa es·*traa*·daa *road map*
maquiagem ⓕ maa·kee·*aa*·zheng *make-up*
máquina ⓕ *maa*·kee·naa *machine*
— de lavar roupa de laa·*vaarr* ho·paa *washing machine*
— de vender passagem de *veng*·derr paa·*saa*·zheng *ticket machine*
mar ⓜ maarr *sea*
maracujá ⓜ maa·raa·koo·*zhaa passionfruit*
maravilhoso/maravilhosa ⓜ/ⓕ maa·raa·vee·*lyo*·zo/maa·raa·vee·*lyo*·zaa *wonderful*
marca ⓜ **passo** *mar*·kaa *pa*·so *pacemaker*
março *maar*·so *March*
maré ⓕ maa·*re tide*
margarina ⓕ maarr·gaa·*ree*·naa *margarine*
marido ⓜ maa·*ree*·do *husband*
marmelada ⓕ maarr·me·*laa*·daa *marmalade*
marron maa·*hong brown*
martelo ⓜ maarr·*te*·lo *hammer*
mas maas *but*
massa ⓕ *maa*·saa *pastry*
massagem ⓕ maa·*saa*·zheng *massage*
massagista ⓜ&ⓕ maa·saa·*zhees*·taa *masseur*
massas ⓕ pl *maa*·saas *pasta*
matar maa·*taarr kill*
mecânico/mecânica ⓜ/ⓕ me·*ka*·nee·ko/ me·*ka*·nee·kaa *mechanic*
medicina ⓕ me·dee·*see*·naa *medicine*
médico/médica ⓜ/ⓕ *me*·dee·ko/ *me*·dee·kaa *doctor*
meditação ⓕ me·dee·taa·*sowng meditation*
meia ⓕ *may*·aa *sock*
— calça *kow*·saa *pantyhose*

meia-noite ① *may·aa·noy·te* midnight
meio ⓜ **ambiente** *may·o ang·bee·eng·te* environment
meio expediente *may·o es·pe·dee·eng·te* part-time
meio-dia ⓜ *may·o dee·aa* noon
mel ⓜ *mel* honey
melancia ① *me·lang·see·aa* watermelon
melão ⓜ *me·lowng* cantaloupe • melon • rockmelon
melhor *me·lyorr* best • better
membro ⓜ&① *meng·bro* member
menina ① *me·nee·naa* girl
menino ⓜ *me·nee·no* boy
menos *me·nos* less
mensagem ① *meng·sa·zheng* message
menstruação ⓤ *mengs·troo·aa·sowng* menstruation
mentiroso/mentirosa ⓜ/ⓤ *meng·tee·ro·zo/meng·tee·ro·zaa* liar
mercado ⓜ *merr·kaa·do* market
mercearia ① *merr·se·aa·ree·aa* convenience store
mergulho ⓜ *merr·goo·lyo* diving
mês ⓜ *mes* month
mesa ① *me·zaa* table
mesmo/mesma ⓜ/① *mes·mo/mes·maa* same
metade ① *me·taa·de* half
metal ⓜ *me·tow* metal
metro ⓜ *me·tro* metre
meu/minha ⓜ/① *me·oo/mee·nyaa* my
mexido/mexida ⓜ/① *me·shee·do/me·shee·daa* scrambled
mexilhão ⓜ *me·shee·lyowng* mussel
microondas ⓜ *mee·kro·ong·daas* microwave
mídia ① *mee·dyaa* media
milhão ⓜ *mee·lowng* million
milho ⓜ *mee·lyo* corn
milímetro ⓜ *mee·lee·me·tro* millimetre
militar *mee·lee·taarr* military
mimado/mimada ⓜ/① *mee·maa·do/mee·maa·daa* spoiled
minhocas ① pl *mee·nyo·kaas* worms
mínimo/mínima ⓜ/① *mee·nee·mo/mee·nee·maa* tiny
minuto ⓜ *mee·noo·to* minute

mirante ⓜ *mee·rang·te* lookout
missa ① *mee·saa* mass (Catholic)
misturar *mees·too·raar* mix
mochila ① *mo·shee·la* backpack
modem ⓜ *mo·deng* modem
moedas ① pl *mo·e·daas* coins
molas ① pl *mo·laas* spring (coil)
mole *mo·le* soft-boiled
molestamento ⓜ *mo·les·taa·meng·to* harassment
molhado/molhada ⓜ/① *mo·lyaa·do/mo·lyaa·daa* wet
molho ⓜ *mo·lyo* sauce
   — de pimenta *de pee·meng·taa* chilli sauce
   — de soja *de so·zhaa* soy sauce
   — de tomate *de to·maa·te* tomato sauce
monastério ⓜ *mo·naas·te·ryo* monastery
monge ⓜ *mong·zhe* monk
montanha ① *mong·ta·nyaa* mountain
montanhismo ⓜ *mong·ta·nyees·mo* mountaineering
monumento ⓜ *mo·noo·meng·to* monument
morango ⓜ *mo·rang·go* strawberry
morar *mo·raarr* live (somewhere)
mordida ① *morr·dee·daa* bite (dog/insect)
morno/morna ⓜ/① *morr·no/morr·naa* warm
morrer *mo·herr* die
morro ⓜ *mo·ho* hill
morto/morta ⓜ/① *morr·to/morr·taa* dead
mosquiteiro ⓜ *mos·kee·tay·ro* mosquito net
mosquito ⓜ *mos·kee·to* mosquito
mosteiro ⓜ *mos·tay·ro* mosque
mostrador ⓜ **de velocidade** *mos·traa·dorr de ve·lo·see·daa·de* speedometer
mostrar *mos·traarr* show
motocicleta ① *mo·to·see·kle·taa* motorbike
motor ⓜ *mo·torr* engine
mountain bike ⓜ *maa·oong·tayng bai·kee* mountain bike
móveis ⓜ pl *mo·vays* furniture

Muçulmano/Muçulmana ⓜ/ⓕ
moo·sool·*ma*·no/moo·sool·*ma*·naa
Muslim
mudo/muda ⓜ/ⓕ moo·do/*moo*·daa
mute
muesli ⓜ *moos*·lee *muesli*
muito/muita ⓜ/ⓕ *mweeng*·to/
mweeng·taa *(a) lot · very*
mulher ⓕ moo·*lyerr woman*
— **de negócios** de ne·*go*·syos
business person
multa ⓕ *mool*·taa *fine (payment)*
mundo ⓜ *moong*·do *world*
músculo ⓜ *moos*·koo·lo *muscle*
museu ⓜ mo·se·oo *museum*
música ⓕ *moo*·zee·kaa *music*
músico/música ⓜ/ⓕ *moo*·zee·ko/
moo·zee·kaa *musician*
mustarda ⓕ moos·*taar*·daa *mustard*

N

na frente de naa *freng*·te de *in front of*
nacionalidade ⓕ naa·syo·naa·lee·*daa*·de
nationality
nada naa·daa *nothing*
nadar naa·*daarr swim*
namorada ⓕ naa·mo·*raa*·daa *girlfriend*
namorado ⓜ na·mo·*raa*·do *boyfriend*
namorar naa·mo·*raarr date (a person)*
não nowng *no · not*
não-fumante nowng·foo·*mang*·te
non-smoking
nariz ⓕ naa·*rees nose*
nascer ⓜ **do sol** naa·*serr* do sol *sunrise*
natureza ⓕ naa·too·*re*·zaa *nature*
naturopatia ⓕ naa·too·ro·paa·*tee*·a
naturopathy
náusea ⓕ *now*·se·aa *nausea*
navio ⓜ naa·*vee*·o *ship*
nebuloso/nebulosa ⓜ/ⓕ
ne·boo·*lo*·zo/ne·boo·*lo*·zaa *foggy*
necessário/necessária ⓜ/ⓕ
ne·se·*sa*·ryo/ne·se·*sa*·ryaa *necessary*
negativo/negativa ⓜ/ⓕ ne·gaa·*tee*·vo/
ne·gaa·*tee*·vaa *negative*
negócios ⓜ pl ne·*go*·syos *business*
nenhum ne·*yoom none*

nenhum deles ne·*yoom de*·les *neither*
neto/neta ⓜ/ⓕ *ne*·to/ne·taa *grandchild*
neve ⓕ *ne*·ve *snow*
nódulo ⓜ no·doo·lo *lump*
noite ⓕ *noy*·te *evening · night*
Noite ⓕ **de Natal** *noy*·te de na·*tow*
Christmas Eve
noiva ⓕ *noy*·vaa *fiancee*
noivado ⓜ noy·*vaa*·do *engagement*
noivo ⓜ *noy*·vo *fiance*
nome ⓜ *no*·me *name*
— **Cristão** ⓜ krees·*towng*
Christian name
norte ⓜ *norr*·te *north*
Noruega ⓕ no·roo·*e*·gaa *Norway*
nós nos *we*
nosso/nossa ⓜ/ⓕ *no*·so/no·saa *our*
nota ⓕ *no*·taa *banknote*
notícias ⓕ pl no·*tee*·syaas *news*
Nova Zelândia ⓕ *no*·vaa ze·*lang*·dyaa
New Zealand
novamente no·vaa·*meng*·te *again*
novela ⓕ no·*ve*·laa *soap opera*
novembro no·*veng*·bro *November*
novidades ⓕ pl no·vee·*daa*·des *news*
novo/nova ⓜ/ⓕ *no*·vo/no·vaa *new*
noz ⓕ noz *nut*
nublado/nublada ⓜ/ⓕ
noo·*blaa*·do/noo·*blaa*·daa *cloudy*
número ⓜ *noo*·me·ro *number*
— **da placa** daa *plaa*·kaa *license plate*
number · numberplate
— **do passaporte** do paa·saa·*porr*·te
passport number
— **do quarto** do *kwaarr*·to
room number
nunca *noong*·kaa *never*
nuvem ⓕ noo·*veng cloud*

O

objetivo ⓜ o·bee·zhe·*tee*·vo *goal*
oceano ⓜ o·se·*a*·no *ocean*
óculos ⓜ pl *o*·koo·los *glasses (spectacles)*
— **de natação** de naa·taa·*sowng*
goggles (swimming)
— **de ski** de es·*kee* *goggles (skiing)*
— **de sol** de sol *sunglasses*

ocupado/ocupada ⓜ/ⓕ oo·koo·*paa*·do/
o·koo·*paa*·daa busy

oeste ⓜ o·*es*·te west

oficina ⓕ o·fee·*see*·naa garage • workshop

óleo ⓜ *o*·lyo oil

olho ⓜ *o*·lyo eye

ombro ⓜ pl *ong*·bro shoulder

onda ⓕ *ong*·daa wave

onde *ong*·de where

ônibus ⓜ o·nee·boos bus

ontem *ong*·teng yesterday

ópera ⓕ *o*·pe·raa opera

operação ⓕ o·pe·raa·*sowng* operation

operador/operadora ⓜ/ⓕ o·pe·raa·*dorr*/
o·pe·raa·do·raa operator

operário/operária ⓜ/ⓕ o·pe·*raa*·ryo/
o·pe·*raa*·ryaa factory worker

opinião ⓕ o·pee·nee·*owng* opinion

oportunidade ⓕ o·porr·too·nee·*daa*·de
chance

oportunidades ⓕ pl **iguais**
o·porr·too nee·*daa*·des ee·*gwaa*·ees
equal opportunity

oposto/oposta ⓜ/ⓕ o·*pos*·to/o·*pos*·taa
opposite

optometrista ⓜ&ⓕ o·pee·to·me·*trees*·taa
optometrist

ordinário/ordinária ⓜ/ⓕ
orr·dee·*naa*·ryo/orr·dee·*naa*·ryaa
ordinary

orelha ⓕ o·*re*·lyaa ear

orgasmo ⓜ orr·*gaas*·mo orgasm

original o·ree·zhee·*now* original

orquestra ⓕ orr·*kes*·traa orchestra

os EUA ⓜ pl os e·*waa* the USA

osso ⓜ *o*·so bone

ostra ⓕ *os*·traa oyster

ótimo/ótima ⓜ/ⓕ o·*tee*·mo/o·*tee*·maa
great

ou o or

ouro ⓜ *o*·ro gold

outono ⓜ o·*to*·no autumn • fall

outro/outra ⓜ/ⓕ *o*·tro/*o*·traa other

outubro o·*too*·bro October

ovário ⓜ o·*vaa*·ryo ovary

ovelha ⓕ o·*ve*·lyaa lamb • sheep

ovo ⓜ *o*·vo egg

oxigênio ⓜ ok·see·*zhe*·nyo oxygen

P

pacote ⓜ pa·*ko*·te packet

padaria ⓕ paa·daa·*ree*·aa bakery

padre ⓜ *paa*·dre priest

pães ⓜ pl *payngs* bread rolls

pagamento ⓜ paa·gaa·*meng*·to payment

pagar paa·*gaarr* pay

página ⓕ *paa*·zhee·naa page

pai ⓜ pai father

painel ⓜ **de marcação** pai·*nel* de
maarr·kaa·*sowng* scoreboard

país ⓜ paa·*ees* country

pais ⓜ pl paa·*ees* parents

Países ⓜ pl **Baixos** paa·*ee*·zes bai·shos
Netherlands

palácio ⓜ paa·*laa*·syo palace

palavra ⓕ paa·*laa*·vraa word

palito ⓜ **de dentes** paa·*lee*·to de *deng*·tes
toothpick

panela ⓕ paa·*ne*·laa pan

pano ⓜ **de limpeza** *pa*·no de
leeng·*pe*·zaa wash cloth (flannel)

pão ⓜ *powng* bread
— **integral** eeng·te·*grow*
wholemeal bread

papel ⓜ paa·*pel* paper
— **higiênico** ee·zhee·e·nee·ko
toilet paper

papelada ⓕ paa·pe·*laa*·daa paperwork

papelaria ⓕ paa·pe·laa·*ree*·aa stationery
shop

Paquistão ⓜ paa·kees·*towng* Pakistan

par ⓜ *paarr* pair (couple)

para paa·*raa* for
— **baixo** bai·sho downhill
— **cima** see·maa uphill
— **sempre** seng·pre forever

parabrisa ⓜ paa·raa·*bree*·zaa windscreen

parada ⓕ **cardíaca** paa·*raa*·daa
kaarr·dee·aa·kaa cardiac arrest

parapeito ⓜ paa·raa·*pay*·to ledge

paraplégico/paraplégica ⓜ/ⓕ
paa·raa·*ple*·zhee·ko/paa·raa·*ple*·zhee·kaa
paraplegic

parar paa·*raarr* stop (cease)

parecido/parecida ⓜ/ⓕ
paa·re·*see*·do/paa·re·*see*·daa *similar*

parede ⓕ paa·*re*·de *wall (outer)*

parlamento ⓜ paarr·laa·*meng*·to
parliament

parque ⓜ *paarr*·ke *park*

— **nacional** naa·syo·*now* *national park*

parte ⓕ *paarr*·te *part (component)*

partida ⓕ paarr·*tee*·daa *departure* • *match (sport)*

partido ⓜ paarr·*tee*·do *party (politics)*

partir paarr·*teerr* *depart (leave)*

Páscoa ⓕ *paas*·kwaa *Easter*

passada (semana) ⓕ paa·*saa*·daa
(se·*ma*·naa) *last (week)*

passado ⓜ paa·*saa*·do *past*

passageiro/passageira ⓜ/ⓕ
paa·saa·*zhay*·ro/paa·saa·*zhay*·raa
passenger

passaporte ⓜ paa·saa·*porr*·te *passport*

passar paa·*saarr* *pass*

pássaro ⓜ *paa*·saa·ro *bird*

passas ⓕ pl *paa*·saas *raisin* • *sultana*

passo ⓜ *paa*·so *step*

pasta ⓕ *pas*·taa *briefcase*

— **de dentes** de *deng*·tes *toothpaste*

patinação ⓕ paa·tee·naa·*sowng*
rollerblading

pato/pata ⓜ/ⓕ *paa*·to/*paa*·taa *duck*

paz ⓕ pas *peace*

pé ⓜ pe *foot*

peça ⓕ pe·*saa* *play (theatre)*

pedaço ⓜ pe·*da*·so *piece*

pedal ⓜ pe·*dow* *pedal*

pedestre ⓜ pe·*des*·tre *pedestrian*

pedido ⓜ pe·*dee*·do *order (command)*

pedinte ⓜ&ⓕ pe·*deeng*·te *beggar*

pedir pe·*deerr* *ask (for something)* • *order*

pedra ⓕ *pe*·draa *rock* • *stone*

pegar pe·*gaarr* *get*

— **carona** kaa·ro·naa *hitchhike*

peito ⓜ *pay*·to *chest* • *breast*

peixaria ⓕ pay·sha·*ree*·aa *fish shop*

peixe ⓜ *pay*·she *fish*

peixeiro/peixeira ⓜ/ⓕ pay·*shay*·ro/
pay·*shay*·raa *fish monger*

pele ⓕ *pe*·le *skin*

pensão ⓕ peng·*sowng* *boarding house*

penhasco ⓜ pe·*nyaas*·ko *cliff*

pênis ⓜ *pe*·nees *penis*

pensar peng·*saarr* *think*

pensionista ⓜ&ⓕ peng·syo·*nees*·taa
pensioner

pente ⓜ *peng*·te *comb*

pepino ⓜ pe·*pee*·no *cucumber*

pequeno/pequena ⓜ/ⓕ pe·*ke*·no/
pe·*ke*·naa *little* • *small*

pêra ⓕ *pe*·raa *pear*

perder perr·*derr* *lose*

perdido/perdida ⓜ/ⓕ
perr·*dee*·do/perr·*dee*·daa *lost*

perdoar perr·do·*aarr* *forgive*

perfeito/perfeita ⓜ/ⓕ
perr·*fay*·to/perr·*fay*·taa *perfect*

performance ⓕ perr·forr·*mang*·se
performance

perfume ⓜ perr·*foo*·me *perfume*

pergunta ⓕ perr·*goong*·taa *question*

perguntar perr·goong·*taarr*
ask (a question)

perigoso/perigosa ⓜ/ⓕ pe·ree·*go*·zo/
pe·ree·*go*·zaa *dangerous*

permissão ⓕ perr·mee·*sowng* *permission* • *permit*

— **para trabalhar** paa·raa
traa·baa·*lyaarr* *work permit*

perna ⓕ *perr*·naa *leg*

perto *perr*·to *near*

perú ⓜ pe·*roo* *turkey*

pesado/pesada ⓜ/ⓕ
pe·*zaa*·do/pe·*zaa*·daa *heavy*

pesar pe·*zaarr* *weigh*

pesca ⓕ *pes*·kaa *fishing*

peso ⓜ *pe*·zo *weight*

pesos ⓜ pl *pe*·zos *weights*

pêssego ⓜ *pe*·se·go *peach*

pessoa ⓕ pe·*so*·aa *person*

pessoas ⓕ pl pe·*so*·aas *people*

petição ⓕ pe·tee·*sowng* *petition*

petróleo ⓜ pe·*tro*·lyo *petrol*

pharmacista ⓜ&ⓕ faarr·maa·*sees*·taa
chemist

piada ⓕ pee·*aa*·daa *joke*

picareta ⓕ pee·kaa·*re*·taa *pickaxe*

pico ⓜ *pee*·ko *peak (mountain)*

pifar pee·*faarr* *break down*

pikles ⓜ pl *pee-*kles *pickles*
pilha ① *pee-*lyaa *battery*
pílula ① *pee-*loo-laa *pill • Pill (the)*
pimenta ① *pee-*meng-taa *chilli • pepper*
pimentão ⓜ *pee-*meng-*towng capsicum •
pepper (bell)*
pinça ① *peeng-*saa *tweezers*
pintor/pintora ⓜ/① *peeng-torr*/
*peeng-*to-raa *painter*
pintura ① *peeng-*too-raa *painting*
piolho ⓜ *pee-*o-lyo *lice*
piquenique ⓜ *pee-*ke-*nee-*ke *picnic*
piscina ① *pee-see-*naa *swimming pool*
pista ① *pees-*taa *track (sport)*
— **de corrida** de ko-*hee-*daa *racetrack*
pistáchio ⓜ *pees-*taa-shyo *pistachio*
planalto ⓜ *pla-now-*to *plateau*
planeta ⓜ *pla-ne-*taa *planet*
plano/plana ⓜ/① *pla-*no/*pla-*naa *flat*
planta ① *plang-*taa *plant*
plástico/plástica ⓜ/①
*plas-*tee-ko/*plas-*tee-kaa *plastic*
plataforma ① *plaa-*taa-*forr-*maa *platform*
pneu ⓜ *pee-*ne-oo *tyre*
pó ⓜ *po powder*
pobre *po-*bre *poor*
pobreza ① po-*bre-*zaa *poverty*
poché po-*she poached*
pochete ① po-*she-*te *bumbag*
poder po-*derr can*
(be able/have permission)
poder ⓜ po-*derr power*
poesia ① po-e-*zee-*aa *poetry*
pólen ⓜ *po-*leng *pollen*
polícia ① po *lee-*syaa *police*
política ① po-*lee-*tee-kaa *politics*
político/política ⓜ/① po-*lee-*tee-ko/
po-*lee-*tee-kaa *politician*
poluição ① po-*loo-*ee-*sowng pollution*
pomelo ⓜ po-*me-*lo *grapefruit*
ponte ① *pong-*te *bridge*
ponto ⓜ *pong-*to *point*
— **de controle** de kong-*tro-*le
checkpoint (border)
— **de ônibus** de o-*nee-*boos *bus stop*
popular po-poo-*laarr popular*

por porr *per*
— **perto** *perr-*to *nearby*
— **que** ke *because • why*
pôr do sol porr do sol *sunset*
porcentagem ① porr-seng-*taa-*zheng
per cent
porco/porca ⓜ/① *porr-*ko/*porr-*kaa
pig • pork
porta ① *porr-*taa *door*
portão ⓜ porr-*towng gate (airport, etc)*
— **de partida** de paarr-*tee-*daa
departure gate
porto ⓜ *porr-*to *port (sea)*
pós barba ⓜ pos *baarr-*baa *aftershave*
positivo/positiva ⓜ/① po-zee-*tee-*vo/
po-zee-*tee-*vaa *positive*
possível po-*see-*vel *possible*
postagem ① pos-*taa-*zheng *postage*
posto de gasolina *pos-*to de
gaa-zo-*lee-*naa *service station*
pouco/pouca ⓜ/① *po-*ko/*po-*kaa
little (not much)
praça ① *praa-*saa *square (town)*
praia ⓜ *prai-*aa *beach*
prancha de surfe *prang-*shaa de
*soorr-*fee *surfboard*
prata ① *praa-*taa *silver*
prateleira ① praa-te-*lay-*raa *shelf*
prato ⓜ *praa-*to *plate*
precisar pre-see-*zaarr need*
preço ⓜ *pre-*so *price*
— **da entrada** daa eng-*traa-*daa
admission price
prédio ⓜ *pre-*dyo *building*
prefeito/prefeita ⓜ/①
pre-*fay-*to/pre-*fay-*taa *mayor*
preferir pre-fe-*reerr prefer*
preguiçoso/preguiçosa ⓜ/①
pre-gee-*so-*zo/pre-gee-so-zaa *lazy*
prender preng-*derr arrest*
preocupado/preocupada ⓜ/①
pre-o-koo-*paa-*do/pre-o-koo-*paa-*daa
worried
preparar pre-paa-*raarr prepare*
presente ⓜ pre-*zeng-*te
gift • present (time)
— **de casamento** de kaa-zaa-*meng-*to
wedding present

presidente ⓜ&ⓕ pre-zee-*deng*-te
president

pressão ⓕ pre-*sowng* pressure
— **arterial** aar-te-ree-ow *blood pressure*

presunto ⓜ pre-*zoong*-to *ham*

preto e branco *pre*-to e *brang*-ko
B&W (film)

preto/preta ⓜ/ⓕ *pre*-to/*pre*-taa *black*

primavera ⓕ pree-maa-*ve*-raa
spring (season)

primeira classe ⓕ pree-*may*-raa *klaa*-se
first class

primeira ministra ⓕ pree-*may*-raa
mee-*nees*-traa *prime minister*

primeiro/primeira ⓜ/ⓕ
pree-*may*-ro/pree-*may*-raa *first*

primeiro ministro ⓜ pree-*may*-ro
mee-*nees*-tro *prime minister*

principal ⓜ&ⓕ preeng-see-*pow* *main*

prisão ⓕ pree-*zowng* *jail • prison*

prisioneiro/prisioneira ⓜ/ⓕ
pree-zyo-*nay*-ro/pree-zyo-*nay*-raa
prisoner

privado/privada ⓜ/ⓕ
pree-*vaa*-do/pree-*vaa*-daa *private*

problema ⓜ **de coração** pro-*ble*-maa de
ko-raa-*sowng* *heart condition*

produzir pro-doo-*zeerr* *produce*

professor/professora ⓜ/ⓕ pro-fe-*sorr*/
pro-fe-*so*-raa *lecturer • teacher*

profundo/profunda ⓜ/ⓕ
pro-*foong*-do/pro-*foong*-daa *deep*

programa ⓜ pro-*gra*-maa *program*

projetor ⓜ pro-zhe-*torr* *projector*

pronto/pronta ⓜ/ⓕ
prong-to/*prong*-taa *ready*

proprietário/proprietária ⓜ/ⓕ
pro-pree-e-*taa*-ryo/pro-pree-e-*taa*-ryaa
landlord/landlady

proteção ⓕ **contra sol** pro-te-*sowng*
kong-traa sol *sunblock*

proteger pro-te-*zherr* *protect*

protegido/protegida ⓕ pro-te-*zhee*-do/
pro-te-*zhee*-daa *protected*

protestar pro-tes-*taarr* *protest*

protesto ⓜ pro-*tes*-to *protest*

provador ⓜ pro-vaa-*dorr* *changing room*

provisões ⓕ pl pro-vee-*zoyngs* *provisions*

próximo/próxima ⓜ/ⓕ
pro-see-mo/*pro*-se-maa *next*

pular poo-*laarr* *jump*

pulga ⓕ *pool*-gaa *flea*

pulmão ⓜ pool-*mowng* *lung*

punho ⓜ *poo*-nyo *wrist*

puro/pura ⓜ/ⓕ *poo*-ro/*poo*-raa *pure*

puxar poo-*shaarr* *pull*

Q

quadra ⓕ *kwaa*-draa *court (tennis)*
— **de tênis** de *te*-nees *tennis court*

quadraplégico/quadraplégica ⓜ/ⓕ
kwaa-draa-*ple*-zhe-ko/
kwaa-draa-*ple*-zhe-kaa *quadriplegic*

qualidade ⓕ kwaa-lee-*daa*-de *quality*

qualificações ⓕ pl
kwaa-lee-fee-kaa-*soyngs* *qualifications*

qualquer kwow-*kerr* *any*

quando *kwang*-do *when*

quanto *kwang*-to *how much*

quarentena ⓕ kwaa-reng-*te*-naa
quarantine

quarta-feira ⓕ *kwaarr*-taa-*fay*-raa
Wednesday

quarto ⓜ *kwaarr*-to *bedroom • room •
quarter*
— **de casa** de kaa-*zow* *double room*

quase *kwaa*-ze *almost*

que ke *what*

quebrado/quebrada ⓜ/ⓕ
ke-*braa*-do/ke-*braa*-daa *broken*

quebrador ⓜ **de gelo**
ke-braa-*dorr* de *zhe*-lo *ice axe*

quebrar ke-*braarr* *break*

queda ⓕ *ke*-daa *fall (down)*

queijaria ⓕ kay-zhaa-*ree*-aa *cheese shop*

queijo ⓜ *kay*-zho *cheese*

queimado/queimada ⓜ/ⓕ
kay-*maa*-do/kay-*maa*-daa *burnt*
— **de sol** de sol *sunburnt*

queimadura ⓕ kay-maa-*doo*-raa *burn*

quem keng *who*

quente *keng*-te *hot*

querer ke-*rerr* *want*

questão ⓕ kes-*towng* *question*

quieto/quieta ⑩/① kee·e·to/kee·e·taa
quiet

quinta-feira ① kween·ta·*fay*·raa *Thursday*

quinzena ① keeng·ze·naa *fortnight*

quiroprático/quiroprática ⑩/①
kee·ro·*praa*·tee·ko/kee·ro·*praa*·tee·kaa
chiropractor

R

rabanete ⑩ haa·baa·*ne*·te *radish*

rabo ⑩ *haa*·bo *tail*

racismo ⑩ haa·*sees*·mo *racism*

radiador ⑩ haa·dee·aa·*dorr* *radiator*

rainha ① haa·*ee*·nyaa *queen*

rápido/rápida ⑩/①
haa·pee·do/*haa*·pee·daa *fast*

raquete ① haa·*ke*·te *racquet*

raro/rara ⑩/① *haa*·ro/*haa*·raa
rare (uncommon)

raspador ⑩ haas·paa·*dorr* *razor*

ratazana ① haa·taa·*za*·naa *rat*

rato ⑩ *haa*·to *rat*

razão ① haa·*zowng* *reason*

realista he·aa·*lees*·taa *realistic*

recarregador ⑩ **de bateria**
he·kaa·he·gaa·*dorr* de baa·te·*ree*·aa
jumper leads

receber he·se·*berr* *welcome*

recentemente he·seng·te·*meng*·te
recently

recibo ⑩ he·*see*·bo *receipt*

reciclar he·see·*klaar* *recycle*

reciclável he·see·*klaa*·vel *recyclable*

reclamar he·klaa·*marr* *complain*

recomendar he·ko·meng·*daarr*
recommend

recursos ⑩ pl **humanos** he·*koor*·sos
oo·*ma*·nos *human resources*

recusar he·koo·*zaarr* *refuse*

rede ① *he*·de *hammock • net*

redondo/redonda ⑩/①
he·*dong*·do/he·*dong*·daa *round*

reembolso ⑩ he·eng·*bol*·so *refund*

referência ① he·fe·*reng*·syaa *reference*

reflexologia ① he·flek·so·lo·*zhee*·aa
reflexology

refrigerante ⑩ he·free·zhe·*rang*·te
soft drink

refugiado/refugiada ⑩/①
he·foo·zhee·*aa*·do/he·foo·zhee·*aa*·daa
refugee

regional he·zhyo·*now* *regional*

registro ⑩ **de carro** he·*zhees*·tro de
kaa·ho *car registration*

regra ① *he*·graa *rule*

regras ① pl *he*·graas *policy*

rei ⑩ hay *king*

reiki ⑩ *hay*·kee *reiki*

relacionamento ⑩ he·laa·syo·na·*meng*·to
relationship

relações ① pl **públicas** he·la·*soyngs*
poo·blee·kaas *public relations*

relaxar he·la·*shaarr* *relax*

rélica ① he·*lee*·kaa *relic*

relicário ⑩ he·lee·*kaa*·ryo *shrine*

religião ① he·lee·zhee·*owng* *religion*

religioso/religiosa ⑩/① he·lee·zhee·o·zo/
he·lee·zhee·o·zaa *religious*

relógio ⑩ he·*lo*·zhyo *clock • watch*

remo ⑩ *he*·mo *rowing*

remoto/remota ⑩/①
he·*mo*·to/he·*mo*·*taa* *remote*

renda ① *heng*·daa *lace*

repelente ⑩ **em aspiral** he·pe·*leng*·te eng
aas·pee·*row* *mosquito coil*

repolho ⑩ he·*po*·lyo *cabbage*

república ① he·*poo*·blee·kaa *republic*

requerimento ⑩ **de bagagem**
he·ke·ree·meng·to de baa·*gaa*·zheng
baggage claim

reserva ① he·*zerr*·vaa
reservation (booking)

reservar he·zerr·*vaarr*
book (make a booking)

resíduo ⑩ **nuclear** he·*zee*·doo·o
noo·kle·*aarr* *nuclear waste*

resíduo ⑩ **tónico** he·*zee*·dwo tok·*see*·ko
toxic waste

resolução ① he·zo·loo·*sowng* *workout*

respirar hes·pee·*raarr* *breathe*

resposta ① hes·*pos*·taa *answer*

restaurante ⑩ hes·tow·*rang*·te *restaurant*

retornar he·torr·*naarr* *return*

reverenciar he·ve·reng·see·*aarr* *worship*

revisão ① he·vee·*zowng* review
revista ① he·*vees*·taa *magazine*
reza ① he·*zaa* prayer
rico/rica ⑩/① *hee*·ko/*hee*·kaa rich (wealthy)
rin pl heeng *kidney*
rio ⑩ *hee*·o river
rir heerr *laugh*
risco ⑩ *hees*·ko risk
ritmo ⑩ *hee*·tee·mo *rhythm*
rock ⑩ *ho*·kee rock (music)
roda ① *ho*·daa wheel
rodoviária ① ho·do·vee·*aa*·ryaa
  bus station
romântico/romântica ⑩/①
  ho·*mang*·tee·ko/ho·*mang*·tee·kaa
  romantic
rosa *ho*·za pink
rosto ⑩ *hos*·to *face*
rota ① *ho*·taa route
  — de bicicleta de bee·see·*kle*·taa
  bike path
  — de caminhada de kaa·mee·*nyaa*·daa
  hiking route
roubar ho·*baarr* rob • steal
roubo ⑩ *ho*·bo rip-off
roupa ① pl *ho*·paa clothes
  — de banho de *ba*·nyo bathing suit •
  swimsuit
  — de cama de *ka*·maa bedding
  — de baixo de *bai*·sho underwear
roxo/roxa ⑩/① *ho*·sho/*ho*·shaa purple
rua ① *hoo*·aa street
  — principal preeng·see·*pow* main road
rubéola ① hoo·*be*·o·laa rubella
rugby ⑩ *hoo*·gee·bee rugby
ruim hoo·*eeng* bad
ruínas ① pl hoo·*ee*·naas ruins
rum ⑩ hoom rum

S

sábado ⑩ *saa*·baa·do Saturday
saber saa·*berr* know
sabonete ⑩ saa·bo·*ne*·te soap
saco ⑩ *saa*·ko bag
  — de dormir de dorr·*meerr*
  sleeping bag

saguão ⑩ saag·*wowng* foyer
saia ① *saa*·yaa skirt
saída ① saa·*ee*·daa exit
sair saa·*eerr* go out with
sais ⑩ pl **de hidratação** sais de
  ee·draa·taa·*sowng* rehydration salts
sal ⑩ sow salt
sala ① **de espera** *saa*·laa de es·*pe*·raa
  waiting room
sala ① **de trânsito** *saa*·laa de *trang*·zee·to
  transit lounge
salada ① saa·*laa*·daa salad
salaminho ⑩ saa·laa·*mee*·nyo salami
salão ⑩ **de beleza** saa·*lowng* de be·*le*·zaa
  beauty salon
salário ⑩ saa·*laa*·ryo salary • wage
salmão ⑩ sow·*mowng* salmon
salsicha ① sow·*see*·shaa sausage
sandália ① sang·*daa*·lyaa sandal
sangue ⑩ *sang*·ge blood
santo/santa ⑩/① *sang*·to/*sang*·taa saint
sapataria ① saa·paa·taa·*ree*·aa shoe shop
sapato ⑩ saa·*paa*·to shoe
sarampo ⑩ saa·*rang*·po measles
sardinha ① saarr·*dee*·nyaa sardine
saúde ① sa·*oo*·de health
sauna ① *sow*·naa sauna
se se *if*
secar se·*kaarr* dry
seco/seca ⑩/① *se*·ko/*se*·kaa dried • dry
secretário/secretária ⑩/① se·kre·*taa*·ryo/
  se·kre·*taa*·ryaa secretary
seda ① *se*·daa silk
sedento/sedenta ⑩/①
  se·*deng*·to/se·*deng*·taa thirsty
seguir se·*geerr* follow
segunda-feira ① se·*goong*·daa·*fay*·raa
  Monday
segundo ⑩ se·*goong*·do second (time)
segundo grau ⑩ se·*goong*·do grow
  high school
segundo/segunda ⑩/①
  se·*goong*·do/se·*goong*·daa second
seguro ⑩ se·*goo*·ro insurance
  — social so·see·*ow* social welfare • dole
seguro/segura ⑩/①
  se·*goo*·ro/se·*goo*·raa safe
seios ⑩ pl *say*·os breasts

sela ① se·laa *saddle*

selo ⓜ se·lo *stamp*

sem seng *without*

— chumbo shoong·bo *unleaded*

semana ① se·ma·naa *week*

sempre seng·pre *always*

sensível seng·see·vel *emotional · sensible*

sensual seng·soo·ow *sensual*

sentar seng·taarr *sit*

sentimentos ⓜ pl seng·tee·meng·tos *feelings*

sentir seng·teerr *feel*

— falta fuw·taa *miss (feel absence of)*

separado/separada ⓜ/① se·paa·raa·do/
se·paa·raa·daa *separate*

ser serr *be (ongoing)*

seringa ① se·reeng·gaa *syringe*

sério/séria ⓜ/① se·ryo/se·ryaa *serious*

serviço ⓜ militar serr·vee·so mee·lee·taarr *military service*

serviço ⓜ postal rápido serr vee·so
pos·tow haa·pee·do express mail*

setembro se·teng·bro *September*

seu/sua ⓜ/① se·oo/soo·aa *your*

sexo ⓜ sek·so *sex*

— com proteção kong pro·te·sowng *safe sex*

sexta-feira ① ses·taa·fay·raa *Friday*

sexy sek·see *sexy*

shiatsu ⓜ shee·aa·tee·zoo *shiatsu*

shopping centre ⓜ sho·peeng seng·terr *shopping centre*

show ⓜ show *concert*

sim seeng *yes*

simples seeng·ples *simple*

sinagoga ① see·naa·go·gaa *synagogue*

sinal ⓜ de trânsito see·now de
trang·zee·to *traffic light*

sintético/sintética ⓜ/① seeng·te·tee·ko/
seeng·te·tee·kaa *synthetic*

sinuca ① see·noo·kaa *pool (game)*

sistema ⓜ de classes ses·te·maa de
klaa·ses *class system*

skate ⓜ ees·kay·te *skateboarding*

slide ⓜ ees·lai·de *slide (film)*

snorkel ⓜ ees·norr·kel *snorkelling*

snowboarding ⓜ snow·borr·deeng *snowboarding*

sobre so·bre *about · above · on*

sobremesa ① so·bre·me·zaa *dessert*

sobrenome ⓜ so·bre·nó·me
family name · surname

socialista so·see·aa·lees·taa *socialist*

sogra ① so·graa *mother-in-law*

sogro ⓜ so·gro *father-in-law*

sol ⓜ sol *sun*

soldado ⓜ&① sol·daa·do *soldier*

solteiro/solteira ⓜ/①
sol·tay·ro/sol·tay·raa *single*

solto/solta ⓜ/① sol·to/sol·taa *loose*

somente so·meng·te *only*

sonho ⓜ so·nyo *dream*

sonolento/sonolenta ⓜ/① so·no·leng·to/
so·no·leng·taa *sleepy*

sopa ① so·paa *soup*

sorte ① sorr·te *luck*

sortudo/sortuda ⓜ/①
sorr·too·do/sorr·too·daa *lucky*

sorvete ⓜ sorr·ve·te *ice cream*

sorveteria ① sorr·ve·te·ree·aa
ice-cream parlour

souvenir ⓜ soo·ve·neerr *souvenir*

sozinho/sozinha ⓜ/①
so·zee·nyo/so·zee·nyaa *alone*

subir soo·beerr *climb*

suborno ⓜ soo·borr·no *bribe*

sub-títulos ⓜ pl soo·bee·tee·too·los
subtitles

suco ⓜ soo·ko *juice*

— de laranja de laa·rang·zhaa
orange juice

Suécia ① soo·e·syaa *Sweden*

suéter ① soo·e·terr *jumper · sweater*

suficiente soo·fee·see·eng·te *enough*

Suíça ① soo·ee·saa *Switzerland*

sujo/suja ⓜ/① soo·zho/soo·zhaa *dirty*

sul ⓜ sool *south*

supermercado ⓜ soo·perr·merr·kaa·do
supermarket

surdo/surda ⓜ/① soor·do/soor·daa *deaf*

surfar soorr·faarr *surf*

surfe ⓜ soor·fee *surfing*

surpresa ① soor·pre·zaa *surprise*

sutiã ⓜ soo·tee·ang *bra*

T

tabaco ⓜ *taa-baa-ko* tobacco
tabaconista ⓜ *taa-baa-ko-nees-taa* tobacconist
talco ⓜ *tow-ko* baby powder
talheres ⓜ pl *taa-lye-res* cutlery
talvez *tow-ves* maybe
tamanho ⓜ *ta-ma-nyo* size
também *tang-beng* also • too
tampa ⓕ *tang-paa* plug (bath)
tampão ⓜ *tang-powng* tampon
tampões de ouvido ⓜ *tang-powng de o-vee-do* earplugs
tangerina ⓕ *tang-zhe-ree-naa* mandarin
tapete ⓜ *taa-pe-te* rug
tarde ⓕ *taarr-de* afternoon
taxa ⓕ *taa-shaa*
— **de aeroporto** *taa-shaa de aa-e-ro-porr-to* airport tax
— **de câmbio** *taa-shaa de kang-byo* exchange rate
— **de serviço** *taa-shaa de serr-veee-so* service charge
táxi ⓜ *taak-see* taxi
teatro ⓜ *te-aa-tro* theatre
tecido ⓜ *te-see-do* fabric
técnica ⓕ *te-kee-nee-kaa* technique
técnico/técnica ⓜ ⓕ *te-kee-nee-ko/te-kee-nee-kaa* coach
teimoso/teimosa ⓜ ⓕ *tay-mo-zo/tay-mo-zaa* stubborn
teleférico ⓜ *te-le-fe-ree-ko* chairlift (skiing)
telefonar *te-le-fo-naarr* telephone
telefone ⓜ *te-le-fo-ne* telephone
— **público** *poo-blee-ko* public telephone
telegrama ⓜ *te-le-gra-maa* telegram
telescópio ⓜ *te-les-ko-pyo* telescope
televisão ⓕ *te-le-vee-sowng* television
temperatura ⓕ *teng-pe-raa-too-raa* temperature
tempestade ⓕ *teng-pes-taa-de* storm
tempo ⓜ *teng-po* time • weather
tempo integral *eeng-te-grow* full-time
têmpora ⓕ *teng-po-raa* temple
tênis ⓜ *te-nees* tennis
— **de mesa** de *me-zaa* table tennis

tentar *teng-taarr* try (attempt)
ter *terr* have
terça-feira ⓕ *terr-saa-fay-raa* Tuesday
terceiro/terceira ⓜ ⓕ *terr-say-ro/terr-say-raa* third
terminar *terr-mee-naarr* finish
término ⓜ *terr-mee-no* finish
Terra ⓕ *te-haa* Earth
terra ⓕ *te-haa* land
terremoto ⓜ *te-he-mo-to* earthquake
terrível *te-hee-vel* terrible
tesoura ⓕ *te-zo-raa* scissors
teste ⓜ *tes-te* test
— **de gravidez** de *graa-vee-dez* pregnancy test kit
tevê ⓕ *te-ve* TV
tia ⓕ *tee-aa* aunt
tigela ⓕ *tee-zhe-laa* bowl
time ⓜ *tee-me* team
tímido/tímida ⓜ ⓕ *tee-mee-do/tee-mee-daa* shy
típico/típica ⓜ ⓕ *tee-pee-ko/tee-pee-kaa* typical
tipo ⓜ *tee-po* type
tirar *tee-raarr* take (photo)
toalha ⓕ *to-aa-lyaa* towel
— **de rosto** de *hos-to* face cloth
— **higiênica** *ee-zhee-e-nee-kaa* sanitary napkin
tocar *to-kaarr* touch • play (guitar) • ring (phone)
tofu ⓜ *to-foo* tofu
tom ⓜ *tong* tune
tomada ⓕ *to-maa-daa* plug (electricity)
tomate ⓜ *to-maa-te* tomato
tonto/tonta ⓜ ⓕ *tong-to/tong-taa* dizzy
torcedor/torcedora ⓜ ⓕ *torr-se-dorr/torr-se-do-raa* supporter (sport)
torcimento ⓜ *torr-see-meng-to* sprain
torneira ⓕ *torr-nay-raa* faucet • tap
tornozelo ⓜ *torr-no-ze-lo* ankle
torrada ⓕ *to-haa-daa* toast
torradeira ⓕ *to-haa-day-raa* toaster
torre ⓕ *to-he* tower
torta ⓕ *torr-taa* pie
tosa ⓕ *to-zaa* crop
tossir *to-seerr* cough

trabalhador/trabalhadora ⓜ/ⓕ **de obra**
traa·baa·lyaa·*dorr*/traa·baa·lyaa·do·raa
de o·*braa labourer*

trabalhador/trabalhadora ⓜ/ⓕ **manual**
traa·baa·lyaa·*dorr*/traa·baa·lyaa·do·raa
maa·noo·*ow manual worker*

trabalhar traa·baa·*lyaarr work*

trabalho ⓜ traa·*baa*·lyo *work*
— **de casa** de *kaa*·zaa *housework*
— **em bar** eng baarr *bar work*

traduzir traa·doo·*zeerr translate*

traficante ⓜ&ⓕ traa·fee·*kang*·te
drug dealer

tráfico ⓜ *traa*·fee·ko *traffic*

tranca ⓕ *trang*·kaa *lock*
— **de bicicleta** de bee·see·*kle*·taa
bike lock

trancado/trancada ⓜ/ⓕ
trang·*kaa*·do/trang·*kaa*·daa *locked*

trancar trang·*kaarr lock*

transporte ⓜ trans·*porr*·te *transport*

traseiro ⓜ traa·*zay*·ro *bottom (body)*

trave ⓕ **de roda** *traa*·ve de ho·daa
spoke (wheel)

travellers cheques ⓜ pl traa·ve·*ler she*·kes
travellers cheques

travesseiro ⓜ traa·ve·*say*·ro *pillow*

trem ⓜ treng *train*

trilha ⓕ *tree*·lyaa *mountain path*

triste *trees*·te *sad*

troca ⓕ *tro*·kaa *exchange*

trocado ⓜ tro·*kaa*·do *loose change*

trocar tro·*kaarr change · exchange*

troco ⓜ *tro*·ko *change (coins)*

tudo *too*·do *everything*

tudo/tuda ⓜ/ⓕ *too*·do/*too*·daa *all*

tumor ⓜ too·*morr tumour*

túmulo ⓜ *too*·moo·lo *grave*

turista ⓜ&ⓕ too·*rees*·taa *tourist*

U

último/última ⓜ/ⓕ *ool*·tee·mo/*ool*·tee·maa
last

ultrasom ⓜ ool·traa·*song ultrasound*

uma vez *oo*·maa vez *once*

uniforme ⓜ oo·nee·*forr*·me *uniform*

universidade ⓕ oo·nee·verr·see·*daa*·de
university · college

universo ⓜ oo·nee·*verr*·so *universe*

urgente oorr·zheng·te *urgent*

usuário/usuária ⓜ/ⓕ **de drogas**
oo·zoo·*aa*·ryo/oo·zoo·aa·ryaa de
dro·gaas *drug user*

útil oo·*til useful*

uvas ⓕ pl oo·vaas *grapes*

V

vaca ⓕ *vaa kaa cow*

vacina ⓕ vaa·*see*·naa *vaccination*

vagão ⓜ **de dormir** va·*gowng* de
dorr·*meerr sleeping car*

vagão ⓜ **restaurante** vaa·*gowng*
hes·tow·*rang*·te *dining car*

vagarosamente vaa·gaa·ro·zaa·*meng*·te
slowly

vagem ⓕ **chinesa** vaa·zheng shee·*ne*·zaa
snow pea

vagina ⓕ vaa·*zhee*·naa *vagina*

vago/vaga ⓜ/ⓕ *vaa*·go/*vaa*·gaa *vacant*

vale ⓜ *vaa lo valley*

validar vaa·lee·*daarr validate*

valor vaa·*lorr value (price)*

van ⓕ *van van*

vapor ⓜ vaa·*porr stream*

varanda ⓕ vaa·*rang*·daa *balcony*

vários/várias ⓜ/ⓕ *vaa*·ryos/*vaa*·ryaas
many

vazio/vazia ⓜ/ⓕ vaa·*zee* o/vaa·zee·aa
empty

vegetariano/vegetariana ⓜ/ⓕ
ve·zhe·taa·ree·*a*·no/ve·zhe·taa·ree·*a*·naa
vegetarian

veia ⓕ *ve*·aa *vein · candle*

velho/velha ⓜ/ⓕ *ve*·lyo/*ve*·lyaa
old · stale

velocidade ⓕ ve·lo·see·*daa* de *speed*
— **do filme** do *feel*·me *film speed*

vender veng·*derr sell*

venenoso/venenosa ⓜ/ⓕ
ve·ne·*no*·zo/ve·ne·no·zaa *poisonous*

ventilador ⓜ veng·tee·laa·*dorr*
fan (machine)

vento ⓜ *veng*·to *wind*

ver verr *look • see*
verão ⓜ ve-*rowng* *summer*
verde *verr*-de *green*
verdureiro/verdureira ⓜ/ⓕ
   verr-doo-*ray*-ro/verr-doo-*ray*-raa
   greengrocer
vermelho/vermelha ⓜ/ⓕ
   verr-*me*-lyo/verr-*me*-lyaa *red*
Véspera ⓕ **de Ano Novo** *ves*-pe-raa de
   a-no *no*-vo *New Year's Eve*
vestido ⓜ ves-*tee*-do *dress*
vestígio ⓜ ves-*tee*-zhyo *trail*
vestir ves-*teerr* *wear*
via ⓕ **aérea** *vee*-aa aa-e-re-aa *airmail*
viagem ⓕ vee-*aa*-zheng *journey • trip*
   — de negócios de ne-*goo*-syos
   business trip
viajar vee-aa-*zhaarr* *travel*
vício ⓜ *vee*-syo *addiction*
   — de drogas de *dro*-gaas
   drug addiction
vida ⓕ *vee*-daa *life*
vidente ⓜ&ⓕ vee-*deng*-te *fortune teller*
vidro ⓜ *vee*-dro *glass • jar*
vigiar vee-zhe-*aarr* *watch*
vilarejo ⓜ vee-laa-*re*-zho *village*
vinagre ⓜ vee-*naa*-gre *vinegar*
vinha ⓕ *vee*-nyaa *vineyard*
vinho ⓜ *vee*-nyo *vine • wine*
   — espumante es-poo-*mang*-te
   sparkling wine
violão ⓜ vee-o-*lowng* *guitar*
vir veerr *come*
virar vee-*raarr* *turn*
vírus ⓜ *vee*-roos *virus*

visitar vee-zee-*taarr* *visit*
vista ⓕ *vees*-taa *view*
visto ⓜ *vees*-to *visa*
vitamina ⓕ vee-taa-*mee*-naa *vitamin*
voar vo-*aarr* *fly*
você vo-*se* *you*
vocês pl vo-*se* *you*
vodka ⓕ vo-dee-*kaa* *vodka*
vôlei ⓜ vo-*lay* *volleyball (sport)*
   — de praia de *praa*-yaa *beach volleyball*
volta ⓕ *vol*-taa *ride (car)*
volume ⓜ vo-*loo*-me *volume*
vôo ⓜ *vo*-o *flight*
votar vo-*taarr* *vote*
voz ⓕ voz *voice*

whisky ⓜ oo-*ees*-kee *whisky*
windsurfe ⓜ wind-*soorr*-fee *windsurfing*

xadrez ⓜ shaa-*dres* *chess*
xampú ⓜ shang-*poo* *shampoo*
xarope ⓜ shaa-*ro*-pe *cough medicine*
xícara ⓕ *shee*-kaa-raa *cup*

zangado/zangada ⓜ/ⓕ
   zang-*gaa*-do/zang-*gaa*-daa *angry*
zodíaco ⓜ zo-*dee*-aa-ko *zodiac*
zoológico ⓜ zo-o-lo-*zhee*-ko *zoo*

INDEX

D

E

F

G

What kind of traveller are you?

A. You're eating chicken for dinner *again* because it's the only word you know.

B. When no one understands what you say, you step closer and shout louder.

C. When the barman doesn't understand your order, you point frantically at the beer.

D. You're surrounded by locals, swapping jokes, email addresses and experiences
  – other travellers want to borrow your phrasebook or audio guide.

If you answered A, B, or C, you NEED Lonely Planet's language products ...

- **Lonely Planet Phrasebooks** – for every phrase you need in every language
  you want
- **Lonely Planet Fast Talk** – essential language for short trips and weekends away
- **Lonely Planet Real Talk** – downloadable language audio guides from
  www.lonelyplanet.com to your MP3 player

... and this is why

- **Talk to everyone everywhere**
  Over 120 languages, more than any other publisher
- **The right words at the right time**
  Quick-reference colour sections, two-way dictionary, easy pronunciation,
  every possible subject - and audio to support it

Lonely Planet Offices

Australia
90 Maribyrnong St, Footscray,
Victoria 3011
☎ 03 8379 8000
fax 03 8379 8111
✉ talk2us@lonelyplanet.com.au

USA
150 Linden St, Oakland,
CA 94607
☎ 510 893 8555
fax 510 893 8572
✉ info@lonelyplanet.com

UK
72-82 Rosebery Ave,
London EC1R 4RW
☎ 020 7841 9000
fax 020 7841 9001
✉ go@lonelyplanet.co.uk

www.lonelyplanet.com